The Values of Community Archaeology: A Comparative Assessment between the UK and US

Faye A. Simpson

BAR International Series 2105
2010

Published in 2016 by
BAR Publishing, Oxford

BAR International Series 2105

The Values of Community Archaeology: A Comparative Assessment between the UK and US

ISBN 978 1 4073 0646 9

BAR Publishing is the trading name of British Archaeological Reports (Oxford) Ltd.
British Archaeological Reports was first incorporated in 1974 to publish the BAR
Series, International and British. In 1992 Hadrian Books Ltd became part of the BAR
group. This volume was originally published by Archaeopress in conjunction with
British Archaeological Reports (Oxford) Ltd / Hadrian Books Ltd, the Series principal
publisher, in 2010. This present volume is published by BAR Publishing, 2016.

Printed in England

BAR
PUBLISHING

BAR titles are available from:

BAR Publishing
122 Banbury Rd, Oxford, OX2 7BP, UK
EMAIL   info@barpublishing.com
PHONE   +44 (0)1865 310431
FAX   +44 (0)1865 316916
www.barpublishing.com

TABLE OF CONTENTS

LIST OF FIGURES

LIST OF TABLES

ACKNOWLEDGMENTS

All my thanks to my supervisors, Dr Alan Outram and Prof Mick Aston, and my former supervisor Dr Howard Williams, for all their advice, time and patience over the last few years.

My heartfelt love and thanks to my parents Douglas and Jennifer Simpson, for the unwavering support and encouragement, I would not have been able to do this without them.

A huge thank you to all the people who have given me advice and support; with special thanks to Gerry Wait, Yvonne Marshall, Tim Schadla Hall and Tim Copeland. To my friend Tim Morley for telling me I could do it, and knowing what was best. Also to many of my former colleagues at the Portable Antiquities Scheme and Museum of London for providing valuable contributions and insights to this research, and to all of Time Team for keeping me sane, digging and providing a relevant distraction and balance away from the books. To the HLF, for funding this fellowship without which this research would never of been possible. And finally to all the community members and archaeologists who have contributed to this research, thank you.

ABSTRACT

Does community archaeology work? Worldwide over the last decade, there has been a boom in projects utilising the popular phrase 'community archaeology'. These projects take many different forms, stretching from the public-face of research and developer-funded programmes to projects run by museums, archaeological units, universities and archaeological societies. Many of these projects are driven by the desire for archaeology to meet a range of perceived educational and social values in bringing about knowledge and awareness of the past in the present. They are also motivated by the desire to secure adequate funding for archaeological research. However, appropriate criteria and methodologies for evaluating the effectiveness of these projects have yet to be designed. This research sets out a methodology based on self-reflexivity and ethnology. It focuses on community excavations, in a range of contexts both in the UK and US. It assesses the values these projects produce for communities and evaluates what community archaeology actually does.

It concludes that community archaeology frequently fails to balance the desired outcomes of its stakeholders. It suffers from its short-term funding and, therefore, often lacks sustainability, which hampers its ability to produce and maintain values. Evaluation of projects should be qualitative as well as quantitative in establishing the cost effectiveness of projects. Subsequently, recommendations are made for future community archaeology project designs.

INTRODUCTION

1.1 Definition of Community Archaeology

Community Archaeology is the engagement of a community (usually geographically determined), with their local archaeology (including tangible and intangible heritage). Community archaeology projects facilitate the community to become involved in the process of archaeological investigation.

In reality the word community disguises the numerous communities that exist within a geographically constructed community. Furthermore, the phrase 'community' has a political context, creating an idea of unity and identity, an entity, which appears on the surface to be stable. For instance, the phrase community archaeology is used to describe the project at Hungate, York, where the site was being developed from a brownfield site into a residential area. It had not since the 1930s had a community. Here the phrase 'community' was used as a form of identity creation, while in reality the community was a specific group of people interested in experiencing archaeology, rather than a geographically determined, and homogenous community.

Furthermore, community archaeology has and is used to justify archaeology's role in society. Community Archaeology has come to represent a way of doing archaeology with, or for, the public, rather than just by and for the professionals (Cressey et al 2003, 2). Yet, when using the term archaeologists are referring to one specific community group, i.e. amateurs, rather than the community as a whole. For instance, the community archaeology excavation at Wittenham Clumps, Oxfordshire, implies involvement of the whole community, whilst in reality all those people involved are members of the existing amateur archaeology community (Ryan Watts, pers. comm.). Sometimes the use of the word 'community' disguises a lack of diversity, and a division within society regarding interest in archaeology.

1.2 Types of Community Archaeology

The breadth of and in some cases lack of the definition of 'community archaeology', means that an immense variety of projects fall under this banner; ranging from school outreach projects, providing educational resources in schools, to field walking projects, finds identification and outreach like the Portable Antiquities Scheme and excavation projects. Despite this potential for diversity within community archaeology projects, the majority of these projects still focus on excavation, and have failed to promote non-intrusive archaeological research methods, perhaps believing they do not offer the same appeal as excavation.

1.3 History of Community Archaeology in the UK

Prior to the 1970s, archaeology and engagement with the public/community was between the professionals and amateurs. During the 70s and 80s this changed to professionals and the wider public, and then in the 90s and into the 21st century between professionals and the 'community'. The 'public' was an all-encompassing phrase, more about inclusion of everyone with few limits, whereas the 'community' was more defined, with limitations often relating to specific local groupings. This change in terminology, and the development of community archaeology, was directly related to changes in government agendas, as well as relating to changes in archaeological theories, and the development of the 'archaeological' profession.

During the 1970s a Labour government was in power, with a political focus on social inclusion and education. Subsequently there was an increase in government support for university extramural classes, and other educational provision such as higher national diplomas in practical archaeology (Aston forthcoming; Beavis and Hunt 1998, 7). This decade saw the first use of the phrase

1

community archaeology by Liddle (1981), and concepts relating to communication and public archaeology being formally discussed (McGimsey 1972). At this stage community archaeology had not been acknowledged as a sub-discipline, but many of its principles were being applied in an *ad hoc*, and localised manner to archaeological education initiatives, principally led by universities. The social and educational values of archaeology were acknowledged, and these new courses were seen to move archaeology away from its upper and middle class origins (Start 1999).

The Conservative government of the 1980s and early 1990s, focused on economics, policy and local government responsibility for budgets. It increased regulations attached to heritage, created quangos and privatised public sector organisations (Parker Pearson 2001). 1983 saw the formation of English Heritage, from the Historic Buildings and Monuments Commission for England, by a National Heritage Act (Lock 2004, 56). It began work in 1984 sponsored by Department of Culture, Media and Sport (Lock 2004, 56). Such quangos considered the costs and benefits of archaeology, and acted as advisors to the government as to its value.

The 1980s saw archaeological projects used by the Manpower Services Commission as job creation schemes for the long term unemployed, providing funding for field units for research excavations if they employed, and trained the unemployed (Start 1999, 51). Sutton Hoo, used labour from this scheme to excavate its burial mounds and trained many future archaeologists, including Time Team's Helen Geake who works for the Portable Antiquities Scheme (Start 1999, 51). This indicated a realisation, both by the government and archaeologists, that archaeology had values that extended beyond knowledge creation.

In 1990 the government issued PPG16, with its 'developer pays' ethos, which encouraged privatisation and professionalisation of archaeology. The government handed over some of its responsibilities for archaeology to the commercial sector, fostering the belief that archaeology should pay for itself. For instance, many local council-based field units had to become financially self-sustaining from contract income. Furthermore, university departments cut many extramural classes, as they were not considered sufficiently profitable (Aston forthcoming).

In 1994, the Heritage Lottery Fund (HLF) was set up by parliament; money raised from the National Lottery was used to give grants to heritage projects. Officially HLF was seen as a non-departmental public body, to whom the Secretary of State for Culture, Media and Sport issued policy directives (www.hlf.org.uk/English/AboutUs). This funding body is responsible for decisions to fund archaeology projects that had previously received government grants. In the same period professionalisation of archaeology had decreased amateur and direct public

involvement in the archaeological process. Where amateurs had once played a vital role in research and rescue projects they were no longer able to, and, in some circumstances, the new 'professionals' did not want them to as it undermined their paid employment prospects. It was within this new environment that the increased need for public archaeology was identified.

From 1997 the New Labour government has been in power, with a social agenda of sharing resources and a focus on 'education, education, education' and widening participation (Lock 2004, 56). This theory of education underpinning social betterment, and creating identity, was highlighted by the previous university grants systems being abolished, in favour of increasing financial support through loans and subsidies for students from lower socio-economic backgrounds to study at university (though the effectiveness of this is debatable). This focus on equality and education for all came with financial incentives for organisations, providing funding for archaeological research, and saw the University of Reading and University of Bournemouth launch their, 'Inclusive, Accessible, Archaeology Programme', which encouraged and enabled students with disabilities to study archaeology at university.

This period saw the funding of the Portable Antiquities Scheme (PAS) in 1997 by the HLF, which was supported by the government, and described as the 'largest community archaeology project in the UK', which, by 2007, became funded centrally by the government, and administered by the Museums, Libraries and Archives (MLA).

The 21st century continued under Labour leadership, but with increasing financial pressure caused by the war in Iraq and Afghanistan, the 2012 Olympics and the 'credit crunch,' the government focus shifted from 'public' to 'community', with the word community used to create a unified identity, something museums were seen as playing a key role in. During the late 1990s and early 21st century community archaeology thrived, meeting social and education agendas of the government, with large-scale community archaeology projects like Dig Manchester and Shoreditch Park, London receiving HLF grants. The number of community archaeologists also increased with many employed through these grants, but some were also employed through direct organisational funding, including museums such as the Museum of London. Furthermore, field units including Wessex Archaeology, were beginning to see the benefit of community outreach to their public profile (Smith 2004), and by 2008 there was a professional training day on community archaeology held at Oxford University.

The larger organisations created by Thatcher's government were doing less well, seen as failing to meet government agendas of social inclusivity. By 2008 English Heritage's funding had been cut by 1/3, and MLA's government funding had also been effected,

2

directly impacting national community archaeology programmes like PAS, who were forced to lay off some of their staff, and who's central office is still under review. The pressure of Olympic funding saw diversion of lottery resources and the HLF budget was cut by 1/3 by 2008. This is bound to have an effect on the continued growth of community archaeology projects, especially as many are coming to the end of their grant periods.

1.4 Why Investigate Community Archaeology?

Community archaeology claims to offer the public an opportunity to become engaged with the interpretation and understanding of the past (Dalley 2004). It has been claimed that it is this proactive approach, one of interaction and participation in the archaeological process, which creates tangible and intangible values from the past for the people in the present. These espoused values range from educational to economic, political and social; however, the extent to which these values have been successfully achieved has yet to be critically analysed. This is the primary function of this research, with particular reference to community excavations.

1.5 How to Investigate the Values of Community Archaeology?

To date, few academics have critically assessed the values and the outputs of community archaeology. This is especially true of the UK, where there has yet to be critical engagement with this relatively new sub-discipline of community archaeology (Marshall 2002). Critical discourse was initiated in the New World; and many of the ideas behind this research were driven by post-colonial and indigenous rights debates (Potter 1994). As such the approach taken was strongly linked to anthropology, which has directly influenced the methodology of their research (Potter 1994, 23; Pope and Mills 2007)

It has been claimed that in order to gain a more comprehensive understanding of the value of heritage, specifically community archaeology, we must move away from statistical rigidity to a more flexible, anthropological model of assessment (Dalley 2004, 19; Marshall 2002; Greer *et al* 2002; Potter 1994; Carman 2002, 167). This draws on ideas from other disciplines, including psychology, sociology, and anthropology, in order to take a critical approach to this sub-discipline and its values (Potter 1994; Walker 1988, 50). Such understanding could put community archaeology in a stronger position to influence political culture and funding towards the subject, rather than the political culture controlling community archaeology (Walker 1988. 55).

In order to critically assess the value of community archaeology excavations and see if context (e.g. political, social, economic and location) affects values, a range of case studies have been selected from the UK and US. These were Shoreditch Park (London), Grosvensor Park (Chester), Hungate (York) and Brayford (Devon) in the UK; Mitchell (South Dakota), Muncy (Pennsylvania), and Annapolis (Maryland) in the US. The same methodology was applied to all these case studies, which was based on ethnological study, anthropological assessment, and self-reflexivity. This fieldwork aimed to examine themes and contrasts between these projects.

1.6 Hypothesis

Over recent years the amount of investment in community archaeology, particularly in the UK, has inexorably increased. The majority of the money invested comes from public funds and, as such, community archaeology projects should be held publicly accountable for the cost effectiveness of that investment (Swain 2007; Carver 2002). Recently, MLA have commissioned qualitative rather than quantitative surveys of some of the largest community archaeology projects in the UK, including the PAS, yet the HLF does not require such assessment of the values attained by its projects, which cost millions of pounds each year, rather, it relies purely on quantitative assessments of projects' outputs.

Key Questions:

- Do community archaeology projects offer values to the community beyond the professional or academic spheres?

- Do community archaeology projects offer value for money?

- Is excavation key to sustaining, maintaining and creating values? Does practical involvement in excavation have a greater impact on the values of archaeology?

This research will provide new qualitative evidence as to the effectiveness, and accountability of community archaeology projects.

It is believed that engagement in the archaeological excavation process is key to achieving and maintaining the values espoused by community archaeology projects (Holtorf 2006). This research aims to test the validity of this assertion, and furthermore compare theoretical aims and actual values achieved.

2. THE ORIGINS AND DEVELOPMENT OF COMMUNITY ARCHAEOLOGY IN THE UNITED KINGDOM

On the public forum of Wikipedia it is claimed the definition of community archaeology is simple; it is 'archaeology for the people by the people' (2007; Reid 2008). I will argue that community archaeology is anything but simply 'archaeology for the people by the people,' and this phase is misleading and dangerously naïve. Community Archaeology's use, and often abuse, is linked to complex issues of ethnicity, politics, nationalism and identity, and is deeply routed in philosophical thought and archaeological theory.

2.1 Introduction

The concept of 'community archaeology', under its broadest definition, creates an archaeological dialogue with the wider public. It was established in archaeological thought long before the first use of the term in academic literature by Walker (1988) and Liddle (1989) in the United Kingdom, and Greer (1995) in Australia (Dalley 2004). Mortimer Wheeler (1954) makes it clear that:

> "… it is the duty of the archaeologist to reach and impress the public and to mould its words in the common clay of its forthright understanding" (Wheeler 1954, 224).

He advocates the importance of communicating knowledge in an understandable and appropriate manner. This idea was revolutionary in many academic archaeology circles, where people were happier to keep the knowledge to themselves. In practice, the communication that Wheeler (1954) suggested took another thirty years to be implemented significantly into archaeological practice. Prior to this, communication with the wider community was sporadic, being done as and when it suited archaeologists. It was the idea of communication advocated by Wheeler (1954) that has become one of the principal objectives of community archaeology projects worldwide, to the extent that Moser *et al* (2002, 202)

listed it as one of the seven key methodological elements that make up community archaeology projects.

The limitation of Wheeler's (1954) concept was that it was still based on the idea of the archaeologist as the expert, controlling the dissemination of knowledge and translating academic thought rather than opening up dialogue. So, with this in mind, the concepts behind community archaeology are not new, but what is new is the attempt by some professionals and policy makers to shift the power and control of the past to the community.

This idea of communicating archaeology has, in the last fifty years, taken on a new dimension, with increased media coverage (Schadla-Hall 2004, 263; Clack and Britain 2007) and the growth in the museum sector (Cunliffe 1981, 192) with its outreach work, including education programmes (Henson 2004). Subsequently, communication became a more two-way process. No longer was it merely about communicating *to*, but rather *with* the public. Communication involved an open dialogue, discussion and consultation, rather than just the archaeologists telling the public what they had found. It is this modern concept of communication that is the basis of community archaeology.

2.2 Philosophy, Archaeology, Theory and Politics

To understand and be able to analyse community archaeology critically, it is vital to deconstruct the core theoretical strands that interweave through this complex new 'paradigm'. At community archaeology's core are fundamental philosophical and ethical concepts.

The development of the concept of community in archaeology has been influenced by the shifting theoretical paradigms that govern archaeological practice. Theory is everywhere (Johnson 1999), and subsequently it is at the very basis of community archaeology, forming the links between the ideas and concepts that are at its core, and the implications of these to practice. To understand how community archaeology came into being, including its transition from thought to practice, it is necessary to deconstruct the philosophical principles and recent, consecutive governments' philosophical allegiances that influenced archaeological theory and practice on a general level (Table 2.1).

Table 2.1 Indicating processual and post-processual archaeological paradigms and their correlation with political philosophical principles (Ideas taken from Blackburn (2006))

Processual	Post-Processual
Traditionalist	Post-Modernists
Realists	Idealists
Objectivists	Subjectivists
Rationalists	Social constructivists
Universalists	Contextualists
Positivist/ Absolutist	Relativist
Truth	No Truth

2.3 Processual Archaeology

The movement to processual archaeology was governed by positivist philosophical principles, the idea progressing towards the truth about the past, as supported by scientific 'facts' (Blackburn 2006; See Table 2.1). It is a rational and objective stance, taking a sceptical view of 'tangible' evidence and the factual interpretation of the physical past. It is one based on conviction of ideas and decisions, founded on modernist concepts. It is the opposite of the relativist stance, abhorring its concept of *anything goes*. Rather progression towards truth is attainable through tangible 'scientific' evidence and hypothesis testing.

This processual scientific approach had implications for public involvement and engagement with archaeological sites. Copeland (2006) described it as enabling simplified and less confusing versions of the past, whilst Hems (2006) suggested that what it produced were constructed facts, which in turn meant an official and inflexible view of the site as it 'was'. The past was divorced from its context in the present, taking no account of how it influenced the way people live today. It was rigid and exclusive. It could be suggested that this approach segregated the community from archaeological interpretation.

Processual archaeology controls interpretation, and therefore could be responsible for the segregation of the public from the process of archaeology. In some cases, hard-line scientific practice can lead to the exclusion of the people it aims to serve. The belief was that archaeology was a science, increasing the belief that archaeology was a professional discipline that could only

be understood with training and technologies outside the reach of most people (McGimsey 1972).

This approach remains one that is still supported as an approach to public involvement and one that is claimed to be less open to political manipulation. (Anthony 1996). As McDavid (2006), amongst others, argues, this is a matter of archaeologists striving to gain a balance between establishing professional standards and the duty to communicate with the public. Because of public funding, it could be argued that the public has a right to know the outcomes of archaeological work, but the above approach led to archaeologists dictating what the public were told, without dialogue.

2.4 Politics, Philosophy and Processualism from a United Kingdom Perspective

The absolutist (as opposed to relativist) philosophical paradigm could be linked with the Conservative leadership in the United Kingdom particularly during the 1980s. It is the understanding of the principles behind absolutism and positivism that can help understand the development of processual archaeology in the UK, but also the changing practice of archaeology, moving towards increased professionalism. Whether intentional or not, the introduction of Planning Policy Guidance document 16 in 1990 (Wainwright 2000, 909) further supported professional control, excluding a number of amateur groups that had been previously involved in rescue archaeology.

During the Conservative government's leadership in the UK from 1979, and specifically in the 1980s, there were specific trends in the way archaeologists approached the public (Pluciennik 2001). Thatcher's government sought to decentralise control and privatise government organisations, and this directly related to the push for economic reform of the country. This decentralisation had a direct impact on the heritage as the centrally controlled, administered and funded Department of the Environment was devolved many of its former roles in 1983 and various quangos, for example English Heritage and English Nature. This shift away from direct control by the government merely masked the mounting bureaucracy and increased government control of heritage agendas (Hunter 1996, 28). This period was one of globalisation, financial boom, and a wider disparity between classes, especially in terms of economic wealth. Ever since, there has been a need to justify archaeology in terms of economics, politics and society (Fowler 1992) and this has only intensified within recent Brownite politics. In essence this has required a translation of the past to the present and to the future. Market principles have been used to justify archaeology as a leisure activity for social betterment (Bowden 1991, 141). This justification produced the need for a recognised profession in archaeology, and this economic impetus and decreased government funding led the development of Planning Policy

Guidance 16, with archaeology becoming a business, and large organisations, for example English Heritage, making the past a tourist industry, charging for access to national sites, including Stonehenge (Skeates 2000).

Under Thatcher's and later under Major's governments with the 'back to basics campaign', there was a heritage push for the cultivation of traditional' values, with archaeology, once again being supported by politicians to justify this idea of continuity of values, and the solid moral fibre of the United Kingdom (Thomas. J. 2004, 193).

The heritage 'industry' (Bowden 1991, 141), under this government control claimed that the interest for the past was never greater (Lowenthal 1989), as it had enabled public archaeology through public choice, and reassessment of what was important. However, Parker Pearson (2001) argues that the mounting bureaucracy of quangos led to increased exclusion of the public. Others argue that this exclusion was counter-balanced by an increase in local archaeological societies, appearing to suggest more inclusion in archaeology (Schadla-Hall 2004, 262; Manley 1999, 110). It has been asserted by Manley (1999, 111-112) that in reality such volunteer organizations had increased exclusion through social elitism, forming very insular groups of people, with specific interests. This suggests that diversity in involvement and interest could potentially disappear.

2.5 Philosophy and Post-Processual Archaeology

The movement to post-processual archaeology was influenced by relativism and the relativist slogan of "there are not facts, only interpretation" (Nietzche 1967). It is methodologically based on embraceing multiculturalism, intangibles and tangibles, therefore, no absolute truth (Blackburn 2006). This was based on social constructivist, and contextualist viewpoints. It was claimed that this facilitated the acceptance of external ideas in the interpretation of archaeology, through taking an anthropological, sociological and therefore inter-disciplinary approach to the subject, but also the reconsideration of public involvement in archaeology (Binford 1983; Hodder 2001, 1; Smith 2004). This approach was by some perceived as having had positive effects on archaeology (Smith 2004); it enabled the opening up of archaeology to broader audiences and increased the exposure of the subject to a wider community. It led to political recognition, in the form of government white papers and public speeches (Lammy 2006), of public desires for preservation and presentation of archaeological remains, which, in turn, led to increased regulations and policies relating to archaeology. Eventually this placed archaeology firmly in the political and public funding sphere, highlighted by the government support and funding of the Portable Antiquities Scheme in 2006, which has been regarded as the largest and one of the most successful community archaeology programmes in the UK (www.finds.org.uk).

This approach also required archaeologists to consider values attached to the past outside their own sphere of thought, and that the value of the past was not solely related to physical remains. This recognition of different interpretations enabled the tangible evidence (archaeological record) to be translated into the intangible values of present communities and subsequently legitimise the past in the present (Munjeri 2006). Furthermore, this new broadening of approaches enabled a two-way communication between archaeologists and the community, that allowed indigenous and local communities more involvement in what some regarded a less politically determined approach to the past (Lowenthal 1985).

This philosophical paradigm is also based on ethics, the rights of people to gain access to and be part of knowledge production. These principles have guided the instigation and methodology of community archaeology projects, and these have been discussed at some length in literature relating to the practice of community archaeology in non-western contexts (Fredericksen 2002; Greer *et al* 2002). These principles for community archaeology appear to be directly linked to the indigenous rights movement in archaeology, which became prominent in both academic and heritage management in the early 1990s and it was also at this time that community archaeology started to appear in the academic literature in Australia (Greer 1995). The discussions related to the rights of the indigenous and/or native 'communities' to be involved in decisions relating to the treatment of 'heritage' on 'their' land (Layton 1989). Despite the fact the UK is less affected by indigenous rights issues, this political movement non-the-less influenced the practice of archaeology, in its dealings with the public.

It could be suggested that the development of community archaeology in Australasia and North America was a response to the growing legislative guidelines that surrounded the practice of archaeology in the field and these guidelines were a bi-product of 'post-colonial guilt' (Copper 2006). These guidelines including the ICOMOS Burra Charter (1999), the Australian Heritage commission 'Ask First' document (2002), and NAGPRA (1990) amongst others, were related to the ethics of doing archaeological work, and the importance of archaeologists communicating their work and engaging with indigenous 'communities' prior to, during and after their work is complete.

Contrary to the above, it could be argued that this new approach allowed archaeology to become easier to manipulate politically, as the controls and scientific standards of archaeology declined. Furthermore, the archaeological profession lost sight of what was important to archaeology, including preservation and protection of the physical heritage, with these multiple interpretations confusing the public rather than educating and informing them (Hems 2006). This relativist approach has been blamed for a decline in public tradition and culture, corroding morals and leading to a belief in nothing. In general, values became viewed in the same light as beliefs and accepted without question, as they were personal (Blackburn 2006, 4). This meant that no decisions could be made about what was important in heritage and archaeology, as everyone had equally valuable views: 'the dogma of self belief'. During this period there was a lack of conviction due to a lack of belief in absolute values within the heritage profession. There was a belief that there was not truth within society, and subsequently the public and the archaeologists became confused as to their roles, and what archaeology was, and its relevance in modern society.

2.6 Politics, Philosophy and Post-Processualism from a United Kingdom Perspective

In the United Kingdom the relativist philosophical paradigm was one which influenced the leadership of the Labour government. With the shift in power from Conservative to Labour government in 1997, their focus was on politically and socially embracing multiculturalism (this forms the primary component of the relativist stance), and this brought changes to heritage agendas (Pluciennik 2001).

Labour claimed to be socialist, with every 'citizen' equal. There was the development of the idea of the active citizen, and citizenship, which was about personal choices, and a more socially inclusive agenda (Merriman 2004, 4). Archaeology was directly influenced by internal political changes and political agendas, even if there was not a formal political archaeological agenda. There were agendas of inclusivity, community and more socially-determined spending, with the Heritage Lottery Fund becoming the principal funding body for the heritage sector, taking away much of the financial burden and direct responsibility away from the government. It was in reality a new quango; whilst finances came from private money (a percentage of lottery sales), the agendas were largely controlled by the government. Money was therefore allocated to projects based on their inclusively and wider public values. Power was increasingly being taken away from government quangos like English Heritage, which by 2003, saw its budget cut by almost a third, with claims being made that it was insular, and failed to represent the people, in many senses regarded as too authoritarian (Taylor 2007, 42).

The change of government from Conservative to New Labour in 1997 had direct impacts on the practice of archaeology (Pitts 2007). Local government's control of spending on heritage was reduced due to financial pressure, in preference for more centralised control of funds, and therefore more government control over the heritage sector. This meant projects like Leicestershire's community archaeology programme were cut, and jobs were combined in order to make heritage more cost effective; the local benefits were overlooked (Liddle pers. comm). Furthermore projects now had to qualitatively justify themselves through social inclusivity (Swain 2007, 284).

This centralisation of heritage during the 90s related to the Labour government's additional European 'agenda' of a 'European identity'; archaeology moved away from the development of research based on local archaeology in order to establish a more federal identity, based on common European origins (Pluciennik 2001). This included European funding for archaeological research on the Bronze Age in Europe, which saw extensive research to link the European nations in prehistory. By 1999 the Council of Europe had set up the Europae Archaeologiae Consilium, which has a pan-European advisory role in the management of archaeological heritage.

The government had an implicit agenda for archaeology, one of education and subject to wider public accountability (Lock 2004). The heritage industry was required to justify the government funding archaeology received (Acenture 2006, 6; Schadla-Hall 1999, 152). This brought about a new focus on the 'value' of heritage to a wider social sphere (Hewison and Holder 2006; Swain 2007, 284), one that had to be understood in terms of diverse 'communities' of people and coming from the grass roots up (Selkirk 1997). Archaeology had become a public service rather than just a luxury and leisure activity, one that required justification beyond a simple cost benefit principle (Carman 2003, 45).

It was under relativist Labour agendas that community archaeology first appeared in political literature. Its first appearance was in 2003, when the All Party Parliamentary Archaeological Group, under guidance from the Council for British Archaeology, published its guidelines on the state of archaeology in the United Kingdom (APPAG 2003). In this document there was a section entitled 'Community Archaeology and Tourism', which set out the values of community archaeology, and furthermore encouraged this as a valuable local asset (2003, 45, 50). It was three years later when community archaeology was first mentioned in government documents, such as English Heritage's (2006) 'Heritage Counts', which had a section dedicated to community archaeology. Community archaeology became a prominent component in political speeches. The previous ministers for culture, David Lammy (2006) and Tessa Jowell (2006), both highlighted and supported the benefit of 'community archaeology projects'. As a result the Department of Culture, Media and Sport funded the Portable Antiquities Scheme, which was described as 'the country's largest community archaeology project' (Museum, Libraries and Archives 2005).

Despite the appearance of 'community archaeology' in political literature none of these sources has ever defined what it meant. Who is the community they are referring to? Furthermore, what does community archaeology involve? The broadness of this definition is reflected when one analyses Heritage Lottery Fund projects. If one surveys web-based research of projects falling under the banner of 'community archaeology', hundreds of projects fall under the categorisation of community archaeology ranging from the restoration of a country house, to a community theatre, to the more traditionally accepted activity of archaeological excavation. It appears community archaeology's definition in the political arena is not governed by strict categorisation. It can be described as meaning anything relating to heritage, which, however intangible, involves the 'community.'

In reality, the development of community archaeology in the political arena could serve as a smoke-screen to distract attention from an actual decline of public participation in archaeology; it could be argued that the public interest in archaeology was inadequately catered for by the archaeological profession. The use of the phrase 'community archaeology' serves to mask some people's belief of what archaeology has become: 'you can look, you can touch, but it's getting harder to join in' (Parker Pearson 2001, 226). Recent heritage literature by the government and professional archaeologists has shifted from referring to amateur archaeologists to describing them as the public, and, more recently, the community, including all people who are not within the archaeological profession. It is interesting to note that many amateurs would still view themselves as being archaeologists, and actually might resent simply being viewed as general members of the community. This indicates the political level at which outreach and engagement works.

2.7 Summary

It is suggested that the development of community archaeology has been helped by a shift from 'processual' to 'post-processual' archaeology, along with political changes in the United Kingdom. It was spurred on by worldwide debates in post-colonial contexts; principally indigenous rights movements, and ethical considerations required for working with such communities. Therefore, it has also been about a philosophical shift in the balance of power and control.

Community archaeology claims to mediate power and control between groups that exist within the hypothetical and vague framework of the community (Banks 1997, 1). These groups could be categorised into academics, professionals, amateurs, interested public and uninterested public. Each of these can have agency in the creation of community archaeology projects. Many of these groups, principally through professional and amateur interplay, attempt to have a commonality of values in support for community archaeology. Often these views are then mistaken for the views of the community as a whole, masking the divisions and maintaining control by specific groups rather than balancing it.

3. THE CHARACTER AND PARAMETERS FOR COMMUNITY ARCHAEOLOGY IN UNITED KINGDOM TODAY

3.1 What is Community Archaeology?

"Archaeology 'is a minority interest" (Fowler 1986, 6)

Academically, 'community archaeology' has been broadly defined as partnerships between archaeologists and the communities (Marshall 2002). They are about opening up dialogues between the archaeologists (the minority) and the communities they work within (the majority). The intention of this approach is to enable the creation of more appropriate and culturally relevant interpretations of the past. Critically, the approach requires the archaeologist to relinquish at least 'partial control of the archaeological process to the communities' (Marshall 2002).

The development of community archaeology could stem from, academic discourse rather than heritage manage-ment. Theoretically, it reflects a post-colonial and post-processual mindset towards archaeological interpretation first advocated in academic literature (Hodder 2001; Trigger 1996). It is the practical implication of this discourse though that has been at the forefront of heritage management policy for the last twenty years, rather than academic debate. Academics have, in the past, shied away from discussing community or public archaeology; it has failed to be regarded as academically valuable, instead of being seen as a woolly, unscientific, though worthy little add on, if one has time. It has been linked to anthropology and social sciences, rather than archaeology.

Community archaeology promotes a more flexible, open and anthropological approach to heritage management, which is contextually specific. Perhaps this is why academic archaeologists (particularly in Europe and non colonial contexts) have failed to enter into this debate, whilst, in the new world, concepts and thoughts about the past that relate to contemporary controversies are incorporated into the interpretation and practice of

archaeology. This was especially true in the practice of archaeology in Australia and America, where, due to native rights issues, and non western concepts of time and space, has required archaeology to have closer links to anthropology than purely academic history or science. Marshall (2002) comments on the lack of community archaeology papers submitted from Europe to the journal *World Archaeology*. This does not, by any means, reflect a lack of thought, rather that community archaeology is to many Europeans confusing because its contextual and relativist implications work against scientific rigidity, and often involves letting the community, many with new world beliefs of time and space, interpret the archaeology. This causes tensions as it involves relinquishing control by archaeologists of some of what they are trained to do.

It has been suggested that community archaeology stemmed from political circumstances in the post-colonial world, requiring heritage managers to consider indigenous concepts of the past and incorporate their beliefs and ideas of ownership into the management of archaeology. This requires consideration of the ethics of working with different groups of people to produce an archaeology that is relevant to the multiple values that are placed on it. Yet community archaeology has yet to truly enter the academic arena, it is still very much a sub-discipline that is associated and debated in the heritage management field. Even in the Australasian world, with all its aboriginal rights issues, it has yet to be seen as relevant enough for academic debate or commercial appropriation.

3.2 Approaches

Approaches to the broad meaning of community archaeology have been divided into two categories. Firstly, that of a top down approach (Selkirk 1997), where archaeologists with pre-determined research agendas enter into consultation within the communities they intend to work with. This approach is perceived as being ethically accountable, as it takes into consideration the community in a reflexive approach to interpretation and communication of archaeological findings. Within this approach, community archaeology's scope is very broad, and is still managed by professional archaeologists and subsequently this is the most common application of 'community archaeology' in both the United Kingdom and worldwide. An example of this type of work is Moser *et al's* (2002), work in Qusier, Egypt. The publication of this research has provided a case study which many other projects use as a model. This is, in part, due to the methodological guidelines that Moser *et al* (2002) set out in their *World Archaeology* paper, listing the seven conceptual methods for implementing successful and sustainable community archaeology projects (Moser *et al* 2002, 202):

1. Communication and collaboration with local community

2. Employment and training for local community

3. Public presentation in an appropriate and accessible manner of findings to local community.

4. Interviews and oral history conducted with local community in order to aid interpretation and make archaeology more relevant in the present

5. Education resources produced to enable continued education after the end of the archaeological project.

6. Photographic and video archive in order to record maximum information in the most relevant medium.

7. Community controlled merchandising, to provide economic and continued economic support in area.

Whether specifically acknowledged or not, these principles are apparent in numerous other community archaeology projects, including the work of Pope and Mills (2007), with native communities in Canada and 'Dig Manchester' in the United Kingdom (Tully 2007). This approach is often one in which archaeologists fight against balancing processual scientific rigidity, with involving the community in a more anthropological, post-processual and flexible approach.

This approach engages the community by involving them in part of the process of archaeology, mainly that of finds processing, the presentation of the results and, in some circumstances, excavation. It does, therefore, not require the community to be involved in the entirety of the archaeological process and archaeologists are selective in what the community are 'able' to be involved in. The community, to some extent, are still excluded in the setting of the initial research agendas; ultimately the archaeologists, the outsiders, are still in control and have the control of the past. One has to question whether this externally-controlled archaeology is really 'community archaeology' or could it be more appropriate defined as 'community consultation archaeology', or merely an archaeological public relations exercise.

The second approach, 'community based archaeology,' has been advocated by Greer (1995; 2002) amongst others, in recent years. This approach is one in which all aspects of the archaeological project are controlled, at least in part, by the community themselves. The community sets the research agendas, although the archaeologists advise in this process, and all aspects of the project are controlled through consultation with the community. Often archaeologists, in these circumstances, are working for the communities. This approach is also referred to as a bottom-up approach (Marshall 2002; Faulkner 2000). This approach is more flexible in its methodology than the seven principles of the top-down approach, it does, though, have similar aims. Both approaches focus on communication, with the agenda, and methodology being set by local people as appropriate to their values, rather than primarily the research values of the archaeologists (Moshenska *et al* 2007).

An example of this bottom up approach is Liddle's (1989) work with amateurs in Leicestershire, where the County Council set up a community archaeology programme in response to the calls from amateur archaeological societies wanting to be more proactive in their local historical and archaeological heritage. The archaeologists supported rather than controlled the local community, although at times the balance of power shifted back to the archaeologists. Some of the Sedford projects rather than promoting democracy became personal projects, where the community merely served a purpose in doing research. Communities and archaeologists are in danger of becoming political and academic pawns, involving potential conflict. Therefore there is need for a definitive ethical code of conduct for such work.

Crosby's (2002) work in Fiji provides an example of how archaeologists can be used for a communities' political and economic purposes. The archaeologists were commissioned and subsequently controlled by the community. The local community wanted economic benefit as well as reinforcing control over their traditions, land and cultural beliefs through archaeology (Crosby 2002, 375). Therefore the archaeologists were "allowing the community to make heritage what they will, not merely paying lip-service to the idea of community archaeology" (Crosby 2002, 376), yet this led to the manipulation of archaeological data to serve a purpose. This case study opens the debate as to why there is a need for wider academic debate about community archaeology. This may also require self-awareness from community archaeologists, as to the dangers and ethics of their work, and the conflicts and misuse of relinquishing control, which could serve partisan political agendas.

At La Trobe (Australia) there was political and economic motivation for appearing to relinquish control to local/indigenous communities (Murray 1998). It was claimed that indigenous communities were given control of the work on Bend Road, Eastlink Freeway project, Melbourne, and were used as the archaeological labour force, but in reality control was never fully relinquished. When the community requested to sieve the soil to recover all sacred objects, they where not given permission by the archaeologists and developers, on the grounds of time constraints and cost implications (Murray. pers. comm.).

It is questionable whether community archaeology can really ever be bottom up, and democratic. When one analyses the community archaeology projects in the United Kingdom, it appears that all projects, even when initiated within the community, are instigated and controlled by a minority of interested parties within the community, i.e. amateur groups or a locally resident archaeologist, rather than the whole community. This brings us back to the Fowlers concept of archaeology as a 'minority interest' (1986, 6).

Community archaeology projects have come to include both the tangible and intangible, moving away from the traditional western comforts of the visual and physical being the primary concern of archaeology (Munjeri 2008). Approaches to community archaeology are complex, and they can often, despite consultation and communication, have very different agendas and values for the community and the archaeologists. It has been advocated that the focus of community archaeology should be about weaving these together, accepting different viewpoints, values and interpretations, and accepting the community's right to appropriate the archaeological findings (Fredericksen 2002).

3.3 'Public Archaeology' or 'Community Archaeology'

Community archaeology first appeared in archaeological discussion, in the field archaeology magazine RESCUE, in an article by Liddle (1981, 8). He was commenting on the practicalities of involving the public in field archaeology and the potential benefit, but even Liddle was unsure why he used the phase community archaeology (Liddle pers. comm.). The phrase 'community archaeology' took a further ten years to appear in a formal academic discussion in the United Kingdom (Walker 1988; Start 1999), and did not appear in practice until 1995 with the opening of the Archaeological Resource Centre in York (Jones 2004; 1995).

The first book entitled *'Public Archaeology'* (McGimsey 1972), was based on an American perspective of archaeological practice, under the more general banner of 'Cultural Resource Management'. This recognised the need of archaeologists to provide a public service, through public awareness of, and engagement in, archaeological work, but perhaps most importantly the

need to encompass the public's values and ideas (McGimsey 1972).

Two interesting points arise from this, firstly the length of time these ideas took to trickle into archaeological practice and, secondly, that the United States were some ten years ahead of the United Kingdom in the practical application of public/community archaeology programmes. An early example from the US is in Alexandria, Maryland, where in 1976 Pamela Cressey initiated work an urban community archaeology programme, although it was not until 1987 that is was formally credited with this title (Cressey *et al* 2002, 2). Interestingly, academic discussion of public archaeology in the United States, was also well ahead of the UK. In Maryland University graduate programmes involving public archaeology date back to the 1980s (Leone *et al* 1987), whilst in the UK the first formal public archaeology programme started in 1999 at the Institute of Archaeology, University College London.

The analysis of the literature discussing the practice of public archaeology suggests a similarity in many of the core concepts that underpin both public archaeology and community archaeology (McGimsey 1972; 1984; Jameson 2004; Merriman 2004). It could be asserted that community archaeology developed out of public archaeology, one phrase merely replacing the other. The reasoning behind this change from 'public' to 'community' has yet to be assessed academically, and both are used interchangeably. It could be suggested that the change was related to a shift in the political climate. The government attempted to show an increased awareness and inclusion of peoples' views and implying they had more influence over politics. *'Public'* was replaced with the more politically appealing, and governmentally friendly, all-encompassing buzzword *'community'*, which aimed to indicate homogeneity of aspirations of the whole community. This movement also represented a desire for a more active role for people outside the archaeology profession and an attempt to move away from the misrepresentation of public archaeology as merely a form of outreach rather than true collaboration. Where once there were university courses, conferences, books and journals entitled 'public archaeology', in the last four years there was a shift towards the use of 'community archaeology', with in 2006, a plethora of conferences on the subject, at the University of Manchester, University College London, and sessions run at TAG, EAA and IFA. Despite this change, the agendas of community archaeology are still largely similar to those of public archaeology.

3.4 Legislation

The process of 'doing' archaeology, and specifically archaeological excavation, has become increasingly exclusive in nature. There has been an exclusion of the public (the majority) by the minority (the archaeological profession; Fowler 1986, 7). This exclusion has ironically led to a plethora of new guidelines advocating an increase in inclusion. To date, these seem too merely to serve as a smoke-screen, behind which the archaeological profession can hide its failure to be inclusive and give the amateurs what they most desire: 'to dig'.

The international guidelines are carefully worded and appear to advocate inclusivity whilst in reality keeping control and power in the hands of 'professional' archaeologists. The Delhi Convention (1956) was drawn up believing that the preservation of monuments from past required the respect and affection from the peoples themselves (1956). This was to be achieved through developing common principles and standards, driven by research and science. Yet, in reference to involvement of these peoples, it advocated only for 'the participation of students in *certain* excavations.' Carefully placed words were added giving archaeologists an excuse and/or justification for exclusion of the public and subsequently from the people that this convention was supposed to represent and understand. The Valletta Convention (1992: 9, ii) appears to promote a more balanced relationship with increased inclusivity: "to promote public access to important elements of its archaeological heritage", yet earlier in article 3 it requires that government agencies "ensure that excavations and other potentially destructive techniques are carried out only by qualified, specially authorised people", again advocating that professionally trained archaeologists are the only people capable of excavating, and subsequently, rather than promoting active public engagement, it merely suggests access to the process.

When one scrutinizes the heritage guidelines in the United Kingdom it is apparent that, although by no means the most publicly exclusive country, it is still falls short of the democratic inclusivity Australasian guidelines suggest. Therefore, despite the increased provision in documents, including Valletta, to justify public exclusion on grounds of suitable qualification, it has moved away from socially elitist exclusivity, and is directing itself, if only slightly, towards more democratic inclusivity.

> *"The archaeologist should be prepared to allow access to sites (but) at suitable times and under controlled conditions, within limitation laid down by the funding agency or by the owners, or the tenants of the site or by considerations of safety and well being of the site"* (IFA 1995, 16)

There are legitimate limitations to public access related to health and safety or protection of the heritage, but frequently these are misused by archaeologists as get out clauses, enabling them to eliminate public participation on site. Despite being advocated for, public involvement is not the primary consideration of many archaeologists in the field.

Increased exclusion could be accounted for by the introduction of Planning Policy Guidance 16 in 1990, which altered the practice of archaeology beyond recognition. Whilst local planning committees still rule on PPG16 related planning conditions, the work is now undertaken by commercial units that are often not local and may exclude local professional, amateur and academic groups. There is also significant non-local influence from quangos and other large funding bodies, e.g. HLF, for public funded archaeology. With PPG16 also came mounting bureaucracy which is part of the reason for the increasing exclusion of the public (Parker Pearson 2001).

The archaeological community is coming under increasing pressure to justify its public spending, and the rights of the taxpayers ("the community") are becoming increasing prominent, especially in a time when public spending and funding for arts is decreasing, with English Heritage's, Heritage Lottery Fund's and MLA's budgets being cut by approximately a third (English Heritage 2006; Faulkner 2008). The government increasingly questions the right of archaeology to receive funding, when the claims of social responsibility could be perceived as overstated, and, in reality, archaeologists like many others in the arts and humanities sectors have been carrying out significant work with public money to fulfil their personal or professional research agendas, rather than taking into account those of the wider community; critically this could include the University of Exeter's Community Landscape Project, which was funded by the HLF, but was in practice instigated and designed to meet the personal research agendas of the academic project managers. For almost thirty years archaeologists have discussed and recognised the need for the practice of archaeology to be more externally mindful, and providing a public service rather than just a knowledge base (McGimsey 1972).

The archaeology profession is coming under increasing scrutiny to justify expenditure and 'value' of their work to the majority, by both governments (Lammy 2006) and often even the public themselves (community member. pers comm.). The need for 'community' involvement in heritage is taking prominence in heritage literature (English Heritage 2006; APPAG 2003). Despite this recognition there is still an overt failure and reluctance by many archaeologists to involve the community in the entirety of the archaeological process, including excavations. Even with this general failure to be inclusive, the archaeological profession is still making claims that archaeology lacks sufficient funding from the Department of Media, Culture and Sport (Catling 2007). Archaeologists need much stronger justifications for such claims when the subject is still failing, in the majority of cases (with the possible exception of the media, e.g. Time Team), to involve and engage the people who are paying for the archaeology.

4. VALUES, IDENTITY AND PRACTICE IN COMMUNITY ARCHAEOLOGY

4.1 Community Archaeology and Identity

The deconstruction of community archaeology requires as a prerequisite an understanding of what is meant by community. Ascherson (2000) suggests this still needs further definition; at present the boundaries are blurred. The archaeological literature (Ascherson 2000; Marshall 2002; Schadla Hall 1999; Smith and Waterton 2009) has failed to define 'communities' in terms of what they constitute, so, in one respect have failed to define what and for whom community archaeology is intended.

In essence, is there a point in using the term without defining the boundaries more clearly? It could be that the boundaries are ones that archaeologists impose to differentiate themselves from the general public (Swain 2007). This categorisation can produce its own problems, a 'them and us' mentality', creating the idea of division and increasing the potential for conflict. This directly contrasts with the naive but often politically and academically accredited ideal of one homogenous group of people sharing ideas, desires, and beliefs. If this concept of homogeneity were to become widely accepted there would be no acknowledgement of cultural diversity within communities, or the agency of individuals, who's differing values bring much to the activity of community archaeology.

The academic literature suggests that people view the past differently (Smith 2004; Carman 1996; 2003); and all these differences should be incorporated in the interpretation and presentation of the past, especially as these views are a reflection of personal values and, therefore, highly emotive (Schadla Hall 2004; Hodder 2000; 1986). Encompassing these different values allows archaeology to become more accessible to a wider, and more diverse, audience (Hodder 2000). This is a morally valid argument, and the understanding of different values is essential to understanding how archaeology is understood and interpreted. This is not to suggest that some generalisations should not be made, just that these should not be based on the idea that all individuals share

values as a single homogenous 'community', or, perhaps controversially, that all values and interpretations are equally valid (Schadla Hall 2004).

Some values and views are dangerous and conflicting, for example values placed on the past relating national and ethic identity (Meskell 1998; Erikson 1993; Banks 1997). Numerous case studies have proved these can have fatal consequences (Meskell 1998; Dennell 1997; Härke 2002; Arnold & Hessmenn 1993). An obvious and widely documented example of this is Nazi abuse of archaeology to genocidal ends (Härke 2002; Arnold & Hessmenn 1993, 70). It was not just the archaeological evidence that was manipulated to support nationalist agendas, but academics also became political pawns, often willingly, as funding, staff, research and curriculum were all controlled by the Nazi state (Arnold & Hessmenn 1993, 71)

More recently, the case of Ayodhya, India, highlighted the fatal consequences of religious exploitation of heritage (Hassan 1995, 874). In this case, the deliberate political use of the past by professional archaeologists for religious agendas caused riots and deaths (Layton & Wallace 2006, 65; Tierney 1998). A battle ensued between academic archaeologists, Hindus and Muslims, each claiming rights to the site of Ayodhya through the use of the material remains. More importantly it became a matter of which religion held more legitimacy through longevity of existence within the region (Serrill 1998). In 1993 this debate led to the Muslim temple, which allegedly stood on the earlier Hindu temple, being razed to the ground during riots that killed hundreds of people (Tierney 1998). During the World Archaeology Congress in 1994, these tensions formed part of the discussion (even though delegates were formally asked not to discuss the issues surrounding the site), and could be cited as having a direct impact on the site's future (Tierney 1998). As a result, much of the site has been levelled and cordoned off in order to prevent future riots and further research has been restricted (Serrill 1998; Tierney 1998).

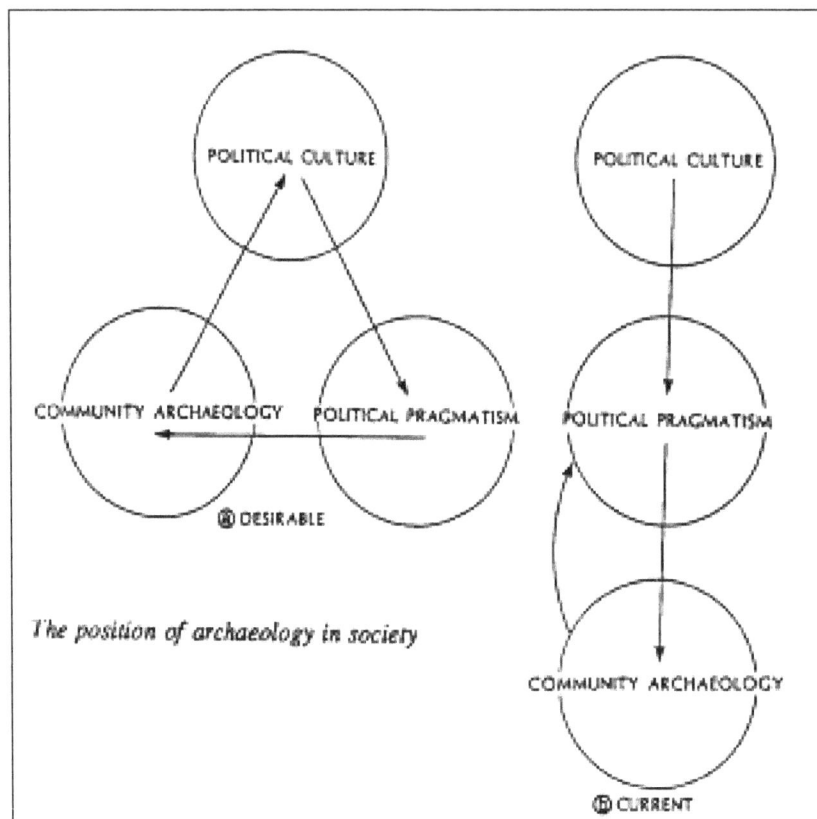

Figure 4.1 Diagram of the position of archaeology in society showing desirable versus current (taken from Walker 1988)

Therefore, ethically and morally, archaeologists have a responsibility towards objective consideration of values (Scarre and Scarre 2006). This aim, often a form of compromise, is essential to enable an understanding and practical management of the past, and therefore also to the running of community archaeology projects. Subsequently, it has to be considered if the Marxist ideal of equality of values is unrealistic, idealistic and potentially dangerous, especially when those values are based on religious or political claims, which include those of Nazi Germany in the 1930s.

In the United Kingdom there have been numerous references to the community in political texts. This is primarily in relation to heritage, and the need to represent 'community' values (Lammy 2006). Each time the phrase 'community' is used it has a political context, creating an idea of unity and national identity, an entity, which appears on the surface to be stable. Therefore, 'community' often appears in these political texts under the banner of 'Britishness' and 'the 'British community' (Lammy 2006; Brown 2006 (http://news.bbc.co.uk/1/hi/uk_politics/4611682.stm). Consequently, it has been suggested that the phrase 'community' has been used as a form of identity creation (Anderson 1983) rather than, as many politicians and academics suggest, as merely identity affirmation (English Heritage 2000; Jones 1997; Erikson 1993, 2). If this is so, community archaeology in

the United Kingdom might be more determined and controlled by political ethos and pragmatism, rather than public views of heritage having influence over political thought and actions (Walker 1988, 55; see figure 4.1).

'Community archaeology', is a politically engineered concept, with broader issues running through its core. Therefore, the context in which the words 'community' and 'community archaeology' are used determine their meaning. Community could, and does, relate to a local, national or international communities, and to both cultural and geographic divisions (Smith and Waterton 2009). Its broadness leaves the definition open to interpretation, confusion and misuse. The term is used to simplify the complexity of identities within a region, and, in doing so, the values placed on the past appear to be more geographically specific. Community archaeology becomes a localised activity with a focus on a specific 'community' of people, whether or not there is a single, cohesive group of residents.

The term community archaeology has become so politicised it has to be questioned whether archaeologists practicing community archaeology merely then serve as the henchmen of the politicians (Layton 1989; Scarre and Scarre 2006) and the communities involved in these projects are merely political pawns. It is important that archaeologists are self-critical and reflexive about why

VALUES, IDENTITY AND PRACTICE IN COMMUNITY ARCHAEOLOGY

they are conducting community archaeology, and the potential implications of their work. Also it is essential not to discount the potential benefit of community archaeology merely because it is politicised.

The focus of recent literature has been on how public archaeology, and in turn community archaeology, has been created by archaeologists, academics and politicians, as an all embracing phrase usually applied to indicate involvement of anyone from outside the archaeological profession in archaeological activities (Merriman 2004; Swain 2007). To archaeologists and politicians, un-public and community-less archaeology focuses on the tangible remains, on projects that are initiated and carried out by people outside the community they work within i.e. by the professionally trained archaeologists. Primarily these are commercial projects that actively exclude the community from the tangible archaeological remains through physical and mental barriers. Yet for those who are not archaeologists, archaeology is simply about their past, their heritage. Archaeology plays a part in everyone's life whether it is tangible or intangible; and it does not matter whether the term 'public' or 'community' is used. The terms community and public archaeology merely serve to reflect the importance that involvement with the past brings to all and so, by labelling the activity, credibility is gained.

4.2 Values of Community Archaeology

As discussed previously, the involvement of the public in archaeology is at community archaeology's core. This can only be enabled through understanding the communities' attitudes and the values they place on their heritage and their archaeology. In order to understand and assess these specific local values it is important to consider the literature relating to the more general analysis of the values attached to heritage.

Academics, including Bender (1998) and Holtorf (2005a; 2006), have suggested that it is vital that archaeologists start to understand the multitude of attitudes towards heritage and the past, not just from an internal professional and political viewpoint, but from an external, dynamic perspective of non-professionals (Hodder 1986). Bender's (1998) work on Stonehenge and Jones's (2004) work in Scotland indicate that this needs to be considered in relation to the public's attitude towards 'their' heritage, encompassing a broader definition of heritage including both the tangible and intangible (Thomas, J 2004). Consideration of multiple values of what the past holds to different people is something that is becoming increasingly prominent in academic and political literature (Jowell 2006; 2005; Holtorf 2005b; Schadla-Hall 2004; Thomas J, 2004).

Hewison (1987) and Lowenthal (1989) were amongst the first to discuss the complexities of people's attitudes to the past. Many of these initial ideas were drawn from

outside archaeology, from disciplines including social anthropology and psychology (Hendry 1999). Although these authors showed an awareness of the potentially different values and attitudes towards the past, they skirted over the complexity of these attitudes and how they could impact on the interpretation and management of archaeology. This idea of complexity in the perception of the past and its values appears to be reflected in theoretical archaeological literature (Binford 1983; Hodder 1986; Shanks & Tilley 1987; Trigger 1989). Academics use this idea to justify not having to explain the multitude of theoretical discourses at the roots of heritage values, particularly those that were outside the realms of the archaeological profession (Lammy 2006).

More recently literature has failed, with the exception of Lipe (1984; 2007), Darvill (1995), Howard (2003), Thomas, R (2004), and to some extent Shennan (1988), to undertake an in-depth discussion of the multitude of attitudes towards heritage, rather they have chosen to focus on one (Layton 1989; Ucko 1989; Smith and Waterton 2009). To date, the debate has primarily focused on nationality and its politics. In more recent years this focus has shifted to the economic value of heritage, in order to make heritage more politically and commercially cost effective (Schadla-Hall 1999), for example Crosby's recent work in Fiji (2002, 362). This work has highlighted the potential for archaeology to increase economic growth through greater work opportunities and a rise in house prices and tourism (Cabe 2004)

There has been an increasing awareness of the value and power of education (Mackenzie & Stone 1990, 4). The value of archaeology in education has been heavily emphasised in numerous articles (Henson 2004; Hills 2001; Schadla-Hall 1999; Pearson 2001), the majority of which have focused on formal learning, rather than the informal learning that is more likely to take place during the visit to heritage site, which is less easily measured. Formal learning is easier to assess, as it is prescribed and taught through classroom methodologies i.e. learning in schools, colleges and universities (see figure 4.2). Informal learning, on the other hand, is learning by watching, doing, thinking and feeling (Whitaker 1995, 7); it is more diverse, flexible and often lacking methodology, subsequently more difficult to assess.

Teaching of the past should be approached with care; education is an important tool for the translation and appropriation of archaeology (Mackenzie & Stone 1990). Formal education has been accused of teaching a false, simplified and stereotypical view of specific groups of people in the past (Mackenzie & Stone 1990, 1). Archaeology is, in the UK, usually taught as part of history, mainly Key Stage 1 and 2 in national curriculum, and subsequently as fact, rather than a jumble of facts, myths and interpretation. There are problems with teaching archaeology as a separate discipline, with theory suggesting that to achieve objectivity it needs to be taught alongside, or together with, other subjects, including

Figure 4.2 Classroom teaching of Archaeology.
(Faye Simpson)

geography and history as part of the national curriculum (Pearson 2001; Henson 2004; Mackenzie & Stone 1990, 11; Henson 1997). This incorporation to date has largely failed (with the exception, for example of Cranborne Chase Ancient Technology Centre) despite efforts from the archaeological community (Henson 2004). On the contrary A-Levels, GCSE's and GNVQ's in archaeology have been dropped in recent years by all but the Assessment and Qualifications Alliance (AQA) examination board (Jones, D. 2004, 41). At, with a present, approximately 82 colleges offering A/AS level Archaeology (Jones, D. 2004, 41; www.hotcourses .com). It is worth mentioning that the IfA are pushing for archaeology to be brought back and have introduced a higher-level NVQ in archaeology. Blame for this rests at least in part through lack of communication from archaeologists to teachers (Henson 2004, 26). This has now been realised and archaeologists are increasingly trying to link the subject into other national curriculum subjects, with the new subject of citizenship being seen as key to this (Henson 2004, 27).

Informal learning which is often unscheduled and impromptu, including the learning you get from visiting an archaeological site or museum in your leisure time, watching an archaeology television programme or attending community archaeology excavations. This has been more successfully recognised than formal learning, in essence, as archaeology is still perceived as a luxury subject (Bahn 1996, 6). Informal learning programmes require less justification, but these are fun and relaxed and therefore appeal to a broader audience (Stone 2004, 8). Despite this, it is worth noting the decline in non-credit-bearing continuing and adult (life-long) learning courses in University in recent years, as these appear financially unattractive to many universities. The overall success of informal educational activities has been indicated in the research by the work done by the Council of British Archaeology's Young Archaeology Club (Stone 2004, 7), which has indicated a growing number and increased

diversity amongst members. This success could be related to YAC's broader aims beyond merely teaching knowledge. It has recognised the multiple values of archaeology and therefore aims to 'developed inquisitive and well rounded young people' (Henry 2004, 99).

Some of the problems and political tensions that have arisen are a direct result of the neglect by many archaeologists in educating through communication, including mass media, to the public about the past and recent archaeological discoveries (Clack & Britain 2007). Hills (2001) suggests a more profitable way forward would be the introduction of the subject in schools, through incorporating archaeology into pre-existing subjects, a way of helping to legitimise ideas about the profession, as well as helping to promote future understanding. Cleere (1984) adds that it also helps promote understanding and respect for the past. In order to attain this, however, there is a need to have sufficient resources, and the funding of such an enterprise appears to have been overlooked by the government and schools boards despite the realisation of its growing importance (Parker Pearson 2001). Perhaps this is because archaeology's inclusion is not seen as important as issues with literacy and numeracy.

Education is one of the areas most studied when investigating the impact and value of archaeology on the public, because it is believed to be the easiest area to assess quantifiably (Pearson 2001; Smardz 2000; Smardz and Smith 2000). Subsequently, the assessment of value has focused on education rather than the broader values of archaeology to the wider community.

4.3 Values Overview

There are innumerable values attached to the heritage, other than politics, economics or education, that are often contextual, interrelated and socially defined by what is perceived as right and acceptable (Darvill 1995, 302). Lipe (1984; 2007) and Darvill (1995; 1999) have produced some of the most seminal, groundbreaking and pioneering work on the values attached to archaeological heritage (Carver 2007, 33).

Lipe (1984) discusses value as a resource, with past values being used in the present for, and associated with, symbolic, informational, aesthetic and economic reasons (see figure 4.3). Therefore, it is the pasts' functionality in the present that is the critical component in the formation of modern day values. He has therefore divided values into broad categories, using a flow diagram that indicates how these values and their interactions with the heritage should work in the presentation, preservation and management of the past. This diagram, as Lipe himself suggests, is overly simplistic and mechanistic; it fails to indicate, firstly, how values feed into each other and, secondly, the relationships between societal institutions and formal research (Lipe 2007, 291). It does, though,

Preserved Cultural Resources — Preserved material from past cultures: Objects, structures, sites, human landscapes — Public understanding of and appreciation for cultural resources

Societal Institutions — Governmental policies, laws, agencies; educational institutions; societies and interest groups; and businesses devoted to cultural resource preservation and study — Books, articles, films, classes, lectures, museum displays about past cultures

Types of Value — Economic — Aesthetic — Associative/symbolic — Informational

Value Contexts — Economic Potential Market factors; costs of development vs. preservation — Aesthetic Standards Stylistic tradition human psychology, etc. — Traditional Knowledge Historical documents, oral tradition, folklore, mythology, etc. — Formal Research History, archaeology, art and architectural history, folklore studies, etc.

Basic phenomena — Cultural Resource Base Objects, structures, sites, human landscapes surviving from the past

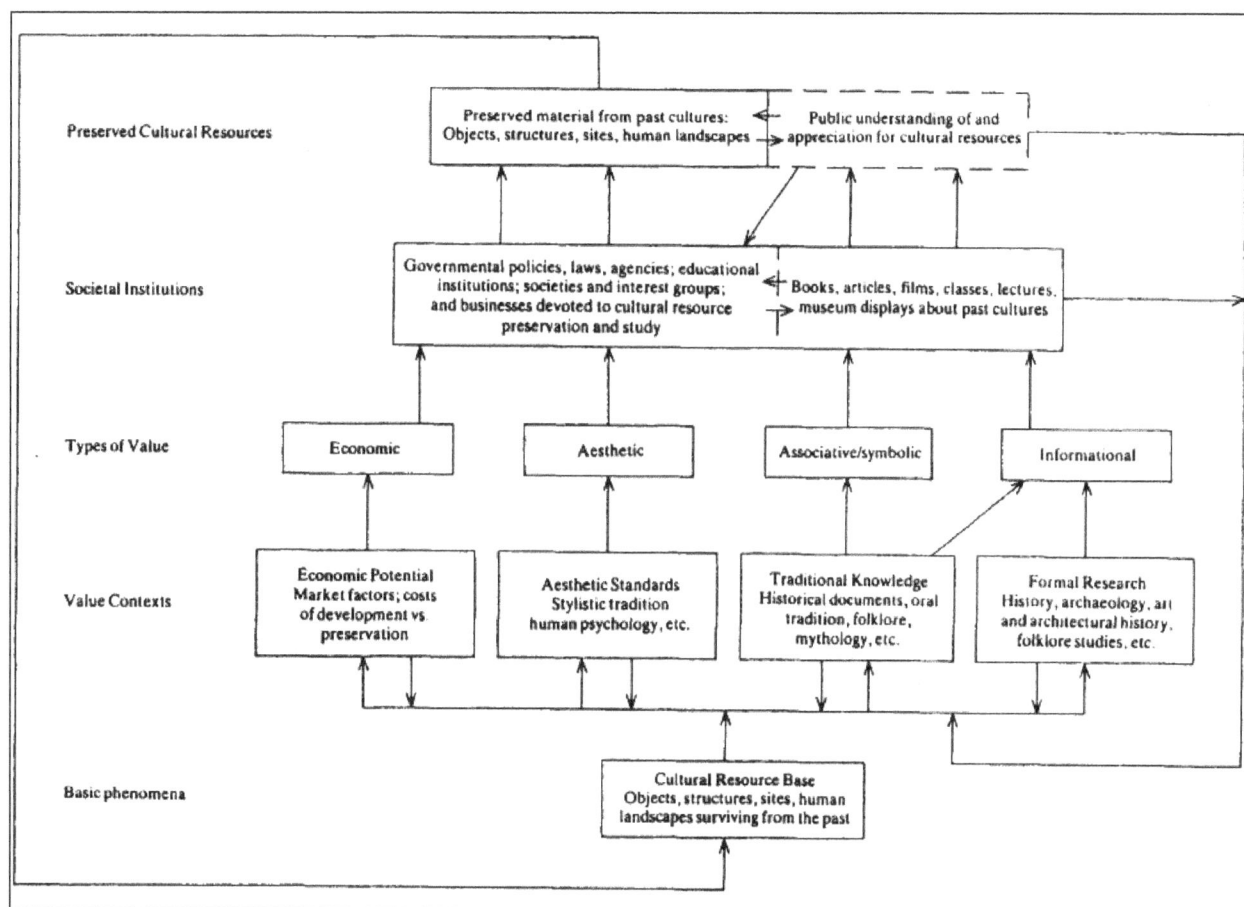

Figure 4.3 Diagram showing values structure (taken from Lipe 2007, 289)

offer a framework and a visual aid to understanding the complexities of values, and how they are part of the system of placing pasts in the present.

Darvill (1995; 1999) builds on Lipe's earlier work (1984) of the identification of values and further divides values into three separate yet interacting systems. Firstly, there is 'use' value, which relates to contemporary construction of the past in the present. These values are tangible and functional, and are therefore often assessed through quantifiable measures, i.e. reduction in crime figures, increased tourism or the production of academic literature (Hewison and Holder 2006). Some examples of these are (after Darvill 1999; Coningham *et al* 2006):

- Archaeological Research: The archaeological resource is used for research, which produces new knowledge about the past, e.g. the excavation of Cumwhitton Norse burial ground, produced internationally important knowledge of Viking age England, and of Viking pagan integration with the Christian native (Simpson 2009).

- Non-Archaeological Scientific Research: Data is collected directly from sites and objects in the past to produce conclusions and knowledge, e.g. the incorporation of archaeological investigations of seismic events in modern risk models (Papazachos *et al.*

1990). Furthermore, archaeological methods can be applied to non-archaeological sites, like forensics to investigate modern day murder scenes (Hunter and Cox 2005).

- Creative Arts: Writers, artists, photographers use and draw inspiration from past monuments e.g. Bernard Cornwall's fictional literature taking inspiration from Stonehenge.

- Education: Archaeological resources provide educational material for schools and higher education i.e. in the form of subject material occasional entering the National Curriculum (Henson 1997) and text books for universities.; Finds handling boxes for schools have been produced by museums and units, such as Canterbury Archaeological Trust (www.canterburytrust.co.uk/schools/catkitpg.htm), and interactive web sites for use in the classroom, such as the Portable Anti-quities Scheme Anglo Saxon Village (www.finds.org.uk)

- Recreation and Tourism: Ancient monuments attract tourists and domestic visitors, and are used as a form of entertainment and recreation activity, e.g. Historic Royal Palace's use of the Tower of London, and English Heritage, of Stonehenge, and, more commercially, Merlin Entertainment Group's use of Warwick

Castle, which along with their archaeological and historical remains provide reconstruction, reinactment, food, and shopping, those encouraging people to visit and stay for the day.

- Symbolic Representation: Archaeological sites, e.g. Stonehenge is used as an iconic image in advertising and logos and for representing the nation.

- Legitimatising Action: Archaeological evidence is often used to support or legitimise political propositions (heritage can be seen to be directly used in government campaigns) (Gathercole and Lowenthal1994), e.g. during the colonial rule of Zimbabwe archaeologists interpreted the Iron Age Settlement to have been built by outsiders (Skeates 2000, 95). After Zimbabwe's independence, the Iron Age settlement site was renamed Great Zimbabwe, and was adopted as a national symbol, becoming the picture on the front of Zimbabwe's currency (Ndoro 1994). It has been used by the politicians on both sides, by colonials as evidence that black indigenous people were incapable of attaining civilisation themselves, and after independence of the great indigenous past before colonial rule, and Zimbabwe's people's right to independence (Skeates 2000, 68).

- Social Solidarity and Integration: Archaeological remains used to bolster social solidarity and promote integration; this is often linked to political usage, e.g. the Museum of London's work, to use archaeological remains at Shoreditch Park, Hackney to promote solidarity and integration of the diverse population, which was used and supported by local government, MP's, the House of Lords and the former Minister for Culture Media and Sport (Atkins and Simpson 2004).

- Monetary and Economic: Looting of archaeological sites for financial gain, i.e., the nighthawking at the Roman cemetery at Kempston, Bedfordshire, (Addyman 1995, 168-9; Skeates 2000, 40). Furthermore, there is selling of illicit artefacts on EBay. Monuments and sites are used to encourage tourism, bolstering local economic, and sites often charge for visits, providing economic support for the maintenance of the site, e.g. York archaeology sites and monuments used in York's Tourism campaign, including the Castle, the walls and Jorvik Viking Centre (Jones 2004; 1995).

The second value system is 'option' value. This is value in the heritage that is produced for future generations, rather than being consumed. These intangible values include stability, timelessness and tradition. It is the value of not knowing the past that creates enigma and mystery. An example of this can be seen in the Druids feeling of connection to Seahenge, and its power to support their claims of timelessness of their beliefs and pagan traditions, even if there is no physical evidence for this (Skeates 2000, 69; Champion 2000).

The third value is 'existence', which provides things with relevance in the present. This is the use of the heritage to produce personal feelings, including wellbeing and contentment. This value is therefore both produced and consumed, perceptual and functional. It creates cultural identity through reference to both the tangible and intangible past, and also creates a resistance to change through the retention of the past and its ideas (Darvill 1999, 303). For example, in Exeter, Devon, the city walls have become connected to civic pride, and a modern symbol of this connection to the past, therefore linked into a feeling of safety and personal identity in the present.

This approach offers promise for the identification of both tangible and intangible values attached to heritage as a whole. It goes some way towards discussing the complexities of evaluation of these values in individual communities (Munjeri, D. 2006). Holtorf (2007) recently suggested that archaeological values are not entirely group, or externally, determined but also created within a specific community and by the individual. This can only be deconstructed through looking at popular perceptions of the past, which can enable an understanding of the individual values of the heritage, its ability to help one to 'find oneself through the creation and affirmation of personal identity from the past' (Holtorf 2005b, 30).

Hewison and Holder (2006, 15) expanded on Darvill's (1995) ideas by deconstructing values into intrinsic, instrumental, and institutional categories. Furthermore, they looked at how values attached to heritage are created by either the public or professionals (see table 4.1 and figure 4.4). This work also touched on which are quantifiable and which are perceived as immeasurable.

Work has so far focused on the identification of the possible outcomes, but has failed to consider how these can be analysed (Hewison and Holder 2006, 27). Heritage literature has suggested that the analysis, and the effectiveness of public and community archaeology on changing the longer term values attached to the past, should take heed of people outside the profession using, for example, public services models (Acenture 2006; Cabe 2006; Hewison and Holder 2006, 27).

In the late 18th century, many academics believed that interest in the past was something innate in everyone, whether consciously or not (Thomas, J. 2004). It was believed by the elite that heritage was something everyone was aware of and, on some level, and therefore needed to be saved for the benefit of all (Cleere 1984). As such, academics claimed that it was their duty to protect this 'heritage', with this being controlled by the minority for the benefit of the majority (Howard 2003). This belief that the heritage was undeniably valuable to everyone, and therefore the State must save and manage it on the public's behalf, led to The Protection of Ancient Heritage act in 1882, with General Pitt Rivers appointed the first inspector of ancient monuments (Cleere 1984, 61). The idea that all people valued their heritage implicitly meant

Table 4.1 Deconstructing and defining values, as identified by Hewison and Holden (2006)

Value	Group	Definition	Example	Quantifiable/ Unquantifiable
Intrinsic (Option, Existence)	Public	Heritage itself, individual experience – intellectual, emotional, spiritual	"This tells me who I am" "This moved me" "This is beautiful"	Unquantifiable
Instrumental (Use)	Professionals/ Policy Makers	Ancillary effect of heritage used to achieve social and economic purposes	Urban regeneration, reduce crime rates.	Quantifiable
Institutional	Professionals	Purposes, techniques that organisations adopt into working practices to 'create' value for people. This value is generated or destroyed by how an organisation engages with their publics.	Working practice and attitudes, notions of for the public good – e.g. antiquarians 19th century English Heritage MLA	Quantifiable

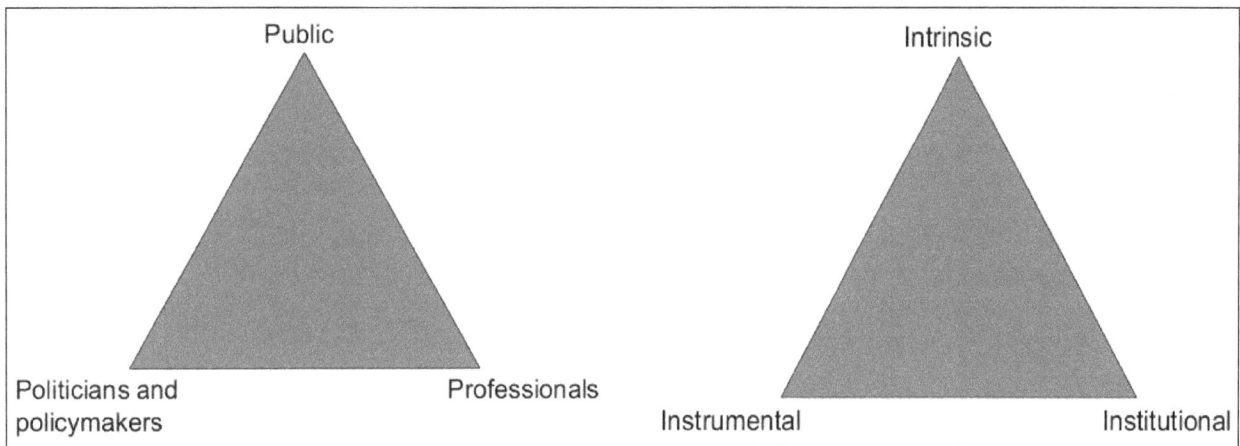

Figure 4.4 The Demos triangle of heritage values and heritage stakeholders (Hewison and Holden 2006, 15-16)

academics needed do no more to investigate that assertion. It could therefore rather simplistically be argued that community archaeology, and the chance to be engaged in archaeology, is something that public would automatically value.

The values and subsequent benefits of public and community archaeology, are becoming increasingly prevalent in academic literature (Howard 2003; Merriman 2004), with the benefits of public and community involvement in archaeology being preached (Ascherson 2000). This has included the use of archaeology as a tool for education (Henson 2004; Thomas, R. 2004), and translating knowledge. There has also been a focus on community archaeology's creation of a 'sense of place' and 'pride' and even its benefits in promoting a sense of community, reducing crime, and providing support for those with mental and physical disabilities: These, though, are externally controlled and promoted values, and not necessarily what is important to the community themselves. More importantly the analysis of this benefit has focused on that which is quantifiable.

The discipline itself is trying to validate this new paradigm of community archaeology. As yet though, no

one has critically accessed what difference community archaeology makes to the community's values and attitudes towards heritage.

4.4 Intangible and Tangible Heritage

'...is history to be considered the property of the participants solely.' (Rustidic 1983, 21)

Many archaeologists, particularly those with western perspectives, claim that the past is created and recreated through its physical discovery in monuments and texts (Smith, L. 2004, 1). If this is the case, then access to physical property controls participation, which is the property of a minority (Cunliffe 1981, 192; Mackenzie and Stone 1990, 11). Alternatively, the past can be regarded as intangible, with 'the spirit taking precedence over substance' (ICOMOS 1995; Smith, L. 2004, 4; Carman 2006). Then history and archaeology should encompass and involve everyone and everything.

It is this concept that is, or at least should be, at the root of community archaeology. The idea of broadening and changing the definition of what archaeology and heritage includes is a shockingly new concept for many professional archaeologists and policy makers. It was not until 1995 and formally in 2003 that it was recognised and accepted that "the intangible had for long been an ignored heritage" (UNESCO 1995, 94). It was in 2003 that UNESCO's strategy for safeguarding intangible cultural heritage (2003) was drawn up and for the first time its importance was recognised. This forced a professional change in the management of heritage. There was a movement away from focusing on the physical values of the past, and preserving and presenting tangible physical remains, to incorporating the intangible values attached to the past in the present. For example, memories, feelings and traditions are used in telling the stories about pasts in the present, and the pasts' interpretation, providing some form of tangibility to these intangible values (Mujeri 2006; Smith, L. 2004, 4). People's relationships with the past and with archaeology were 'seen' as being both intangible, and tangible, both with equal validity, with society's understanding that the tangible can only be understood and interpreted through the intangible (Mujeri 2006, 334). It is these intangible and tangible values and the personal expression of these in physical form that should be at the core of community archaeology. The breath of definition has benefits, but has meant that it has come to mean everything and nothing. This is perhaps why many academic archaeologists are critical of the phrase, and the work which in undertaken in its name.

It could be suggested that the past and, therefore, archaeology should not be prescribed by a westernised mentality, and therefore should not primarily focus on the physical value of the heritage (Carman 2006; 1996). Community archaeology is increasingly not being limited to one particular method or definition, as it is fluid and contextual. Therefore, controlling the past is fraught with problems, as its intangible aspect means it is not the 'sole property' of any elite minority.

4.5 Participatory Fieldwork

By the 19th century the definition of archaeology included 'excavation' as part of the process (Wallace 2001, 12). Today its definition is still restrictive, regarded as "the study of human history and prehistory through the excavation of sites and the analysis of physical remains" (Oxford English Dictionary 2002, 68). A core component of archaeology is the process of excavation and interpretation. It is subsequently interesting then that when archaeologists claim to 'involve' the public or the community or communicate archaeology to a wider audience, they are not generally enabling them to get practically involved in one of the most fundamental activities to archaeology, that of digging.

In recent years, after the decline of amateur excavations and volunteering on archaeological digs, television, including Channel Four's archaeology programme Time Team, is the closest most people will get to experiencing

excavation, watching 'archaeologists' excavating a site from the comfort of their sofas on a Sunday evening (see figure 4.5). High viewing figures (approximately 2.6 million) suggest that, for many members of the public this is sufficient involvement (Piccini and Henson 2006, 14; Taylor 1994), perhaps leading to the supposition that most people do not want to actively participate, but rather enjoy being armchair archaeologists. Alternatively it could be proposed that people are content with this because there is little or no awareness of the alternatives with the exception of some select amateur societies and academic institutions that provide volunteer places on excavations (Ascherson 2003). Critically, TV could be described as creating the illusion of engagement in the subject, but it does not engage people in their past on a physical level. It has, without doubt, been successful in bridging some of the boundaries between archaeologists and the wider community and offered the public an opportunity to experience something new (Jordan 1984; Silberman 1999; Clack and Britain 2007), yet it provides entertainment on a voyeuristic level. This may have been ground breaking ten years ago, but a lack of change in format, or successful new programmes being commissioned, could mean that rather than archaeologists building on the public's potentially increased interested, and possible demand for more interaction, there has been a failure to meet possible public demands and values (Clark and Britain 2007; Gathercole, Stanley and Thomas 2002).

Figure 4.5 Picture of Time Team Excavation:
Lincolns Inn, London. (Faye Simpson)

Interestingly, and possibly of significance, is the recent BBC television programme Restoration, which did not use excavation to communicate and engage audiences in archaeology and heritage. Instead it focused on public restoration, historical and archaeological buildings, and moved away from more tried and tested factual and documentary style programmes like Time Team. Its high viewing figures indicate this non-excavation programme can be successful in engaging and entertaining the public, therefore, potentially indicating the public's interest, values and understanding of archaeology is underestimated

In the last twenty years, there has been a growth in the analysis of the public's perception of archaeology. Statistical research by Lucas (2004) and Merriman (1991) indicates that archaeology is primarily associated with digging. Archaeology's popular image is one of discovery, and of physicality, all of which are positive, and offer an experience and a chance of fulfilling a dream (Lucas 2004, 19). These perceptions are based on stereotypical notions of archaeology, drawn from mass media, but this 'disneyfication' and fantasy is what gives archaeology 'archaeopeal' (Holtorf 2005b; 2006) Yet, despite the growing literature and awareness of what the public want and the building of a positive, if somewhat stereotypical, image of archaeology, some academics and professional archaeologists have criticised the media as misrepresenting a profession (Gathercole et al. 2002) and undermining its painstaking methodology. Such critics want to move away this disneyification, and treasure hunting to a more 'professional' and responsible, portrayal of the entire archaeological process, not just excavation. This would involve a degree of control regarding who is involved in archaeology and what the public see.

Holtorf (2006, 4) suggests that using research from other disciplines can provide evidence and understanding of why excavation could be regarded as so fundamentally important to people, leading him to conclude that excavation is at the very essence of why archaeology is important to people. The deconstruction of recent sociological theories, including Gerhard Schulze's 'The Experience Society' (1993), provides evidence of the changing values in society, suggesting that as western society becomes increasing financially secure, the need to have new experiences 'experience value' take precedence over the former 'monetary value' (Holtorf 2006, 5). Subsequently, some keen people want to be actively involved in archaeology rather than being worried about the cost. Perhaps this explains why members of public are now willing to pay thousands of pounds to go on an excavation. For instance the Earthwatch project at the mammoth site in Hot Springs, South Dakota, charges people $2950 for 15 days excavation on the site (Figure 4.6; www.earthwatch.org/expeditions/ agenboard.htm).

The concept of archaeology and heritage as entertainment is backed up by a travelometer survey (www.tia.org) of why people visit heritage and historic sites in the USA. It concluded that the main reason was entertainment rather than educational (Slicks 2002, 223). The Popcorn Report (Popcorn 1992), offers further insights into the need of archaeology to provide entertainment, escapism and adventure; Holtorf (2006, 5) suggests that archaeology should and could provide for this. I would suggest it offers insight as to what people will want from archaeology in the future, and it will be far removed from the static museum displays of the 19th century (or even

Figure 4.6 Earthwatch Volunteers excavating mammoth site at Hot Springs, South Dakota (Faye Simpson).

21st century): Could community archaeology excavations offer something exciting, and adventurous?

It has been suggested by psychologists and sociologists (Lev Vygotsky's socio-cultural theory) that a fundamental part of the formation of memory, especially on a personal level, involves something practical (Wallace 2001, 15; Johnson 2000, 73-74). Furthermore, Vygotsky stressed that learning was a social activity and that social learning leads to stronger learning (Wallace 2001, 15) This suggests that the practical process of digging could be a crucial part of forming memories and learning about the about the past, making intangible ideas into tangible evidence. This is the concept of excavations as performances in the landscape and therefore 'theatres of memories' (Holtorf and Williams 2006, 249). This is described by Wallace (2001) as 'the seductions of the soil', where no one is immune to the practical approach. This excavation gives rise to the formation of new memories, giving the past an existence in the present (Wallace 2001, 82) and making the past part of the present and providing memories which will remain in the future (Holtorf and Williams 2006).

Archaeology has deeper psychological connotations; perhaps it is also poignant that Sigmund Freud had a passion for (if not also a minor obsession with) archaeology (www.freudmuseum.co.uk; Freud 1961; 1964). It has been suggested that interpretation and involvement in archaeology and the past was a reflection of the desires of the conscious and unconscious mind (Freud 1961, 64). Building on these concepts it could be proposed that the involvement in archaeology could provide a 'displacement for other concerns' (Wallace 2001, 80). It has also been suggested that being involved in the process of digging can offer a sense of 'finding' oneself (Cunliffe 1981, 193). This idea has symbolic and metaphysical significance, with digging providing a route to self discovery, and that one is 'digging' deep to find our own identities and desires, and understand what lies beneath the surface both of the ground and the soul (Holtorf 2005b, 17). It has been proposed that digging can offer a physical process, something 'tangible,' to the psycho-gical and intangible process of revealing ones own mind. If this is the case, excavation is for some a cathartic and a very personal activity (Holtorf 2005b, 30).

The All Party Parliamentary Archaeology Group claimed in 2003 that 'the public's' perception of the purpose and practice of archaeology however, is too narrowly focused on excavation. Perceptions by the public, reinforced by the media, frequently focus on excavation and discovery, as surveys suggest that is what the public want (Picinni & Henson 2006, 14; Merriman 1991). Yet, despite this assertion, it is still the one-thing archaeologists, whether deliberately or not, exclude the public from. The APPAG report (2003) and others (e.g. Hawkins 2000, 201), suggest that archaeologists should encourage the public to engage in alternative participatory activities, to under-stand the historic environment through its most accessible and tangible elements before they are persuaded to 'reach prematurely for their spades and trowels' (Oswold 2007, 20). This work has included standing building surveys, documentary historical research, geophysical surveying and fieldwalking (see figure 4.7).

Figure 4.7 None excavation at Bow Historical Society, finds drop in and historical research day (Faye Simpson)

Case studies of this type of community project can be seen all over the United Kingdom (www.britarch.ac.uk/communityarchaeology), including at Cawood Castle Garth, in North Yorkshire, where the local archaeology group and villagers are researching garden landscapes and context of the village's development by engaging in oral and social history and standing building surveys (Oswold 2007). At Sandick in Scotland the community has been involved in locating, recording and rebuilding archaeolo-gical sites (Bradley, Dawson and Lelong 2008). Whilst in North Somerset, the CHERT project involves field-walking, and earthwork surveys every weekend (Barry Lane pers. comm.); whilst the XArch project, in Exeter

providing local archaeology and history groups with geophysical survey work and training (see figure 9; Simpson and Williams 2008).

This has been successfully developed in Leicestershire (Schadla Hall 2004), but it is something that has taken 30 years to achieve. This community project has involved extensive field survey, training and stewardship, giving control of archaeology and its maintenance back to the community. This project has supported local archaeolo-gical societies in these activities, but it is questionable still whether it or any archaeology project really does appeal to the wider community, or just a select demographic, who share similar interests.

It could be perceived, through comparison of participants with overall demographic make-up, which these alterna-tives to excavation have yet to achieve wider public interest. Part of the problem stems from the fact that the majority of these projects are initiated for or by a local archaeology or historical society, and that subsequently participation is usually limited to members of these groups, and their particular age and socio-economic demographic (Manley 1996), with occasional provision for local school groups. Perhaps limited participation also stems from the archaeologists failing to promote other parts of the archaeological process as valid alternatives, or perhaps the wider community are not interested in the re-search side of non-intrusive research, as these do not offer the same thrill of discovery and experience as digging.

The importance of excavation should not be overlooked in appealing to wider audiences, especially given that peoples' popular mindset about archaeology is still digging, discovery and treasure. Perhaps archaeologists should stop trying to placate the public with other activities, but offer them everything through a multi-disciplinary approach. Excavation does not have to involve large-scale open-area excavation. Other avenues of giving the public experience of excavating have been attempted, including test pits on gardens; this technique has been used in Time Teams Big Dig at Great Eastan in Leicestershire (2003), in the village of Nether Poppleton, Yorkshire in 2005 (www.channel4.com/history/microsites/T/timeteam/2005_pop.html), Shapwick, Somerset in 1989 (Gerrard and Aston 2007) and more recently in Sedgeford, Norfolk (Moshenska 2005) and Bow, Devon (Figure 4.8)

The Shapwick project involved field walking, standing building survey, geophysical and botanical surveys as well as excavation. A test pit strategy was developed in order to deal with difficulties of excavating a village environment; it was devised in order to investigate the 'blank spaces' in between and underneath people's lawns, the areas which archaeologists are usually unable to investigate (Aston *et al* 1997, 6). The one metre square test pitting strategy enabled completion within a day, maximising spatial coverage and understanding the depth and date of the underlying medieval deposits (Aston *et al*

Figure 4.8 Bow test pit survey (Faye Simpson)

1997). Teresa Hall, who was also involved in the project as an archaeologist, describes the multiple values of this multidimensional approach to archaeological research, in its ability to get villagers communicating and creating a social network (T. Hall pers. comm.). Critical to this project is that it involves gaining respect and trust from the community, which can be time consuming. This technique is perceived as more advantageous to both research and public engagement than a single excavation, as it enables fluidity of research, and changing research agendas. Its methodology of excavating in different people's backyards encourages a wider demographic of people to become involved, and therefore had values to both the archaeologists and within the village community, beyond just the collation of knowledge (Moshenska 2005).

Time Team Big Dig used this approach. Like many projects that allow the public to excavate, it was criticized by professional archaeologists for encouraging people to destroy the archaeological record, especially in areas where the public excavated outside the original programme's supervision, e.g. at Time Team Big Dig in 2003 (Fowler 2004). Yet much of the fieldwork, recording and post excavation evidence suggest this is far from the case in the majority of public excavations, as the professional standards are, on the whole, if supervised and advised sufficiently, of a high standard (Lewis 2006). Therefore, suggesting that archaeologists naively believe that the exclusion of the public from excavation is for a common good of preserving archaeology (Hawkins 2000, 209). This 'professional' archaeological mindset has created tensions both within the profession and outside, and also created the belief that if the public are allowed to dig, it will create a 'generation of pot hunters' (USA) or 'treasure hunters' (UK) which has become an increasing concern amongst professional archaeologists in the USA and UK over the last ten years (Smartz 2000, 239). This suggests why archaeologists are so keen on encouraging alternatives to excavation. This exclusion of the public from excavation, has backfired, and has been blamed for

the creation a generation of glorified 'pot hunters' or 'treasure hunters' in the form of metal detectorists in the United Kingdom (Aston pers. comm. 2007). This idea could be figuratively backed up by the increasing number of metal detectorists in the UK (www.finds.org, see figure 4.9). Exclusion from excavation could be perceived as creating a generation who perceive archaeology as having little personal relevance as the public fail to understand what archaeology does.

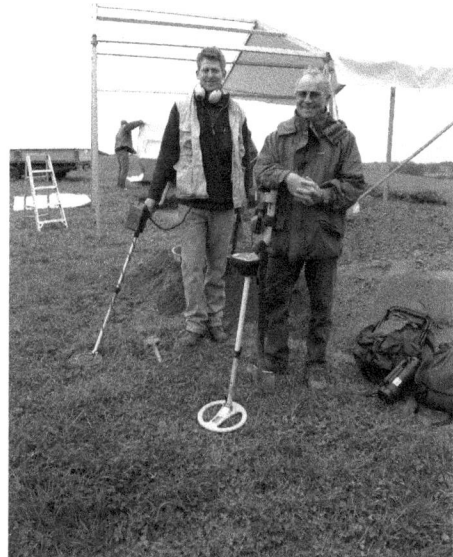

Figure 4.9: Metal detectorists, finding Viking site at Cumwhitton (Faye Simpson).

4.6 Summary

The phrase 'community archaeology' defines a plethora of diverse archaeological outreach projects with often conflicting agendas behind them. The phrase can be seen to have been used politically to create and maintain specific identities, based on the notion of homogeneity of the public.

The values attached to community archaeology are complex, ranging for the tangible to the intangible, which are frequently driven by groups or individuals, whose agendas and feelings attached to the past vary. Archaeological, sociological and psychological literature suggests that excavation plays an important component to the values people attach to archaeology (Holtorf 2005; Slick 2002). It could therefore be asserted that it is this that is vital to the success of community archaeology projects, as it creates and maintains values attached to archaeology, critically providing the public with what they want, and enabling them to experience and be entertained. Critically, this archaeological process of excavation is by no means the only way of engaging the public in archaeology, but usually forms a key component in community archaeology projects.

5. THE ORIGINS AND DEVELOPMENT OF COMMUNITY ARCHAEOLOGY IN THE UNITED STATES

In the last two decades, community archaeology in the United States has become firmly established in federal and state archaeological politics and legislation. It has also been accepted into the professional practice of archaeology, and its academic thought and writing. This chapter aims to examine the changes in political and subsequent philosophical mindsets, within the US, that enabled community archaeology to develop. Furthermore, it hopes to compare the US and UK, including the ideas and core concepts that can assist community archaeology to develop a sound theoretical and methodological basis within the UK.

5.1 Political Overview: Attitudes to Archaeology

It is essential, in the first instance, to discuss politics in the US and its relationship with archaeology, to enable an understanding of how this has shaped the development and practice of community archaeology today. Politics in the US has 'federal', state and local levels, and the relationship between archaeology and politics in the US is complex.

Writing over thirty years ago, McGimsey (1972) touched on the subject of federal and state influence on archaeology, going someway to deconstructing the effect of federal and state finances on the practice of archaeology. More recent research has focused on the political history of federal acts affecting archaeology and outreach, rather than on the deconstruction of the direct effects of changing political mindset on public archaeology (Jameson 2004; Little 2002). Neumann's recent survey of how federal and state laws were passed, including the Historic Environment Act of 1966, offers some insight as to the complexity of political influence on archaeological practice (www.nps.gov/history/sec/protecting/html/201-neumann.htm). This research deconstructed democratic and republican senators' representations in the passing of the bill and indicated a Democratic majority in support of the bill, against what appears to be a Republican opposition (www.nps.gov/

history/sec/protecting/html/201-neumann.htm). These ideas are further consolidated by Jeppson's work on education and public archaeology, discussing the effect of the changes in governments from Democratic to Republican representation in the last decade (Jeppson 2008; Jeppson and Brauer 2007, 231-232). This research indicated an increased support for education and archaeology under the democratic government. These recent studies start to highlight a political division based on political philosophical mindsets attached to archaeology.

5.2 Federal Politics and Community Archaeology

The Republican party is conservative with right wing viewpoints. Demographically majority of Republican voters are white middle class, educated and religious (majority Christian), or white rural working class. Common standpoints include being anti-abortion, nationalist, and are pro-individual, pro-gun and support a small state (Skocpol and Campbell 1995; Wasserman 1995, 221). The Democrats are liberal; 'centre right.' Demographically voters are believed to be more socially and ethnically diverse (Wasserman 1995, 221). The majority of the party are known for appearing to want to balance and redistribute resources to support lower social groups, supporting gay rights, multiculturalism and the pro-choice movement (Wasserman 1995, 221). It could be suggested that these political standpoints directly relate to the attitude of politicians towards heritage, and have a direct impact on federal and state legislation. This affects the practice of archaeology, and enables or hinders the development of community archaeology.

5.2.1 Politics, Philosophy and Processualism from the United States

The 1970s saw Richard Nixon's (1969-1974) and Gerald Ford's (1974–1977) republican presidencies, followed by James Carter's (1977-1981) democratic administration (Wasserman 1995, 58). However, all through the period from 1955 to 1981 there was a democratic congress. It was a period of heightened awareness of the diversity of the American population and tensions relating to 'immigration'. This, coupled with the Vietnam War (which ended in 1974), and the associated anti-war movement, caused widespread public demonstrations and anti-government protests (Wasserman 1995).

This period saw the beginning of public archaeology in the United States, with the first references to public archaeology occurring in academic literature (McGimsey 1972). Before the concept of public and community archaeology was mentioned in academic literature, however, the need for wider communication, a key tenet of community archaeology, was appearing in federal political documents. During the Democratic presidency, of Franklin D. Roosevelt (1933-1945), in 1937 the Historic Sites Preservation Act was signed. It included in it a federal responsibility for all national parks (including the archaeological resources) 'to preserve and promote heritage for the benefit of all the people' (Jameson 2004, 26). Therefore, states such as Florida and Texas, with large proportions of federal land, including forests and national parks, have long traditions of community archaeology work, and developed education programmes.

One such example of this was National Forestry Service land in Minnesota, where, in 1988, George Peter instigated a community archaeology programme, including public archaeology training, and involvement in excavations and research for members of the community (Jameson 2003, 156). This would in 1991, during the Republican presidency be rolled out nationally to over 117 forests in 36 states, under the title of 'Passport in Time' (www.passportintime.com, USFS 2000). The federal support and promotion of such programmes enabled community archaeology in these locations to become sustainable.

The establishment of links between academic, professional and amateur archaeologists, supporting and encouraging local archaeology societies, was previously helped in 1934 by the Historic Preservation Act, and the formation of the Society for American Archaeology (http://www.saa.org/aboutSAA/index.html). Since its establishment, this society has been responsible for producing guidelines and codes of ethics, which encourage archaeologists to work with the public.

The late 1970's saw Carter's Democratic government attempting to rebuild patriotism and national pride (Wasserman 1995). This was attempted through 'empowering' the individual to take control; this was related to the ethos of philosophical relativism. Under this philosophy there was not one, single truth, subsequently communities and individuals should take control of their own past in order to rebuild national pride (http://www.whitehouse.gov/history/presidents/jc39.html). The period saw the direct impact on archaeology of President Carter's interest in, and collection of, prehisto-

ric arrowheads, in the passing of the Archaeological Resources Protection Action of 1979 (Smith and Ehrenhard 2002, 124). It was this act that forced archaeologists to consider the public, and the states to take responsibility for promoting and preserving the archaeological resource (Smith and Ehrenhard 2002, 124). Archaeology was no longer able to work in isolation, but was becoming increasingly tied into Democratic policies of embracing multiculturalism. These federal and state laws encouraged professional archaeologists to accept the multiple values attached to heritage by American citizens, including those of Native Americans, in their research and interpretation. Therefore if working on federal land or federally funded and permitted projects, archaeologists were encouraged to consult all stakeholders, and have a mitigation plan for dealing with the effect of works on the integrity of the historical resource (www2.cr.nps.gov/laws/NHPA1966.htm)

Community (public) archaeology became synonymous with cultural resource management (McGimsey 1972, 5). Cultural Resource Management (CRM) initially developed in the 1960s, but really took off in the 1970s, encompassing a broad range of historic preservation programmes (Jameson 2004, 29; Snead 1999). It developed out of the archaeological management and recording work of the early 1930s salvage and rescue programmes. There was a growing public, professional and federal realisation that legislation was required in order to preserve these archaeological resources from destruction during construction and land development (Jameson 2004, 30). These acts including National Historic Preservation Act (1966), National Environment Policy Act (1969), Protection of Cultural Environment (1971), Archaeological and Historic Preservation Act (1974) have been credited with changing the character of archaeological research and preservation on federal land and federally controlled projects, indicating a growing level of the importance ascribed to preserving the heritage for the public (Jameson 2004, 30). Political support for public archaeology extended to a more local level, with Alexandria in 1976, Annapolis in 1981, funding full-time archaeologists to initiate public archaeology programmes (Cressey, Reeder & Bryson 2003, 2).

This early political and public recognition of the importance of heritage changed views and values attached to archaeology by professional archaeologists. This led to the acceptance of the concept of community archaeology in mainstream archaeological thought, linked directly to a political climate in which archaeologists felt they needed to be, or at least seen to be, ethically responsible (Scarre and Scarre 2006, 12). This related to the increasing number of excavations on public land and visibility of archaeological work in the public domain, which was due to development, caused by growth in the economy (McGimsey 1972; Jameson 2004).

During the 1960s and 1970s archaeology became firmly embedded in anthropology departments within the university system. In 1966 the University of Pennsylvania took the lead and launched its Historical Archaeological course, taught by a National Park Service employee, John. L. Cotton, and aimed at training future professional archaeologists (Pykles 2008, 33). Such courses became commonplace in universities all over America. Prior to this, in the 1930s, archaeology within anthropology departments was limited to a few select universities in North Eastern universities, including Harvard, but these courses placed little relevance on learning the skills to become a professional archaeologist (Jameson 2004, 29; Pykles 2008, 33). This connection to anthropology enabled archaeologists to begin to consider archaeology not just as a scientific discipline working in isolation, but also its relationship with cultural systems. This period saw not only the beginnings of professionalism, and creation of professional jobs in archaeology in federal and state government agencies, but also the birth of the New Archaeology within archaeological practice, combining positivist scientific approaches with ethnology (Willey and Sabloff 1974, 210; Johnson 1999, 49; Pykles 2008, 33).

This shift was in part enabled by the development of CRM, with archaeologists working more closely with politics, being guided by federal acts. CRM increased the amounts of raw archaeological data being discovered, which required professionals and academics to work together to interpret these in a scientific manner, to collect and collate data, looking for patterns and connections that created universal laws and models for behaviour, placing archaeological research in the present. This new dialogue opened up relationships between academics, professionals, and the public; these foundations would enable the development of community archaeology. At least, this was the theory.

5.2.2 Politics, Philosophy and Post-Processualism from a United States Perspective

The 1980s saw Ronald Reagan's Republican presidency (1981-1989). Despite his Republican background, his politics where philosophically seen as more liberal than predecessors. His government supported private economic growth and the individual. In order to build and present national unity, it overlooked multiculturism and future potential problems. They aimed to present the USA as a united and powerful nation, forging forward from the troubles of the 1960s and 1970s, including the Cuban Missal Crisis and the ongoing Cold War. It was a period of rebuilding nationalism, trust in the government, and improving world image. This was done through considerable public spending on creating an idea of power through national monuments and buildings, including the renovating the White House. It was a philosophical period of absolutism, were there was a political movement towards belief in absolute truths. This idea of a unified nation in the present was something that the past could support, and could be used to create (Little 2002).

Federal spending was used to attempt to boost the economy and to unite the states. The focus of this spending was on creating power, through investment in defence and education, but social investment was not seen as a priority against the background of defending the nation again the threats of the Cold War. This national threat was something that was highlighted to the public during Reagan's presidency. Equally important, during this period of hostility, was maintaining and building international relationships and gaining support for the political philosophies of the United States. Therefore, direct investment in heritage and archaeology decreased, as its social benefits were less valued that previously. Subsequently, heritage organisations and monuments had to think of other ways to continue research and preservation that did not require as much direct government funding (White 2002; Slick 2002). In 1987, the George and Martha Washington's Plantation Home in Washington D.C., Mount Vernon, launched their public archaeological programme, which combined initiatives to increase tourism and interest in the site, which would fund further research, including excavation and educational work locally (White 2002, 146). Furthermore, by 1989, the National Trust for Historic Preservation recognised the niche market for heritage tourism, and launched its demonstration project, with its five principles and four key steps to achieving maximum benefit between heritage and tourism (Slick 2002, 220). The importance of heritage was seen in terms of tourism and profit, rather than social value.

This was a critical period in the development of community archaeology, with archaeology becoming interlinked with tourism, the public and politics, and with increasing need to justify its role in society. It was in this period that the phrase 'Community Archaeology' first appeared in print, in an article for the National Trust for Historic Preservation, in 1987. Pamela Cressey used the phrase to define doing archaeology with, or for, the public (Cressey et al 2003, 2).

Another Republican, George Bush (senior), was elected as President from 1989 to 1993. In comparison to Reagan, Bush was more conservative ('right' wing), and his policies focused even more on giving power back to the individual, the concept of 'small state' and the idea of supporting yourself. It saw a heightened philosophical political focus on absolutism, and the idea of a single truth about the past. On the other hand, and perhaps in self-contradiction, the government attempted to make multiple voices into one national voice through federal acts. It subsequently saw, through an act of congress, the establishment of the National Native American Museum, under the 'federally' controlled Smithsonian Institute (http://www.nmai.si.edu/subpage.cfm?subpage=about).
This museum, which opened in 2004 in Washington DC, has been described as an ambitious attempt to educate the public and make Native American Indians part of Americans' 'national' heritage (Volkert, Martin and Pickworth 2004, 2).

The early 1990s possibly saw the most influential effects on archaeological theory from politics. Political intervention through acts of congress enabled the growth of community archaeology, including one of the most significant federal acts, the Native American Graves Protection and Repatriation Act (NAGPRA), signed by Bush in 1990 (Jameson 2003, 45). It forced the profession to rethink its fundamental assumptions about finds, and reconsider archaeological interpretation outside the realms of 'western' science (Watkins 2007, 36). It gave the Native American public a more powerful role in 'their' heritage, opening up archaeology and forcing archaeologists to collaborate and communicate the past to this specific community of people (Jameson 2003, 158). It was, in a sense, an attempt to make archaeology more democratic, with ethical and moral considerations placed before research objectives. There was increased need to justify archaeology in the public domain and to society (Jameson 2003, 160; Scarre and Scarre 2006). NAGPRA could be suggested to have enabled a rhetoric through which facilitated the development of the theories behind community archaeology and its practice.

Between 1993 and 2001, the US had Democrat Bill Clinton as President, and, with fairly relativist philosophical policies once again becoming the focus of attention, it became known as the 'progressive era' (Jeppson 2008, 18). His administration has also been described as 'centralist', the 'third way' and 'new democrat', in similar guise to Tony Blair's New Labour in the UK. Furthermore, it is a political philosophy that stresses technological development and a focus on education. This government wanted more control at a both federal and state level in order to more evenly distribute resources (Jeppson 2008) These Democratic policies were focused around social betterment of lower social and economic classes, with education playing a key role in supporting the social disadvantaged, and balancing the differences between classes. Education was taking centre stage and public 'educational' archaeology flourished in this environment, under the 2001 Democrat policy of 'No Child Left Behind' (www.ed.gov/policy/elsec/leg/esea02/107-110.pdf). This decade saw a plethora of community archaeology programmes both at a local level, such as Baltimore County Public Schools Programme of Archaeology, and at a federal level, for example, The National Forestry Service 'Passport in Time' programme. Educational community archaeology gained funding at both a federal and state level (Jameson 2004; Merriman 2004; Jeppson and Brauer 2003).

This period saw a renewed focus on tourism, with Bill Clinton commenting in 1993, that tourism was vital to the economy, having become a $467 billion industry (Slick 2002, 219). Subsequently, he launched the 'pay to play' philosophy and public private partnerships, in which programmes must be beneficially financially as well as socially (Slick 2002, 219). Research in New Mexico in 1995-6, indicated that 8.2 million of the 19 million visitors came to the state because of archaeological and

historical sites, museums and Indian reservations (McManamon 2002, 33). Subsequently, heritage attractions were regarded as vital players in this tourist economy (McManamon 2002, 33). Similar to the mid 1970s there was a focus on making money, but conversely it was order to redistribute money to the economically deprived, supporting the ethos of 'no child', and no person, left behind.

During the 1990s the Society for American Archaeology played a pivotal role in establishing archaeological ethics, standards, and advice for public archaeology (Society for American Archaeology 1996). In 1995, as part of its annual conference, the SAA had the first formal public archaeology session, which resulted in the book 'Public Benefits of Archaeology' (Little 2002).

It was in the mid 1990s, due to the actions of the 104th Republican congress that the practice of archaeology was forced away from blue sky's research, as the National Endowment for Humanities (NEH) budget was cut (Jeppson and Brauer 2007, 231- 232). This cut in funding also led to the reduction in money for federal historical agency offices, which resulted in the loss of cultural resource jobs (Jeppson and Brauer 2007, 232). Despite interest in the past by the public, and growing visitor numbers to museums congress also decreased funding to national museums, decreasing their research, and interpretation (Jeppson and Brauer 2007, 232). At the same time, at both federal and state level, the government was facing low public approval ratings and, CRM firms were facing increasing incidences of public obstruction during the archaeological mitigation process, with calls for projects to be halted. Public archaeology provided a tool to change these views and meet current government agendas outside the research arena (Jeppson and Brauer 2007, 232). This change in government support and funding forced archaeology to consider its role outside the discipline (Zimmerman 1996; Jeppson 2008). This period saw large CRM project contacts, especially federal ones, begin to have public elements added into the specification as requirements, including consultation, and presentation of results.

In 1995, Sacramento saw the US General Administration planning to build a huge new federal building and courthouse, which required archaeological mitigation work under Section 106 of the National Historic Preservation Act of 1966 (Praetzellis 2002, 52). The federal and state government both recognised the importance of public opinion in the success of this project and used the archaeological work to open up communication with the Chinese community (Praetzellis 2002, 52). It funded both the archaeology mitigation work, and also a public archaeology programme. Subsequently after consultation, public talks, and finds work, the Chinese community put together a permanent exhibition "Uncovering Sacramento's Chinese Pioneers" in the lobby of the new federal building (Praetzellis 2002, 54).

The 21st century was until January 2009, Republican, under the presidency of G.W. Bush, and until 110th congress in 2006 there continued to be a republican majority in congress, which had lasted for twelve years. G.W Bush was known for his right wing, neo-conservative philosophies. This period saw conflicts in spending, where defence spending increased, but taxation did not. This resulted in cuts in other public spending, including archaeology and heritage budgets, and further budget cuts to NEH, the National Advisory Council on Historic Preservation and State Historic Environment Offices (Slocpol and Campbell 1995). The reason for these budget cuts is that heritage is perceived by the Republican government as a luxury rather than an essential. The cuts to the National Advisory Council have led to both archaeological officers being laid off centrally in Washington D.C. and therefore loss of centralised heritage structures to support and advise the various state archaeology programmes (Jeppson pers. comm.). This loss of support consequently forced many states to curtail their activities, including South Dakota and Maryland (Hannus pers. comm. 2007). In Maryland, the Baltimore Country Public Schools Archaeology Programme was forced to close down from autumn 2007, due to lack of funding (Jeppson pers. comm.).

Under G.W. Bush's presidency the American public's psyche appeared to struggle to recognise the benefits of archaeology to the public. This, in some sense, was because the benefits were aimed principally towards the education and social and economic improvement of the lower social classes. Furthermore, it was recognised as something that could help lower social groups and ethnically diverse populations find 'their' identity (Little 2002). This concept was, to the Republicans', something that American public were not willing to support, believing instead that the individual had to make their own success, whether that was educationally, socially or economically. Therefore, archaeology was regarded as a middle class hobby of the educated, rather than appealing to the wider community. The Republican government appeared to focus on the present rather than the past; forging a future for the individuals based on economic strength, and defensive power (Jeppson 2008, Snead 1999).

It was during this Republican government that the 'culture war', became the most heated (Jeppson 2008, 18). This was a war between 'progressive' and 'conservative' factions, 'multiculturalists' and 'traditionalists', 'relativists' and 'absolutists' (Jeppson 2008, 18; Jeppson and Brauer 2007, 231). This debate was further inflamed after 9/11, with right-wing Republicans appearing to take advantage of the general public's distrust of non-western cultures, to push for a more singular past, one in which relativist social ideals were shunned, and a return to traditional history focus in American Education' (Jeppson 2008, 20). This included returning to an educational focus on the American Civil War and European colonial settlement rather than more interpretative and multicultural pasts,

including that of Native and African American histories (Slick 2002).

In January 2009 the Democrat Barack Obama became president of the United States, supported by democratic congress and senate. It will be interesting to observe how this complete change in the government of the United States, and the total control by the democratic party at all government levels, will affect archaeology's role in American society in the future and the development of community archaeology. Room for manoeuvre, however, is limited due to budget deficits resulting from the 'credit crunch'.

5.2.3 Summary

The Democratic leadership and government (i.e. congress) of the 1970s, with a relativist philosophical paradigm, enabled multiple public views and values associated with heritage to be considered on a national level. This change led to the rise of the term 'public archaeology' and, subsequently, 'community archaeology'. It was the Republican leadership and congress in the 1980s and democratic congress of early 1990s that enabled federal acts to be passed that would set the foundation for community archaeology, even if action on the ground took longer. These acts, and the shift in government in the 1990s to the Democrats, enabled a philosophical shift, which was favourable to the post-processual theoretical movement within archaeology. It was an acceptance of these philosophical elements that enabled a methodology to be developed that accepted communicating and working with the public. This gave credence to the idea and practice of community archaeology, even if the American archaeological method, on the whole, remained processual and positivist in nature.

Clinton's presidency saw money invested into archaeology for the public, education and a growth of public archaeology initiatives, including the Baltimore School Programme, which enabled children to come out from the classroom and be taught about archaeology practically, through excavating and processing finds (Jeppson 2008; www.p-j.net/pjeppson/or). G. W. Bush's presidency saw decreased funding for archaeology and heritage, with budget cuts to federal and state public archaeology programmes, which was not a direct result of funding the 'War on Terror', but a deliberate choice of government on how to spend public funds. This has had a direct impact on archaeologists' ability to continue or instigate community projects, especially at state level, without private or commercial support. It is vital that archaeologists remember that neither governments nor presidents work in isolation from each other; each is affected by previous choices, in terms of acts signed, or funding priorities. For example, it could be proposed that it was Clinton's decision to decrease spending on defence, which consequently required Bush to redistribute funds and cut budgets from in federal agencies to finance the defence needed for the 'War on Terror'.

Each successive president and government has had both positive and negative effects on the practice of community archaeology in the United States. It is these changes in governments in the US, their philosophical ethos, and spending priorities, which make it necessary for archaeologists to be more imaginative in finding funding sources to support community archaeology projects.

5.3 State Politics and Community Archaeology

The enormity of the country, its history and the nature of the constitution helps in understanding why the government is organised with, at least on paper, high levels devolved powers to state level, and the federal government appearing to act as an impartial overseer (see

Fig. 5.1 and 5.2). Constitutionally, the federal government is not responsible for states, yet it has become apparent that it is the ruling government who determines the nature and extent of the relationship of federal government with state, even if this is unconstitutional. This interference with state level legislations is achieved primarily through withholding funding from federal projects, such as interstate roads, in states that do not support federal policies. Even so, it has been suggested that state administrations have more of an influence than federal ones on the practice of community archaeology (Smith and Ehrenhard 2002, 124). It is the state control of archaeology, and their ability to carve an individual 'niche' for heritage, for the purposes of tourism, which is argued to be a benefit for empowerment and socially relevant archaeology and stewardship. Although heritage tourism brings in outsiders, this creates a tangible local

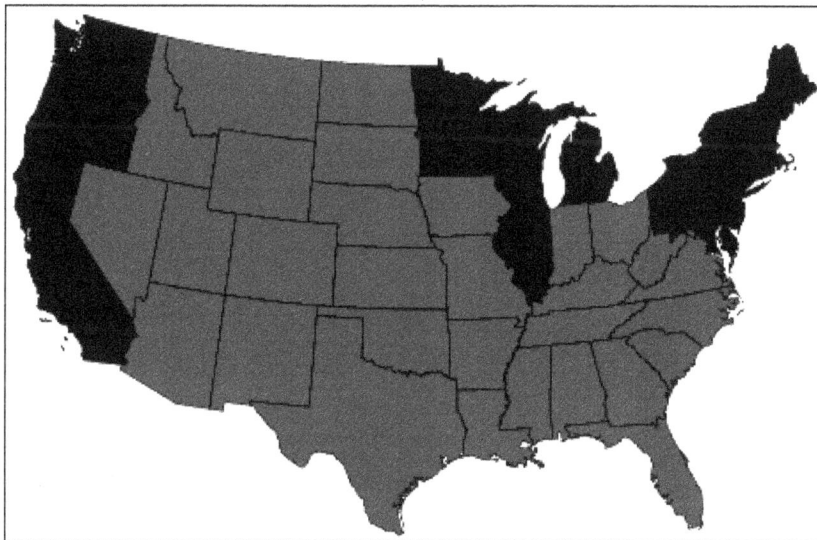

Figure 5.1 Map of US state division of political parties 2004.
Grey: Republican / Black: Democrat (http://www-personal.umich.edu/~mejn/election/2004/)

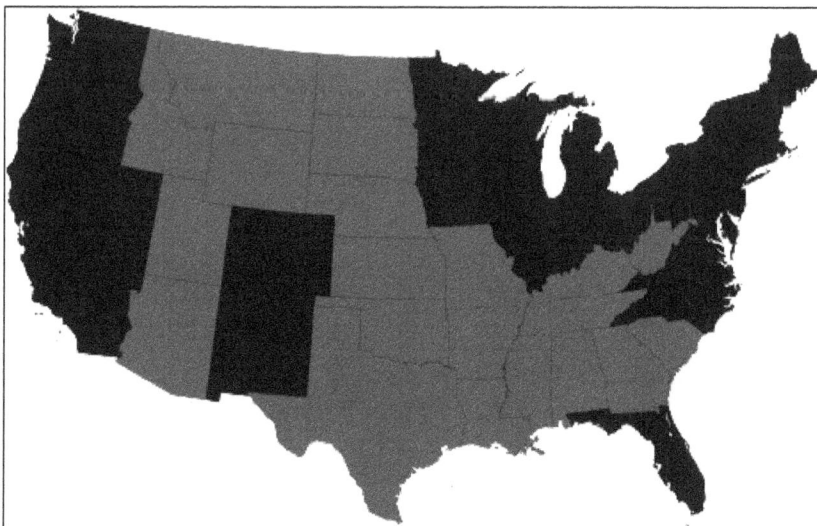

Figure 5.2 Map of US state division of political parties 2008.
Grey: Republican / Black: Democrat (http://www-personal.umich.edu/~mejn/election/2008/)

value, awareness and appreciation towards heritage (Smith and Ehrenhard 2002, 124). Furthermore, much of this money is used to fund educational programmes and outreach locally, for example at Mount Vernon, Williamsburg and Jamestown (White 2002; McManamon 2002). However, it is argued that increased independence of states from federal politics, could result in states and their senators losing sight of the bigger picture, for example national policies and attitudes towards archaeology (Shull 2002, 196). This state isolation could subsequently jeopardise federal funding for research and outreach, by states loosing track of current political trends in what federal authorities support, including community archaeology (Little 2002; Rowlands 1994).

The State Historic Preservation Office (SHPO), which is managed at a state level, but funded federally, acts to preserve, protect and monitor archaeology, and, under requirements of Section 106 of the National Historic Preservation Act of 1966, has a responsibly to 'actively encourage outreach' (Bergman and Doershuk 2003, 95). The level of this 'outreach' is, at the discretion of the state, and dependent upon financial and local support, subsequently outreach on state owned land is highly varied. Many SHPOs have pushed for public interpretation and consideration as part of all major archaeological work. For example in Alexandria, Virginia, and Annapolis, Maryland, public consultation and involvement in archaeological work on state owned land has been accepted and embraced by the local community, and widely supported as a model for the future (Cressey *et al* 2003; Potter 1994). At Alexandria the state archaeologists involved the public in excavations and public exhibitions and created a 'tour de sites' (a bicycle tour of excavations around the city), and a definitive mission statement (Cressey *et al* 2003). Regulations regarding private land are more complex, as unless developments have received financial support from federal or state sources, or require state or federal permits, or the land contains Native American remains, and NAGPRA applies, there no legal of requirements or standards for archaeological work or outreach (Watkins 2007; Ragins 2002, 202).

Local societies have played a prominent, active and often official role within many SHPOs (Praetzellis 2002, 58). This involvement has meant active participation in the selection and registration of archaeological sites for both the National Register (for sites which are deemed nationally important) and National Historic Landmark Register (for sites deemed locally important). This selection is limited to a specific demographic, which make up local societies, which, like the United Kingdom, is primarily white, middle class, and frequently retired people with more spare time. Therefore, sites and monuments nominated for selection and investigation were often determined by a specific demographic and subject to their biases and choices, rather than representing the interests and values of more diverse community. Perhaps this also explains why the majority

of sites on the national register are colonial, civil war and industrial sites, predominantly representing white history.

The National Register is on a publicly accessible web database and is the public's primary access to information about 'their' historic environment (Shull 2002, 197). This local level involvement in registration means that sites registered are increasingly dependent on state level views towards specific types of heritage. The registration of sites by the state comes with financial support from the federal government, with the aim of giving back control of heritage to local people (Shull 2002, 196). This has meant a difference in public archaeology programmes between states, dependent on local politics. This local 'state' control over heritage has meant that public archaeology programmes in many states, for example in Pennsylvania, have been joint projects between State Historic Preservation Officers, archaeologists, and local societies (Moe 2002, 182).

The federal and state governments use landscape, monuments, commemorative days and archaeology to create an official national 'public' memory. Subconscious and conscious choices are made to forget, create and develop a patriotic and nostalgic memory of the past (Shackel 2007, 307). These decisions have affected archaeology, determining which sites received federal and state funding. Principally, to date, these have been colonial and civil war sites, which may explain why Jamestown and Colonial Williamsburg have such high government financial support (Shackel 2007, 325). Furthermore, whole sections of the past, including prehistoric and post civil war archaeologies were less prominently promoted until recent years (Shackel 2007, 308). There is a belief that archaeology plays a role in teaching American people to be 'good American citizens,' and in teaching them the national 'truth.' Therefore, there have been deliberate political choices as to the nature of historical and archaeological topics taught in schools and public education programmes, which have been made by successive federal governments (Moe 2002, 176; Little 2002, 16; Metcalf 2002, 170). Despite the limits set out in the US constitution regarding federal involvement in education, which allow for state control and choice, influence has been acquired through government 'think tanks' and the allocation of grant support for educational programmes and outreach (Jeppson 2008, 21).

The 1980s saw a move away from traditional history-centred approach to the teaching of archaeology to an integrated social studies approach; this led to the creation of state programmes in archaeology including Baltimore County Public School Programme of Archaeology in 1984 (Jeppson and Brauer 2003, 79). This concept of broader, more interpretive and less scientifically rigid teaching flourished in the mid 1990s, and the BCPS programme integrated archaeology into the core curriculum in 167 schools, at K–12 level, which is children at approximately 17-18 year old (Jeppson 2008; Jeppson and Brauer 2003, 61). The subsequent Bush (junior) administration saw a return to archaeology being taught within history, with a traditional, conservative focus of 'people, places and events.' (Jeppson 2008, 28) History focused on traditional stories, including people crossing Bering Strait, occasionally losing flints; of the strange uncultured Aztecs 'eating hearts,' and then a temporal jump to the arrival of Europeans and the civilisation of America (Metcalf 2002, 170). There was little mention of the multiple cultures that made up the American population, or the huge time periods involved, which could have contributed to the modern public's temporal confusion about the past. This change in focus and effect of politics on public archaeology was highlighted that by at end of the Bush administration, when in 2007 the Baltimore Archaeology Programme closed down. This indicates that the teaching of archaeology within schools and, therefore, public views of archaeology and the past were influenced by current political agendas (Metcalf 2002, 177).

5.4 Public Attitudes and Community Archaeology

There has been a long history in the United States of public apathy towards the government and its institutions (Thomas 2002, 130). Despite this, American citizens perceive the government as a 'necessary evil', believing that it is the government's responsibly to provide and protect its citizens through its services (McKay 2001, 1). The American public demand low tax rates, which are substantially lower than UK, yet at the same time they have high expectations (McKay 2001, 3). The general opinion is that people should fend for themselves, based on the idea of the 'individual' and looking after one's own family. This has led to what has been described as a selfish country, being unsupportive to the socially and economically deprived, especially if 'their taxes' are involved (McKay 2001, 3). Philosophically, the citizens feel they should have to do very little themselves to help national problems. Yet this is counter-opposed to the very nature of government in the United States which is based on a democracy in which all people have a say, which is why the States have such power and act to represent their citizens both in the house and the senate (McKay 2001, 3). The basis of the government is that in order to change policies, ideas and strategies, the people must speak up, and it is their governors', representatives' and senators' duty to represent these views to congress and the federal government (www.nps.gov/history/sec/protecting/html/201-neumann.htm). These ideals about the government by the public and the running of the country are therefore paradoxically opposed. Equally, contradictory to this is the apathy and mistrust towards government institutions. Interestingly this is not reflected in the public views of archaeology and heritage institutions, which have maintained interest and public 'trust' (Thomas 2002, 130). Community archaeology is therefore viewed in a positive light by the public and often gains public support, and this support has been used by the government to gain support for other federal organisations, including the National Forestry Commission.

The philosophical mindset of the American citizens, that they expect the government to take responsibly, but also want to have a say, is reflected in their opinions about archaeology and heritage (McKay 2001, 1; Bergman and Doershuk 2003, 94). A national telephone survey of public attitudes to and understanding of archaeology, commissioned by the Society of American Archaeology, concluded that the majority of the American public are interested in and support archaeological work (Ramos and Duganne 2000; McManamon 2002, 37). The majority of respondents believed the value of archaeological sites and objects to be educational (99%), believing them to be an important tool for learning (Little 2002; McManamon 2002, 37). Other perceived contributions of archaeology related to scientific (99%), aesthetic or artistic (94%), personal heritage (93%), spiritual (88%), monetary (73%), and political (59%) values (McManamon 2002, 37). Yet, despite the widespread realisation of the value of archaeological work, the public do not see it as their responsibility to preserve and look after it, nor do they consider it a cost that they should take on (Bergman and Doershuk 2003, 94). This puts American archaeology in a very difficult position for two principal reasons, privately there is a reluctance to pay to visit sites, and privately support research, and, secondly, low tax rates cannot support archaeological projects (McKay 2001, 3).

Interestingly, despite this reluctance to pay directly for heritage, donations to charities and philanthropy towards public facilities relating to heritage, under the banner of 'public archaeology' and 'community archaeology', have been rising in the United States. Many middle class and wealthy individuals donate a percentage of their pay each month, or lump sums to 'do good' and give something back to the community (Versaggi 2007). In what has been described as a 'selfish' economically driven climate, this is a way of feeling morally 'good' about oneself that also provides tax breaks and personal recognition. Community Archaeology has thrived under this current public climate of charity and patronage, as it is seen as a public service and an educational tool, especially for children. Subsequently, as charity is mainly received from white middle class donors, it is that group which appears to benefit the most and have the most influence on community archaeology.

American citizens are selective about what heritage they are interested in and what past they choose to commemorate (Shackel 2007, 307). This relates to independent and personal choices about what people are actually interested in and regard as 'their heritage'. It also concerns multiculturalism and the relatively recent immigration of the majority of the present inhabitants to that enormous country. Perhaps worryingly, some people do not regard, for example, Native Indian archaeology as 'their' heritage. Likewise, Native Indians do not regard 'colonial' archaeology. Community archaeology has enabled some of these multicultural issues to be addressed, encouraging multiple stories about the past to be told together, through consultation and active involvement. The notion of personal relationships to sites through public involvement in the process of archaeology has enabled individuals to relate to sites and open up archaeology to a broader audience by making it personally relevant. The case of the African American burial ground in New York has highlighted how community archaeology can serve individuals and individual communities (Crist 2002; Taylor 2001). In 1991, during the construction of the New Federal Office Building, the remains of 400 formerly enslaved African Americans were uncovered (Taylor 2001). Subsequently members of the community were consulted and empowered to make choices about the project, including its leadership (they requested an African American) and were involved in its interpretation, and finds work (Crist 2002, 101; Taylor 2001). This work facilitated a voice for the African American Community, subsequently; part of the footprint of this building was given over to a memorial park and museum (Crist 2002; Taylor 2001).

Praetellis (2002, 51), from personal observations, briefly touched upon the profound differences between the ways many British people and North Americans view their respective pasts. He discussed these views with reference to time: 'American citizens are much more aware than our British cousins that we are a product of our immediate past' (Praetellis 2002, 52). He concluded that the American public find a greater meaning in the past though personal relevancy and identification with the people of the not so distant past, subsequently there is a greater association and interest in historical archaeology sites, including 19th century sites (2002, 52), this observation is something that Jeppson also highlights (2008). This is an interesting observation, but I would argue this 'rose tinted' supposition disguises a plethora of the political, social, philosophical and psychological reasons for American attitudes to heritage, something that is far more complex.

5.5 Summary

Community archaeology, and the adaptation in theory and philosophy within archaeology that enabled it to develop as a sub-discipline, were spurred on by the indigenous rights movement in the United States. This forced the government and 'professional' archaeologists to be less introspective, and give greater consideration for what individual communities wanted, and the value that archaeology had outside their domain of research.

The growth of community archaeology in the United States has been enabled by federal and state acts encouraging public 'outreach,' and its advancement is linked to the development of cultural resource management (Jameson 2004). Federal and state support for the ethical basis underlying the practice of community archaeology enabled it as a discipline to be accepted and embraced by some academic archaeologists, which was vital for its progression and sustainability. Universities have, in some circumstances, supported and provided a base for community archaeology programmes and their research, including at Bridgehampton University in New York State (Versaggi 2007), and Pennsylvania University (Jeppson 2008). Part of this could also relate to archaeology's location within anthropology departments, being an integral part of social science, rather than being viewed as the 'handmaiden to history' as in the UK. The establishment of community archaeology within academia has enabled it to develop as a theoretical, philosophical and sociological concept. Furthermore, its longevity and active research it is beginning to prove its methodological and theoretical validity.

Regular political changes and the vastness in size of the US make community archaeology and its relationship to politics more complex than in the UK. The federal perspective gives an insight into how and why community archaeology has developed, but it is necessary to deconstruct how politics has affected community archaeology at an individual state and 'local' level in order to understand it properly. This local perspective will be discussed comprehensively in the results chapter, where specific community archaeology case studies in the US will be politically deconstructed in relation to their state's politics, in order to understand philosophical mindsets relating to the past.

6. METHODOLOGY

6.1 Methodologies for Assessing the Impact of Community Archaeology

Some of the most relevant methodological guidelines have come from Kramer and Kramer's (2001, 70) ethnoarchaeology work. It was deemed appropriate to take the lead from ethnographic studies based on anthropological and sociological principles of enquiry. These, to date, have primarily come from new world contexts, principally Australasia (Marshall 2002; Edgeworth 2006).

Sian Jones' (2004) research at Hilton of Cadboll offers some practical and potentially enlightening advice when considering the cross-disciplinary application of anthropological, sociological and ethnographic methodologies. Here these basic principles were used to investigate values, options and perceptions of archaeology in a community context (2004, 7). Consequently the modes employed were focused on participant observation and in-depth, open, qualitative interviews. As Jones (2004) and McClanahon (2006) suggest these modes are becoming increasingly popular in research focusing on the meanings and values that are attached to heritage. To date this type of contextual investigation has primarily been undertaken by anthropologists, as opposed to archaeologists (Bender 1998). Bender takes this idea a step further, by applying an anthropological methodology to understand the multiple values attached to the archaeological remains of Stonehenge in a contemporary context, with an aim of providing appropriate interpretation and management of this highly contentious and evocative place. This type of investigation in archaeology stems from what is described by Hodder (2000; 2001) as a 'reflexive' method, employing an anthropological approach in understanding the value and interpretations of excavations to all stakeholders. This approach facilitates analyses of the roles of excavations in wider social, political, cultural and historic contexts (Hodder 2000). Hodder applies this 'reflexive' methodology during his research excavations of the Neolithic site of Çatalhöyük in Turkey (2000; 2005),

enabling the archaeological excavators to individually interpret their areas of excavation through their personal perspectives. Hodder claims this presents an appropriate approach for the communication of the findings and interpretations, creating a more broadly acknowledgeable value to archaeology (2000; 2005). The basic method applied by Hodder and Bender for contextualisation of archaeology, does offer scope for understanding how to investigate the values of excavation from the viewpoint of those involved in each stage of the project. These methods and approaches can be practically applied to the methodology of investigating the value of community archaeological excavations, which is the principal question of this research.

This anthropologically-based methodology could be described as a post-processual approach as opposed to a more rigid, processual methodology (Edgeworth 2006). In this context, by rigid I mean the use of closed questioning, and formal gathering of empirical and quantifiable data via the medium of pre-constructed interviews. These approaches are usually in the form of multiple-choice questions, which are aimed to produce quantitative information that can readily be subjected to statistical analysis. Examples of such quantitative analysis include Merriman's (1991) museum visitor survey. Quantitative questioning was deemed inappropriate for this present study, except for collating basic demographic information about the participants taking part in the interviews.

The quantitative approach has several fundamental flaws for application in this type of research (Mason 2002). Evidence of these flaws was indicated through the deconstruction of results from the quantitative analysis of Bruce Castle's community archaeology project (Rosenfield 2006). This survey was produced by the Museum of London Access and Learning Department. The questionnaires were handed out to visitors after attending the community archaeology excavation. They had specific objectives and aimed to gauge whether learning outcomes had been achieved, rather than assessing other more unquantifiable, intangible values.

This 'quantitative' approach is based on closed question methodology, in which specific questions produce a limited or predetermined selection of answers, usually focused on market values (McClanahon 2006, 127). This highlighted the approach's inability to allow for openness in responses and a lack of specific detail, which is required for this present, broader study of community archaeology, in order to assess the multiple and often un-quantifiable and interwoven personal values (McClanahon 2006, 127). The quantitative approach lends itself to accentuating predetermined research biases, as it has conscious objectives which affect the formulation of questions. The structure of the questionnaire can guide the participant in the survey to a particular answer and conclusion (Newman 1995, 321). This approach can create tensions, and barriers between the interviewer and interviewee, meaning honesty and openness in answers are potentially problematic. Personal experience also indicates that people are increasingly unwilling to participate in the survey as they feel threatened by the interviewing context or people feel alienated from the questionnaire because they feel the questions are not the right ones; consequently this would produce a bias in the demographic of the people being interviewed and an unfair representation of the community values. The results from quantitative surveys provide numerical estimates of the ideas of the person who designed the survey, simplifying complex concepts and failing to produce meaningful and tangible results. These biases mean that one could question whether this perceived scientific approach is actually scientifically valid, or merely pseudo-scientific. Of course there is variability in the quality of the construction of questionnaires, but very few archaeological surveys have been devised with sufficient understanding of the complexity of the science behind their formulation. But no matter how well formulated these are, they still elicit closed responses.

In summary, these surveys (Rosenfield 2006; Streeter 2006) have failed to tangibly answer questions relating to people's intangible values or beliefs, hence the inappropriateness in this approach for this particular study (see chapter 4). They have, though, highlighted themes that this study wishes to investigate further (see section 6.3):

- Archaeology is mainly associated with excavation; excavation may be a critical component to community archaeology projects and the production of values.

- People enjoy and have fun excavating; this indicates some form of social value.

- Archaeology and excavation are perceived to have educational potential; they are associated with educational value.

To tackle these more complex sociological and psychological issues relating to personal values and perceptions, it is necessary to produce an alternative methodology. This methodology will incorporate traditional demographic information, building from the generalisations that the closed question quantitative approach produces. It will use the generalisations of previous studies to provide a thematic basis to produce open questions, which allow for broader personal value-based answers (Emerson et al 1995, 143; Merriman 1991; Streeter 2006; Treble et al 2007). This approach could be described as producing specific individual responses rather than just numbers and generalisations.

Justification of this approach related to the core aims of the study, which was to increase understanding of the range of perceptions and values attached to community archaeology programmes within the community.

6.2 Aims of the Selected Methodology

It was felt that a qualitative, more flexible methodology was needed in order to understand:

1. The possible broader implications of community archaeology programmes on communities' values.

2. Community Archaeology's influence on the perceptions of archaeology/heritage in general.

3. The perceived and associated relative values of community archaeology, and more specifically community archaeology projects which involve excavation, versus the broader values associated with heritage and archaeology as a whole.

It is argued that questioning alone, even open questioning, would be insufficient to capture wider community's values. Some closed questioning was deemed appropriate in order to ascertain contextual relationships of interviewee to the site or area, and enable a summing up of responses. Subsequently, this study will primarily use casual interviews and participatory observations. This will allow for the assessment of the responses from a wider selection of the community, from different contexts, including those who are involved and not involved in the project.

6.3 Research Methods

A number of research methods were used, based on ethnological modes of enquiry (Newman 1995), with the objective of the research aimed at enabling a comprehensive understanding of the values of community archaeology excavations.

a. **Participatory Observation:** During the course of a community excavation the participants, both visitors and officials (meaning those who are proactively involved, or as part of learning programme, either informally or formally) and the staff, were observed. Observations will be made of personal interactions with the site, which were recorded in the form of field notes and photographs.

b. *Interviews:* The interviews were deliberately designed to be informal and conversational; using a semi-structured thematic approach which enabled an organic and flexible conversational style. As Jones (2004) suggests, this style of interview allows people to set their own agenda, and a relaxed situation and environment (including public places and space; such as café, public houses, community centres, to name but a few examples) enables people to be more open and honest with the interviewer (Jones 2004, 8). In many cases it is the relationship between the interviewer and the interviewee that influences the information that is received and its relevance.

These interviews were carried during the community archaeology project, so that organisers can be self-reflexive in their answers. It was deemed more appropriate when interviewing people in an official capacity to take a more structured approach, as this was more appropriate and comfortable for them.

Instead of formal questions the interviews are planned around key themes:

• Perceived values of archaeology, personally or to the community.

• Attitudes and associated values of being involved in excavation.

• How and where knowledge about the past is gained

• Broader attitudes to the past.

• Changes in values placed on archaeology, heritage after being involved in community excavation (if any).

• Future desires for involvement in archaeology

The benefit of an ethnological approach to questioning is that it allows individuals to be taken into account (Newman 1995), rather than suggesting that the community and all its members are homogenous, static, and will respond the same way in the same situation. During the interviews, demographic and biographic information (including age, gender, and proximity of home to site) was gathered. Interviews were recorded in either the form of field notes or digital recording, and these were transcribed.

Ethical guidelines for anthropologists (see the Association of Social Anthropologists Ethical Guidelines for further information on informed consent, http:/teasa.org/ethics. htm) were followed at all times.

6.4 Audit Research Methodology

Seven community archaeology projects were audited, from different geographical localities, four from within the UK and three in the US (Fig. 6.1 and 6.2). The reason for analysing the case studies outside the UK was firstly to give an idea of the different community perceptions of archaeology under different political situations, and also to investigate the effect that the flourishing indigenous rights movement has had on community archaeology in the US. These audit case studies aimed to show variability and diversity in community archaeology approaches.

Audit projects locations will be chosen based on the following criteria:

1. Case studies fell under the definition of Community Archaeology: (see Marshall 2009; and Chapter 1.1). As the definition of community archaeology is so broad and includes a diverse range of projects, this included projects that any member of the community could come along and take part in and furthermore had perceived community outputs.

2. The community archaeology projects included a community archaeology excavation, in order to test the theory that excavation is a core value attachment to archaeology (see Simpson & Williams 2008). The inclusion of a community excavation is perceived as a critical component for this study and is part of the hypothesis regarding changing values of heritage and archaeology through an interactive approach to the archaeological process.

3. Different localities, and hence different kinds of communities, were identified within. This included the assessment of projects in different geographical locations (e.g. urban and rural, see table 6.1). The comparison of the UK and US also highlights differences in the projects and the political, social, economic and cultural contexts in which they operate. The analysis considers how such contexts affect the projects in their entirety, including their aims, perceived values, management structures and the actual impact on community values.

4. All case studies were contemporary, operating during 2006-2009.

5. There was an ability to communicate, and collaborate with the organisers of these projects. This research required the agreement of the organisers to use the project, to visit the site, involve themselves and the rest of the participants in interviews and be able to carry out observations of the site whilst it is active.

6. The project had a diverse range of people actively participating or encouraged to participate in the community archaeology excavation; this diversity is based on age, sex, socio-economic status. This enabled

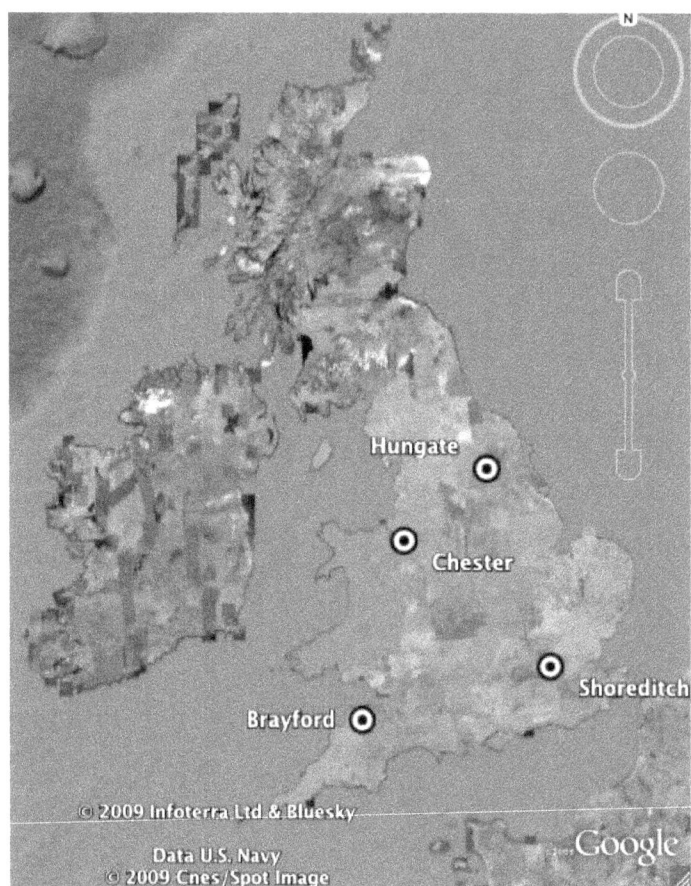

Figure 6.1 Map of UK location of case studies

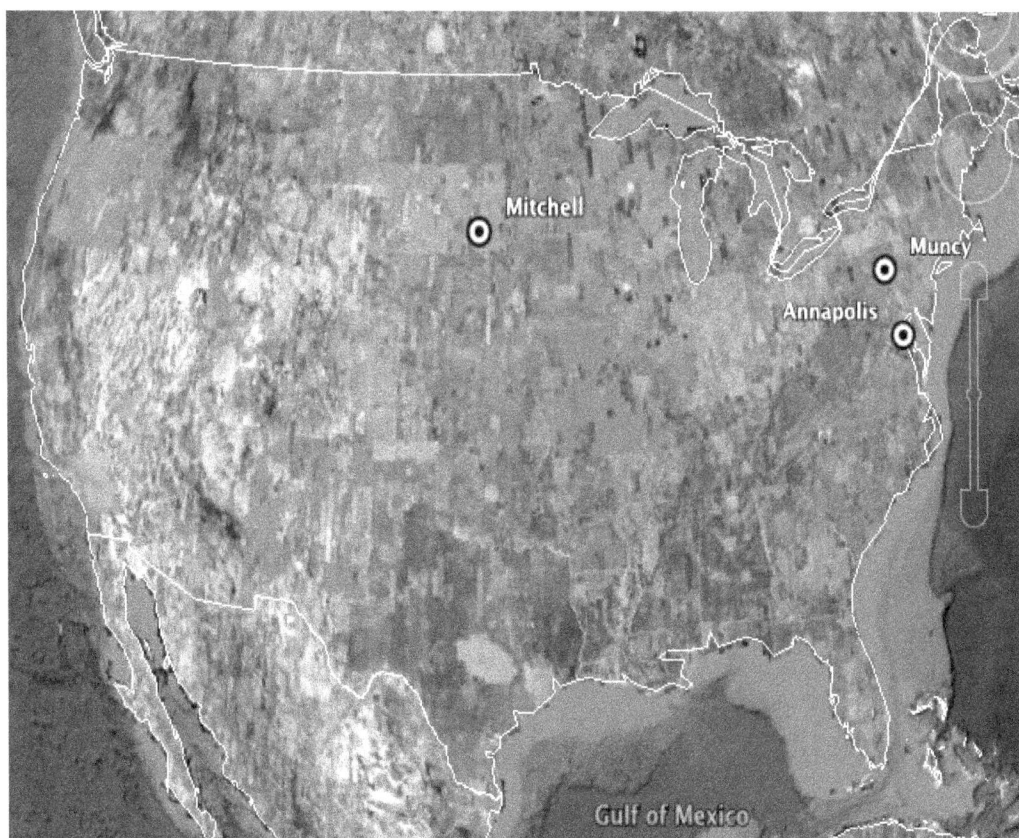

Figure 6.2 Map of Location of US case studies

Table 6.1 Summarising Audit Case Studies

Site Name	Country	Location	Lead Organization.	Funding	Rural/ Urban	Open Public Participation: Excavation	Open Public Participation: Finds Work	Volunteer Participation	Student Training	School Program
Shoreditch	UK	Hackney, London	Museum	HLF	Urban	Yes	Yes	Yes	Yes	Yes
Grosvenor Park	UK	Chester	Council	HLF	Urban	No	No	Yes	Yes	No
Hungate	UK	York, North Yorkshire.	Commercial	Developer	Urban	No	Yes	Yes	No	Yes
Brayford	UK	Devon	University	HLF	Rural	Yes	Yes	Yes	Yes	Yes
Mitchell	US	South Dakota	University	Private/Federal/ University	Urban	No	Yes	Rarely	Yes	Yes
Muncy	US	Pennsylvania	Historical Society	Historical Society	Rural	Yes	Yes	Yes	Yes	No
Annapolis	US	Maryland	Commercial	Developer (city council)	Urban	No	Yes	Yes	Yes	No

Table 6.2 Indicating, contact and web information giving contextual information for site

Site	Contact	Website	Site Period	Date Assessed
Shoreditch	Hedley Swain/ Faye Simpson	http://www.museumoflondonarchaeology.org.uk/English/ComLearn/ComExcavation/ShoreditchPark.htm	19th/20th Century	July 2006
Grosvenor Park	Jane Hebblewhite	http://www.chester.gov.uk/grosvenor_park.aspx	Roman to 17th	June 2007
Hungate	Peter Connelly/ Jon Kenny	http://www.jorvik-viking-centre.co.uk/hungate/index.htm	19th/20th century	April 2008
Brayford	Penny Cunningham	http://www.projects.ex.ac.uk/xarch/Brayford%20Com%20Ex.shtml	Roman	April 2008
Mitchell	Adrien Hannus/ Alan Outram	http://www.mitchellindianvillage.org	Prehistoric, Native American (1000 AD)	July 2007
Muncy	Bill Poulton/ Robin Van Auken	http://www.muncyhistoricalsociety.org/dig/index.html	19th/20th century	August 2007
Annapolis	Mark Leone	http://www.bsos.umd.edu/anth/aia/index.htm	17th-19th century	May 2008

the analysis and understanding of a broad section of the community, and value, producing results that are representative of the community as a whole, as opposed to a socially select group of people.

7. There was access to materials and resources, including access to written reports, project designs, historical records, grant applications, the site and the community. This access and support is essential in order to gain an insight and understanding of the aims of the project as perceived by the organisers (see table 6.2). This was vital as it affected the ability to analyse the values of the project to the community on site, during the community archaeology excavation.

6.4.1 Shoreditch

The community archaeology project of Shoreditch, is located in the borough of Hackney, within Greater London area, and provides an example of a community archaeology project run in the urban location in contrast with the rural locations of Brayford (UK) and Muncy and Mitchell (US). The project was also chosen as it fitted into the research criteria for selecting sites (See above). Furthermore, as project organiser I had access to all the relevant information about grants, aims and objectives of the community project, as well unique access to site during the community excavation of 2005 and 2006.

This project was the pilot case study, in which theories of longevity of involvement in assessment were tested. This case study used both self-reflexivity and ethnological methodology, in part because I was the project manager of this project, setting it up and running it prior to and during the course of the first year of my PhD.

6.4.2 Chester

The community archaeology project at Grosvenor Park, in Chester, was selected for research as a audit case study in part due it geographical location, its urban location offering a contrast between the rural setting of Mitchell and Muncy (US), and Brayford (UK) project.

The project also fitted into the research criteria for community archaeology projects (see above). It was a project that was similar to Mitchell, in which although excavation formed a major component but did not allow the public to actively participate in the excavation process. The project organisers (English Heritage and Chester County Archaeological Services) supported and agreed the use of the project for the research outlined above. This support enabled both access and provision of the information needed to deconstruct the aims of the project. It also provided me with the opportunity to interview the organisers prior to the commencement of the project and to attend the community excavation to carry out further investigation in June 2007.

6.4.3 Hungate

The community archaeology project at Hungate is located in the city of York, and provides an example of a community archaeology project run in an urban location, in contrast to the rural location of Mitchell and Muncy (US), Brayford (UK), and Hartland (UK). Furthermore it offered an interesting contrast with Heritage Lottery Funded projects, as this project was funded by Hungate Regeneration Ltd (Crosby Lend Lease, Evans Property Group and Land Securities Group PLC), and was a project that was integrated within commercial archaeology.

The project was chosen as it fitted into the research criteria for selecting sites (See above). It was a project that compared well with Muncy (US), and Brayford (UK) where excavation formed a major component and was open to all members the community. The project organisers (York Archaeological Trust) supported and agreed the use of their project for the research outlined above. This support enabled both access and provision of the information needed to deconstruct the aims of the project. It also provided me with the opportunity to interview the organisers prior to the commencement of the project and to attend the community excavation to carry out further investigation in January 2008.

6.4.4 Brayford

The community archaeology project at Welcome Farm, Brayford, was selected for research due to its rural location offering a contrast with the urban setting of Chester (UK) and York (UK).

The project also fitted into the research criteria for community archaeology projects (see above). It was a project that was similar to that of Muncy (US), and Hungate (UK). It was a project where excavation formed a major component and was open to all members the community. The project organisers (X-Arch community archaeology project, University of Exeter) supported and agreed the use of the project for research outline above. This support enabled both access and provision of the information needed to deconstruct the aims of the project. It also provided me with the opportunity to interview the organisers prior to the commencement of the project and to attend the community excavation to carry out further investigation in April 2007.

6.4.5 Mitchell

The site of Mitchell Prehistoric Indian Village is located in the state of South Dakota, in the North-Central US. The use of the site's public archaeology programme and excavation as a case study was chosen in part due to its geographical location. The location within the US provides an interesting dichotomy and contrast to that of the studies in the UK because it allows for the analysis of a different political situation and effect of contrasting federal and state laws, and the source of funding on the perceived values of archaeology and heritage.

The site was chosen because it is located in a rural area; providing a contrast with the urban area studies. Crucially, the site fitted the case study criteria (see above). Perhaps one major difference is that it does not allow the public to excavate but does allow them to view the excavation and interact through finds work. This provides a different, non-excavation example of community archaeology projects.

The choice of this site is also related to practical considerations; the site was directed by Dr Alan Outram (University of Exeter) and Prof L. Adrien Hannus (Augustana University, Sioux Falls (US)). Both people had very strong links to the archaeological and local community in the state. This meant easy access to information about the site and financial support for attending the fieldwork in July – August 2007 was supported by the University of Exeter.

6.4.6 Muncy

The Muncy Cannel Archaeology Project located in Pennsylvania (US) was selected for research as a case study to provide a comparative analysis with Mitchell, enabling the analysis of the different values attached participation in excavation rather than that of a non participatory approach.

The project also fitted into the research criteria for community archaeology projects (see above). It was a project that compared well with Hungate (UK) and Brayford (UK) where public involvement in excavation formed a major component of the project. The project organisers (Muncy Historical Society) supported and agreed to the use of the project for the research outline above. This support enabled both access and provision of the information needed to deconstruct the aims of the project. It also provided me with the opportunity to interview the organisers and to attend the community excavation to carry out further investigation in August 2007.

6.4.7 Annapolis

The public archaeology excavation at Fleet Street and Cornwall Street, in Annapolis was selected as a case study in part due to its urban setting, in contrast to Mitchell and Muncy (US), and Brayford (UK).

The project also fitted into the research criteria for community archaeology projects (see above). It was a project that paralleled with Chester (UK), and Mitchell (US) where public access to the excavation formed a major component of the project. The project organisers (University of Annapolis) supported and agreed the use of the project for the research outlined above. This support enabled both access and provision of the information needed to deconstruct the aims of the project. It also provided me with the opportunity to interview the organisers and to attend the public archaeology excavation to carry out further investigation in May 2008.

6.5 Summary of Audit Methodology

The analysis of these case studies, involved informal interviews, as well as participant observation and casual conversations with archaeologists, organisations, and community members. The first day of the two day fieldwork took place during the community archaeology excavation and involved informally structured interviewing of the archaeologists, project managers and directors as to the aims of the project, and their perceived

values of community archaeology excavations to the community. Informal semi-structured interviews (see appendix for guidance) were deemed most appropriate for this group as often their time is limited. It was estimated that these informal interviews were about thirty minutes in length (although will not be tightly upheld) and were recorded on a digital recorder. The context and locality in which the interviews were held was chosen by the interviewee, producing a situation in which they were comfortable and relaxed, and honest in their responses to the open, non-leading questions.

The second day of the fieldwork also took place during the community archaeology excavations, where community members both participating in and not participating in the excavation were interviewed, and observed. These interviews were more informal in structure than the interviews on the first day with organisers. They took place as casual conversations based around themes (as described in the methodology for the core case study), and through observations. Both of these, along with contextual information, were digitally recorded, transcribed and analysed. This research also included examination of literature, Heritage Lottery Fund bids and project designs, offered insights as to the project management and organisation.

The aim of this brief two day study in the field was to gain an understanding of the perceived values by the archaeologists and organisers of the project (i.e. project aims) compared to the values attached to 'community archaeology' by the members of the community themselves.

This critical analysis of community archaeology excavations aims to offer guidance for its future within the UK, and whether there is anything that can be taken from New World approaches that can be applied to the community archaeological approach within UK. Subsequently this research aims to draw from worldwide examples of community archaeology in order to understand perceptions, and the values of a broader demographic of people outside that of amateurs and professionals.

6.6 Political Context of Research

The funding for this PhD and subsequently this research was provided by the Heritage Lottery Fund, through the University of Exeter and the X-Arch community archaeology programme. The research to some extent is determined by my location within the University of Exeter and the British university system, and funding constraints that require the researcher to base their core location for research on community archaeology within the UK.

The funding for fieldwork is restricted to any fieldwork grants obtained from the university, external fieldwork grants, and support from community/public archaeology programmes. This affected both fieldwork location and time spent in the field. The research time was also limited to the duration of a three-year PhD.

6.7 Conditions and Duration of Fieldwork

The duration of the fieldwork is set to two days for each project, although some projects, due to the nature of my role in them, required me to stay on after the research was completed.

Initially I planned to live in these locations for a period, as it has been suggested that this is valuable for anthropological studies (Emerson *et al* 1995), in order to understand the participants, and to be able to observe daily activity and engage in casual daily conversations, and for people to feel comfortable in unstructured interviews. Yet, during my initial studies firstly in Shoreditch, where I lived for three years, and secondly in Mitchell, where I spent a month, and thirdly in Chester, where I merely visited, I noted little difference or evidence of problems with communicating with the public. In some senses a temporary visit enabled me to be less biased and observe from the periphery without being involved in excavation politics.

6.8 Investigator Knowledge

In order to gain an insight into the context, and the values of heritage to the community, it is important to research historical and contemporary literature which provides contextual information for the project research, offering personal insights as to the formation of archaeological values, both tangible and intangible. Archive material, council records, newspaper articles, surveys, local heritage documents, and books were used to develop a contextual understanding of the area. The results of this enabled the development of relevant qualitative fieldwork and were crucial for analysing the results from interviews and field notes. It offered a basis for contextualising the values attached to archaeology and the community archaeological excavations.

It was vital to be aware that personal circumstances and knowledge altered the type of investigations, interpretations and perceptions of interviews and participant observation. It was important to make these clear from the outset of research, and be aware of the biases these could cause in questioning, and conclusions. By identifying these from the outset, and becoming self aware of biases, it enabled the research to take a more balanced and self critical approach to the research.

It is important to mention that the researcher is not a trained anthropologist, rather an archaeologist. It was thus deemed appropriate to do extensive reading and ask advice from trained sociologists and anthropologists. This

was aimed at gaining a better understanding of the appropriate methods of anthropological research in the field, relevant to this specific context, but also in order to understand the ethical considerations of doing anthropological research (see the Association of Social Anthropologists Ethnics Guidelines for further information on informed consent, http://www.theasa.org/ethics.htm). The research was undertaken in accordance with The University of Exeter Research ethical code.

6.9 Number of Households, Individuals: Representation of classes, ranks, statues, role and gender in area

There was no formal demographic selection process for interviews, as the information was not intended to be used for demographic representational statistical analysis. The selection of people for this survey was based on the person's willingness to talk to the interviewer about the core themes of the study. Demographic information was gathered from the individuals participating in the interviews and semi-structured questionnaires, and interviews were carried out in a variety of locations, and selections of as many stakeholders as possible were interviewed.

6.10 Analysis

The analysis of the field notes collated during the ethnological study aimed to produce a coherent ethnography i.e. a thematic narrative. This identified common themes which were interwoven, producing patterns which led to conclusions. These conclusions related to the primary theme of this research.

The extensive field notes, including participant observations and transcribed conversations, were re-read after all the case studies were completed to form a comprehensive view and identify common themes. The analysis involved the careful reassessment and deconstruction of field notes, which involved coding of texts and conversations. Colour-coding was used to identify themes (Emerson *et al* 1995, 172).

The selection of field notes for presentation in this research was based on the following criteria:

- Relevance to primary themes of research

- Ability to illustrate patterns that are relevant to themes

- Capacity for providing an indication of differences and variation of ideas.

- Power to produce an evocative and persuasive tone, which engage and lead the reader into the ideas of the author.

Only a small proportion of the extensive field notes were selected for inclusion in the final text (Emerson *et al* 1995, 170), the rest is available in the appendices. This section of quotes and participatory observation commentary was structured within sub-chapters based on themes, where each excerpt was contextualized, quoted, and analyzed. This analysis deconstructed the excerpt and applied inferences about it relating to the sub-sectional themes (Emerson *et al* 1995, 182). These sub-sectional themes were linked back to the core themes in the discussion chapter.

6.11 Summary

The purpose of this ethnologically-based methodology was to provide a deconstruction of the public and professional values attached to community archaeology, and how these differ dependent on context and approaches. It offers a theoretical framework for deconstructing community archaeology and moves community archaeology on from being a theoretical concept, through evaluating what community archaeology actually does and whether the theoretical concepts of community archaeology work in practice. It offers an understanding of how the interaction of community archaeology and values takes place, and presents recommendations in its conclusions for best future practice.

7. AUDIT OF COMMUNITY ARCHAEOLOGY CASE STUDIES
IN THE UNITED KINGDOM

7.1 Shoreditch

Shoreditch in located in the Greater London borough of Hackney. It is an urban location with a dense population of 208,400, which has a diverse ethnic and racial make up of approximately 44% white, 25% Black Caribbean and African, 9% Asian, 4% mixed, and 3% Chinese (http://www.spiritus-temporis.com/london-borough-of-hackney/demographics-of-hackney.html). This should be compared 6.5% ethnic minority population in the UK as a whole (www.ukinnl.fco.gov.uk/resources/en/pdf/3190535/insight-uk-ethnic-diversity). At the time of the community excavation the site was within a Labour constituency and under a Labour government.

This community excavation was assessed using two different methodologies and two phases of ethnological research, which offered the opportunity for an experiment, and to test the validity of the methodology. In the first phase, during the 2005 and 2006 excavation seasons, the methodology involved informal conversational interviews with both participating and non-participating members of the community, and observations of the activities. Subsequently, a formal interview was conducted with Hedley Swain (Director (HS)), in which a degree of self-reflexivity was encouraged. Further information was gathered through the analysis of the material within the Time Team documentary "Buried by the Blitz" special, based on the community excavation, which recorded interviews with members of the public, and professional and personal opinions of the project.

The second phase occurred after the project was complete; it involved personal self-reflexivity. I set up, directed and managed this project during my employment by the Museum of London as a community archaeologist for Greater London. This offered me the opportunity to engage in critical analysis and provide personal insights, similar to those the other project managers engaged in with me during their interviews in the other case studies.

Local Attitudes to Archaeology

The community of Shoreditch compromises of numerous nationalities, which includes a diversity of ethnic and social groups, which is problematic in terms of creating or enabling homogenous views of the past. This is further complicated as many people rent and/or were not born in the area, or even the UK and their physical connections with the place may be transient, or they may not regard the area's heritage as their own. This is similar to attitudes expressed in Annapolis, as many of the population regarded their heritage to be passed down through oral tradition rather than being related to the physical remains of the place they currently live in.

This lack of continuity in the population was reflected in early discussions about the archaeological project with residents, as many where unaware of the history of the area and, despite the relatively recent addition of a park, they were unaware that it had not always been an open space. Consultations with the residents, Shoreditch Trust and Hackney Council suggested that there were no objections to archaeological projects being undertaken, as long as they involved the community, and did not encroach on the sporting area to the west side of the park. One of the things many residents frequently mentioned, and were confused about, was why the Museum of London would be interested in Hackney, and specifically Shoreditch Park, which was not particularly known for its rich heritage, or archaeological potential.

Context

Shoreditch Park is owned by Hackney Council, and managed by their parks department. On one side of the park is New North Road, the major road linking Islington and North London to the city of London. On all sides there is housing association accommodation in the form of large high-rise town blocks (see Fig. 7.1). In contrast to this lack of wealth, there is also the new luxury

Figure 7.1 Photograph of Excavation in Shoreditch Park
(Faye Simpson)

Gainsborough Studios apartment complex on the north side of the park. This is a heavily built up area, with 27 local primary schools, serving a population of over 200,000. There are issues with high crime rate and young offenders, and Hackney is also being redeveloped for the 2012 Olympics.

History

There was no permanent settlement on the site until 1832, when Smith's map indicated the first housing on the site. It was this period that also saw the area becoming connected with roads, like Dorchester Street, with housing along them. Prior to this, map regression work indicates that the area was used for agricultural and possible market gardens. The OS maps show that the area was by 1891 fully developed with residential housing, shops, factories and churches, which were linked to the spread of the City and London's growing population, which included many immigrants. A census in 1891, by the Salvation Army, indicated that much of the area around Dorchester Street was inhabited by a largely working class population, and much of this growing population appears from the records to be involved in local factory work.

The occupation of the area ended in 1941 when it was destroyed by German bombing, during the Blitz, and in subsequent V1 and V2 rocket attacks. The 1954 OS map of the area clearly indicates that many of the houses in Dorchester Street no longer exist, and much of this area is recorded as open land. In 1966 the OS reveals that much of the land to the east of Dorchester Street was used for 'prefab' housing, around the remains of the pre-war housing. In 1980 these 'prefabs' were demolished and the land was made into a park under the ownership of Hackney Council. Around the edges of the park there are elements of the pre-war landscape surviving in the street furniture (Aitken & Simpson 2005).

Background of the Community Archaeology Excavation

In 2005 and 2006, the Museum of London was funded by the Big Lottery Fund project 'Their Past, Your Future' to create and organise a community archaeology excavation in Shoreditch Park, in commemoration of the 60th anniversary of the end of World War II (Simpson and Williams 2008). The work was directed by the author, for the Museum of London, and grant-managed through the Museum, Libraries and Archives with support from Hackney Council and Shoreditch Trust. The project aimed to explore the nature of the community prior to World War II as well as the effects of the German bombing, a period that remains an important part of the community's remembered history and identity (Simpson and Keily 2005).

Participation

The excavation was open to the public for a three-week period in July 2005, and one week in August 2006. The public could attend drop-in sessions, which were open sessions on weekends, or booked sessions for School and community groups, running from 10.00-12.00 and 14.00-16.00, during the week (see Fig. 7.2). In each session started with an introductory talk on the history of the site, archaeology and health and safety, after which groups of up to thirty people where divided into two groups, which where rotated between finds processing and participation in excavation, this was followed by a debrief session.

Figure 7.2 Photograph of community excavating
at Shoreditch Park (Faye Simpson)

Volunteers from London Archaeological Archives Resource Centre (LAARC) and from the Volunteer Learning Programme (many of which where also members of local archaeology societies) where trained and assisted staff during the project. The project also took on seven undergraduate students from University College London, as part of their summer training excavation.

Espoused Values

Professionals: Part of the attraction and value of this site for the Museum of London was its location in inner-city London, an area known for its socially and ethnically diverse population, high crime rates and a high percentage of socially and economic disadvantaged groups (referred to as groups C2D&E: Aitken & Simpson 2005). Therefore, it had a political value and the project fitted into the Museum of London's Group Diversity Strategy 2005-2010, which aimed to reach new audiences outside the usual museum visitor demographics. These factors enabled the project to have the support from the directors of the organisation, which allowed access to the expertise, staffing, and resources of a large and respected professional archaeological unit and museum.

The project also aimed to "change internal views" (HS) relating to the relevance of archaeology and the importance of outreach for the archaeological profession, including museums. One of the agendas was using this outreach project to "build the capacity of LAARC, to be the focus of community archaeology and outreach and engagement" (HS), a facility already positioned in the heart of the community, and opposite the park, which, to date, the space and resources had been under-utilised.

The excavation of this 19th and 20th century site, fitted into the Museum of London's previously existing research programme: 'The Biographies of London Life Project' (The Archaeology of Londoners (1600-2000)), and it was a site that "John Shepherd (former manager of LAARC) had already done preliminary research on" (HS) based on this research potential. This existing research programme examined 17th to 20th century London through material culture, a period that has been under-researched by archaeologists in the UK, in terms of urban life and society. So, by asking the question "can we really glean anything from digging something this modern" (Tony Robinson (TR)), Shoreditch aimed to be a "real experiment" demonstrating whether this type of site could be of the value in examining the material culture of recent centuries as a primary medium for interpreting the past, rather than as a supporting medium to merely illustrate text-based narratives. "So digging 19th and 20th century is really about trying to prove we can add something to history" (Faye Simpson (FS)). This site was also used as part of the research agendas of Time Team, which became an "experiment to find out if it's possible to detect bomb damage" (FS), and to find out "what is the physical evidence that tells us about these horrific events" (TR). It was hoped the excavation would reveal physical evidence of bomb damage, including craters, evidence of blast damage and burning of the houses.

The aims of the project were as broad, aiming to provide, through excavation, within a socially inclusive and relevant archaeological project that directly engaged local people (Simpson 2005). The project aimed to enable local people to interpret their heritage, and through this

involvement and knowledge, provide them with a sense of pride in their local environment. It aimed to instil a "sense of place, improve the quality of life of the individual…making them feel better about where they live and their place in the world" (HS). It hoped to bring together a diverse community through a common goal and activity, therefore enabling a sense of social cohesion. It aimed through practical experience to provide an educational tool, both for life-long learning and schools, allowing students to learn about World War II, local history and the job of an archaeologist (Simpson 2005).

Public: The hope of many older members of the local community, particularly those who had lived or been brought up in the area, was that this project would raise awareness of the importance of the park to Council and prevent this open space being developed. During the consultation process those that attended commented that they were keen to see some of their history incorporated into the park, and where excited and surprised by the interest in 'their park.' Although it is important to mention that the majority of residents did not attend this informal meeting.

Government: Hackney Council supported the publically motivated aim to create a useful park. By offering an opportunity to turn this under-utilised area into a recreational space, the project also aimed to meet the All Party Archaeology Group and Department of Culture Media and Sport plans to make heritage more inclusive for London communities.

Nationally, it hoped to serve government agendas in, "celebrating the 60th anniversary of Second World War" (HS), which was a project that had been launched by MLA earlier in the Year and it was "struggling to find people" (HS), to support or host the exhibition. The Museum of London offered to accommodate it if the MLA would fund the excavation.

Actual Values

Professionals: The research value of this project was evident from the amount of archaeology that still survived and how this demonstrated that some of the historical records, in particular the bomb damage maps, were not always wholly accurate. The excavation provided evidence of the layout of the houses, supporting historical plans, but, more interestingly, it offered a personal picture of the former residents of Dorchester Street, from toys to the skeletons of pet cats in backyards (Simpson and Keily 2006). As TR said, "this is my kind of archaeology; with a plan from Iris (former local resident) all of a sudden the details of this house are so much clearer".

The excavation provided some of the first evidence for bomb damage in the archaeological record. The walls had separated, bulged and burnt, but that the lack of evidence of bomb damage elsewhere indicated that the historical sources were not always accurate with regard to the scale of bomb damage.

Combining all the evidence "slowly, but surely, the history of these streets is being pieced together in a way that is not possible in ancient sites" (TR). This research did affirm that excavating these contexts provided new evidence: "I think this project is incredibly important as it is excavating a new area of archaeology" (Stewart Anisworth (SA)). It also worked to change professional views of "digging through 19th and 20th century" (FS) archaeology, which was helped by employing commercial professional archaeologists.

For some of professionals, it did not change views of archaeology and the public: "I don't feel it changed views...it proved I was right" (HS) affirming what many in community archaeology already believed, that it was possibly to be "part of the link [between archaeology and the public], [as] archaeology is about the people, [therefore we need to] start doing slightly more archaeology with people" (HS). Furthermore, the research potential, public response and numbers involved provided evidence that it was possible to do modern archaeology and that this work was supported, and to some extent the public felt more comfortable with modern archaeology as they felt an attachment and prior, and personal understanding of the period. "Personally, I feel incredibly comfortable that we provide that modern archaeology, and members of public where very comfortable engaging in modern archaeology" (HS).

Furthermore, like Brayford and Hungate, it indicated that, despite professional worries about maintaining the quality of work whilst doing a community excavation, Shoreditch was able to "maintained professional standards of field-work whilst creating a friendly working environment" (Gabe Moshenska (GM)). This was something that was commented on by the many professional archaeologists and volunteers attending the excavation, even if it took longer than usual. In part, this related to the number of volunteers and professional staff and the ratio with community members, (due to insurance) had to be kept at a 3:1 ratio, similar to that maintained at Hungate. This ratio did limit the number of people able to get involved physically in the excavation, and of a local population of 200,000, only 3,000 in total attended and/or got physically involved. There was a large proportion who did not get physically involved yet who get value from being engaged with the excavation and finds through media involvement, including Time Team and local newspapers.

Those who ran the project did not believe that it changed political views toward outreach, but it did build community archaeology and excavations into agendas for the future: "In terms of the Museum of London the important thing is we demonstrated to ourselves that this was worthwhile, and the key people recognised it, and we kept it going...Now it would be seen as a bad show if that

department didn't do a dig somewhere every summer" (HS). Indeed, that *has* been the case ever since the Shoreditch Project. It forced an archaeology department, who had never done a community archaeological excavation before, to go out and engage in excavation with the public, therefore working as a form of outreach, rather than merely research.

Students: Training 11 undergraduate students in archaeological excavation, was something that was well received as it provided them with a broader knowledge of the past and working with the public; the "young archaeologists [were] brought face to face with people" (TR).

This project also acted to encourage personal research interests: a "valuable element of my research into oral history in historical archaeology" (GM), which provided some supporting evidence for an academic article about oral history and its value in archaeology. Furthermore, it provided a research case study for an MA dissertation (Streeter 2005). This was similar to the educational value for students achieved at Annapolis.

Public: For a period during the community excavation in July 2005 and 2006, when the project was part of Shoreditch Youth Festival, the project did offer a focus for the community. It created a social value and a renewed connection to the past for the residents, "keeping memories alive" (Stewart Anisworth (SA)) through sharing stories of their past. Residents related that during the blitz they "were scared all the time," (Grace Cook), and "all you could see was red" (Gladys Sulliven (GS)). Furthermore, it enabled the verbalisation of pride in their area: "this is important to the community around here, to know their history, even if it's just goes back to the 1840's, 1850's, to them its history, and it's our history" (Ezzie Dye (ED)). The pride and social value appeared to be transferred to this younger generation, in a similar guise to Hungate, there was no vandalism in the park or to the site during the excavation, something that surprised the local police and youth offending team. It was even commented that crime had been reduced, and some of the young offenders became regulars on the site after school.

Its location and support from local charities and community groups, and the involvement of the project in other community activities, including Shoreditch Youth Festival, encouraged a more socially and ethnically diverse participation in the excavation than any of the other case studies. Still, as Streeter (2005, 28) commented, "it was not attracting a diverse range of people, representative of the local area (with the exception of school children)." The ethnic make up of the attendees did no match the ethnic make up of the local area and the majority of the attendants where still white and middle class. This perhaps gives some indication that archaeology is still perceived as irrelevant to diverse ethnic and social groups, who may not regard this type and period of archaeology as part of their heritage. Furthermore, this may highlight issues relating to perceptions of the discipline of archaeology and of archaeologists as elitist.

The oral history component of the project was especially successful in bringing together the community, with the older generations able to share stories about their experiences with younger generations (Moshenska 2007b): "the real thing to me is our young archaeologists here being brought face to face with people for who[m] that archaeology was a living breathing reality" (TR). It was believed that the nature of this site enabled this wealth of information to be shared. "The familiarity of the subject made it easier for members of the public to connect and engage with the subject, this became most clear in the oral history work I carried out" (GM).

Initially, the project had educational value, as Streeter (2005, 28) comments, "the learning outcomes where good". It increased the knowledge and awareness of World War II and "raised awareness of archaeology" (HS). The marketing survey carried out concluded that "children and adults with no prior knowledge picked up a lot of new and interesting information" (Streeter 2005, 28), something supported by local comments like: "Dorchester Street, I didn't even know it was here until the boy came over and cleaned the top of it…it's history right under our nose" (Dean Sullivan (DS)). One of the motivations for bringing school children along was that the Blitz fitted into National Curriculum. The interest of the children and the adults was focused on the finds: "come see what I have found" (Yetty). One teacher commented "it's just like the whole treasure thing, it's like finding treasure, it's interesting to anyone if you dig up a floor and come across things you didn't know were there." In some respects it was the fact that there were "plenty of finds to keep the public happy digging" (TR), rather than they wanted to dig *per se*. There were similar issues at Brayford, where it was claimed that it was the "items that bring the past to life in a way that history books never can" (TR). This type of comment was often heard at Mitchell, too.

The educational value was, in some respects, temporary, even though there were finds handing boxes created for after the project was complete. The take up on these was minimal by schools. It appeared that it was the social value, and entertainment value of this project that was the most successfully achieved: "ask my kid now [and] they would remember having a good time, but if you asked them what they were digging, and all that, they wouldn't remember" (HS). Despite this, the positive experience may be remembered in the future when they are adults and affected their personal decisions regarding visiting archaeological sites and supporting local heritage.

In the survey carried out by Streeter (2005), it was highlighted that the project's enjoyment value was very high. This statement was backed up by comments like "I had lots of fun here" and "I really like this trip" (Streeter 2005, 21). It appears from anecdotal conversations with

the participants that the chance to dig was "fabulously entertaining" (Anonymous (A)). The project's entertainment value, and subsequent social value, was reflected in Time Team's filming of the project as a documentary special during 2005, which attracted viewing figures of over 3 million (see Fig. 7.3). This brought with it support, especially the resources and logistics that the Channel Four television programme facilitated. This included the ability to research and access information and people: "it usually gives you about 10 million pounds of free publicity and marketing, it gives you several tens of thousands worth of research and kit" (HS) and by successfully communicating and disseminating the results of the project to a wide audience, that "really enjoyed the programme" (Yetty), both within and outside the local community. Unfortunately, the programme was screened in later 2006, after the project had completed, and after community interest had waned. Furthermore, the Museum of London was not made aware of the date of screening until a few days before the event, so was unable to utilise the interest to attract more people into the Museum.

Figure 7.3 Photograph of Time Team filming the excavation at Shoreditch Park (Faye Simpson)

The value of this project was high for a select group of people, principally those who experienced digging, "few out of the 1000's people it had a powerful impact on" (HS). For local volunteer diggers and those who attended the project regularly it was successful: "volunteer digger Den is even starting to talk like an archaeologist" (TR). "…you got the two features here and this one over here "(DS), Den goes on to describe how you identify and interpret the archaeological evidence as resulting from bomb damage. It also had an impact on former residents of Dorchester Street, such as being "…both surprised and excited to see their childhood home again" (TR). This raises questions over whether it is better to reach fewer people and provide quality over quantity. It appears that you cannot always have both, and this is something that MLA is debating and researching the moment.

Government: Locally, Hackney Council supported projects that built on the interest generated by Shoreditch, and Hackney Museum set up an exhibition relating to the site and the archaeology of World War II after the excavation was complete. This included much of the material found during the excavation and it was hoped that visitor figures would increase, but the boost was very transient and numbers dramatically declined following the exhibition's opening. The park itself was redeveloped, signs erected and pathways put in which followed the line of old streets hidden beneath the ground. This was a positive, but non-engaging step. It did at least help to remind the public of what is beneath their feet and perhaps of their experiences in the summers of 2005 and 2006.

The project aimed to change external politics relating to the importance of archaeology to communities. It is questionable whether this was achieved in the short timescale of the project. It did raise awareness of community archaeology, and archaeology in general, within the council and wider political players, including visits from the then Minister for Culture, Media and Sport, David Lammy, and some of All Party Parliamentary Archaeology Group, including the local MP, and Council for British Archaeology staff. This did not affect the amount of money given to support further community excavations or continuation of this project. However, David Lammy's suggestions of doing a dig in Tottenham, his local constituency, were taken seriously and did occur in 2006.

7.2 Chester

Chester is a historic cathedral city located the County of Cheshire in North West England (see Fig. 7.4). It is known as one of the best-preserved Roman and medieval walled cities in the United Kingdom, and has a population of just over 80,000 (http://www.chester.gov.uk/council_and_democracy/research_and_intelligence/chester_in_context.aspx). At the time of this case study it was under a Labour-dominated city council, although it fell to Conservative in recent local elections (http://www.chester.gov.uk/council_and_democracy.aspx).

Over a two-day period in June 2007, I undertook formal interviews, casual conversations and participant observations to investigate community aspects of excavations at Grosvenor Park, the Roman amphitheatre and a Visitor Centre located across the road from the amphitheatre. I also conversed with people in the city, in cafés, bars, restaurants, and shops and in the youth hostel, as well as at a local high school with 6th form students. These students were taking part in a geography lesson relating to Grosvenor Park where they were planning to conduct visitor surveys. This class was led by Chester City Outreach Officer, with Jane Hebblewhite (community archaeologist) and myself present in an observing role (I was positioned at the back of the classroom, talking notes).

Figure 7.4 Photograph of Chester City Centre (Faye Simpson)

I carried out formal interviews with Jane Hebblewhite (community archaeologist (JH)), Mike Morris (City Archaeologist (MM)), Garth Richards (local volunteer (GR)) and Dan Gardenier (Excavation Director (DG)) and also held conversational interviews with members of public, staff members, and council employers. I discussed the project with Stewart Ainsworth and Tony Wilmott (English Heritage) prior to a visit to the site, as they were involved in the planning stages of the Grosvenor Park excavations and were directly involved with Chester Amphitheatre Project.

Local Attitudes to Archaeology

In 2007, a survey of local attitudes toward heritage and archaeology was carried out by undergraduate students attending Chester Grosvenor Park excavation (Treble, Smithies and Clipson 2007). The quantitative survey was based on email questionnaires and asking people visiting or passing through the park about the publicly viewable excavation. It found that the local people had a high level of interest in archaeology, but still perceived it as inaccessible, despite the four-year presence of a publicly viewable archaeological excavation at the amphitheatre site. Interestingly, it also concluded that people enjoyed watching the work and thought that the Grosvenor Park excavation was important, but did not want to get actively involved (86%). Furthermore, it found that this dynamic way of presenting information met audience expectations (Treble, Smithies and Clipson 2007, 5).

This quantitative survey provided interesting, if somewhat superficial, insights from the fifth-seven people who filled in the questionnaire. Many of the closed questions were answered with 'yes' or 'no' answers including: 'Did you enjoy watching the excavation?' As such, these answers did not provide much insight into people's values regarding heritage or why they enjoyed the excavation. However, the research can, and does, complement the qualitative research that this study advocates, because it provided a brief overview of opinion from a select demographic.

Conversations with local people indicated that many had a very strong connection with, and a great pride in, their city: "Chester is a magical place" (anon. resident). Furthermore, many felt strongly about the amphitheatre project, and were confused about why this public excavation had stopped and would like to see more digs made public. The attitude towards archaeology was positive, but there was discontent at the lack of work and lack of maintenance (as voiced in letters to county archaeological service) in relation to the amphitheatre.

Despite this, the amphitheatre was not as high the local government agenda, especially considering that over the last five years budgets have been cut, and English Heritage has also cut its financial support to the project. The Archaeological Service, which is still under the control of the City Council, is gradually coming under more financial pressure.

Context and History

The site of Grosvensor Park is owned by the City Council and is located in the city centre. Public archaeology in Chester hit the political, professional and public radar in 2002, when the Chester Amphitheatre Project undertook the first season of a four-year excavation project, funded by English Heritage and Chester City Council, based on initial discoveries dating back to the 1970's. The archaeological work aimed to define and understand Roman Chester and 'inform future management, conservation and display' (Ainsworth and Wilmott 2005). Furthermore, its location in the centre of the city, and at the side of the central ring road, meant that this project could fulfil English Heritage's and Chester City Council's duty to present and make archaeology accessible to the public. The excavation had walkways and displays put around it, so people could observe the work in process. This proved highly successful in terms of both increasing interest and knowledge about Chester's Roman heritage and increasing tourism in Chester.

Excavation in Grosvenor Park aimed to locate 'Cholmondeley's Mansion.' It was believed this was built on what was originally the site of the church of St John, which passed Sir Hugh Cholmondeley after the Dissolution. The ecclesiastical building was destroyed during the Civil War and in the 18th century the mansion was built in its place (Morris 2007, 1; Ainsworth and Wilmott 2005, 29). The building was demolished two hundred years later, when the park was laid out (Ainsworth and Wilmott 2005, 29). Furthermore, excavation would solve a few puzzles about the development of this area of the city from the Roman period to the 19th century (Morris 2007, 1; Ainsworth and Wilmott 2005, 29). A geophysical survey carried out by English Heritage, under the guidance of Stewart Ainsworth, identified a number of features in the west end of the park. These were correlated

with map regression work and historical texts, as indicating the former presence of buildings and 'Cholmondeley's Mansion' (Ainsworth and Wilmott 2005, 30).

Background to the Community Archaeology Project

Grosvenor Park training project and 'publicly viewable excavations' started in June 2007 (see Fig. 7.5). In many respects this project stemmed from the success of the amphitheatre 'public archaeology' project, and the City Archaeologist's and Council's desire to keep the impetus of the amphitheatre project alive. The park, being Council owned land, aimed to provided the focal point for the community to view and experience a new component to the project. It also was seen as an opportunity to research the extent of the Roman activity, enabling the amphitheatre to be placed in a wider context. The work was funded by the City Council, in support of their conservation management plan for the park, and a successful application that had been by Chester City Council to Heritage Lottery Fund in the form of their 'Parks for People' bid (Morris 2007, 1). Subsequently, they were required to find out more about the archaeology and history of the park, in order to inform future activities and development.

Figure 7.5 Photograph of fencing around community excavation in Grosvenor Park (Faye Simpson)

The archaeological intervention itself was comprised of three separate trenches, each investigating a different geophysical anomaly. All of these were located just to the side of public walkways in the park. The trenches were surrounded by Harris fencing and interpretation panel around the outside that allowed for easy viewing by the public.

Participation

The setting was similar to Mitchell in the sense that it allowed the public to watch the process of excavation, although not actively participate. Its primary participatory aim was to provide excavation experience for Chester University archaeology students, along with providing opportunities for local volunteers (the majority of which where local amateurs), many who had worked at the amphitheatre in previous years (see Fig. 7.6). It also provided schoolwork experience students with an opportunity to be involved, but because this was primarily a research project under time constraints, casual involvement by the wider public was very limited.

Figure 7.6 Photograph of volunteers excavating at Grosvenor Park (Faye Simpson)

The finds processing was visible to the public and it took place in the visitor centre across the road. Many of the visitors to the park excavation did not and did not intend to visit this, as it did not seem as exciting to them.

Espoused Values

Professionals: The archaeological work was, to a large extent, based on professional research objectives. On the surface it appeared that the community archaeology aspect was secondary, although still important. In some respects, making it a 'public archaeology excavation' (i.e. marketing it as a training project, volunteer programme and viewable excavations) (Morris 2007, 1) facilitated the funding for the research, which would eventually be of benefit to the public, and enable preservation and presentation of the archaeology to the public.

The project was supported by the Council, who believed it fulfilled their role as a "public service [whose] core role is to try and communicate and make archaeology accessible to the public" (MM). It believed that publicly visible and accessible excavations were a successful way of doing this: 'there is no other way in my experience of enthusing people as much, pound for pound, really" (MM).

Educationally it was hoped that this project would "expand their [the public's] knowledge and values and

make a difference, provide them with what they want and more" (JH). It was also hoped that this would change people's perceptions and "make people aware that we are doing it for them; we are not just digging holes and going away...It will encourage people to go away and do research themselves, even have respect for the environment" (JH).

Another aim was to educate the public about the archaeology of Chester by "imparting a little bit of knowledge in layman's terms, using modern comparisons, and making them think about how things get here" (MM). In other words, the project aimed to get people thinking.

Students: The organisers and archaeologists for the excavation were lecturers attached to the University of Chester's Department of History and Archaeology. In this role they had made a commitment to provide a training excavation for the University's students, which was a core component of their course. Such experience is not often achieved on commercial archaeology projects of university excavations, due to time pressures, health and safety, and insurance issues (for an example of an exception see York case study).

There were also some schoolwork experience students, aged 16-18 involved in the excavation. It was seen by both them and their schools as an opportunity to experience real archaeology and therefore be able to make informed choices about a future career in the subject.

Public: "You never know what their values are" (MM). The Council hoped it, as part of their park redevelopment plan and their 'Parks for People' bid that this public excavation would provide an opportunity to understand and liaise with the public about their values with regard to heritage and the park, itself. The Council also hoped that their outreach staff could incorporate these values as part of the consultation process for the Heritage Lottery Fund bid for the future plans for the park.

Since 2006 and the end of the amphitheatre excavations, there had been (what is described by the organisers of this project) as widespread public demand for the council to provide further viewable excavations, and to somehow maintain the interest in archaeology that the amphitheatre project had sparked.

Many of the public viewed the archaeology and public archaeology projects as a benefit but "...don't think they [the Council] are going to rate archaeology very highly... it comes way down the bottom in providing for people and that sort of thing"(GR). It was hoped that this project would raise the profile of archaeology at local government level and encourage support for archaeology, and future projects including the future plans for development of the Chester amphitheatre project. It aimed to make the local government understand the excavations at the amphitheatre in a wider context, but also to perpetuate the public's interest and passion for archaeology.

Assumptions were made about what the public were interested in and wanted to see. For the organisers it was assumed that the majority wanted to dig or at least experience of seeing excavation would excite them, making them want to learn more about archaeology. It was believed that a public archaeology project would provide people with the opportunity to understand archaeology, and archaeological methods and techniques, better. It was hoped it would provide them with a broader knowledge of the area, and a greater respect for the park though understanding its history and connection to the amphitheatre.

Actual Values

Professional: Having to be in the park, working in a public place, forced many of the archaeologists to re-evaluate their opinions and views towards the public (see Fig. 7.7). For many diggers, the public came to be regarded as a nuisance, and not particularly interested or informed: "When I was digging the trial trenches, homeless people would hang around the place. I found them irritating at first, but when you engaged with them, they are really some of them who are really intelligent, just unfortunate. They respond very positively if you engage with them" (MM). Furthermore, many archaeologists assumed that if you did a dig in the park, then it the excavation would be vandalised by youths, though this did not happen, since many of them came up to the fence and asked questions. Some even wanted to know if there were any jobs, and what a career in archaeology is like. Many of the archaeologists on site actually discussed being surprised about what they learned, and "people would stop...I enjoyed chatting to them" (GR).

Figure 7.7 Photograph of Dan with Dig T-shirt encouraging the public to talk to staff (Faye Simpson)

Students/volunteers: Participation in Chester's public excavations has allowed many of students to get the vital experience, which will enable employment afterwards. This is evident from the fact that many previous students from the amphitheatre dig have been employed at Grosvenor as site supervisors. Many of the volunteers discussed enjoying the project and the friendliness of the students was apparent; they wanted to come back the next year, as many have done in previous years. This could be seen as training the students and amateur volunteers in the process of archaeology, and other transferable skills. For some of the volunteers, the experience of digging has put them off wanting to excavate, yet this experience has led them into finds work: "I didn't ever feel very confident digging; it was difficult archaeology, looking at soil changes." (GR) Other volunteers discussed the more social aspect of digging, rather than the activity of digging itself. It interested them to work in a team and they enjoyed the fact that excavation was a 'great social activity' (JH). The dig provided them with friendships, both in and out of the field, meeting in the winter months in the pub.

Public: The majority of people I stopped and talked to over the days in Chester were genuinely interested in the archaeology. Most frequently they referred to it in to the context of the Roman amphitheatre excavations, or Time Team: "most people were interested in what we were doing" (anonymous archaeologists).

Some of the public walking past the excavation and seeing the 'activity' made them question why they weren't involved, and have got in contact with Jane Hebblewhite and subsequently volunteered: "Coming past it and thinking this is stupid, why aren't I involved?' (GR). Furthermore, it changed their opinion; some were interested in history but knew very little about archaeology: "my interest was in history rather than archaeology, but I enjoyed it, I enjoyed the company" (GR). These people discussed that it was the "activity and not the knowledge that they where interested in, the process rather than the outcome" (JH) which surprised the professionals.

Interestingly, despite the belief by the professionals that too many people wanted to excavate, the majority of people, after watching the process of archaeology, did not want to dig. They were "surprised at how much digging was involved." (Anonymous Volunteer), but they did seem to be interested by watching the excavations and find processing: "love seeing people work" (Anonymous Visitor (AV)), "enjoy watching people doing things" (AV). They found it entertaining, but also very quickly lost interest and wandered off. This was especially the case when it was realised that there was nothing valuable being found: "most of it is scrappy little bones" (AV), and were interested "...but only if there were swords, not pieces of pot on their own, those have no meaning" (AV). Furthermore, many were "disappointed it was not like the telly" (AV). This was supported by the lack of approaches from people wanting to volunteer to dig, which has surprise the organiser who observed that there was "not that pressure for community archaeology excavation that there was last year when the amphitheatre was running" (JH). This suggests several things about this excavation, that its location, finds, type of archaeology and profile have not raised public interest in the same way the amphitheatre. People are not as interested in this type of less visually stimulating excavation, instead wanting to see reconstructions and exciting things like Time Team and "experience the excitement."(AV). Perhaps this is also a benefit to the profession since many of the public, after seeing this experience, questioned the reality of the television portrayal of archaeology, but they were disappointed and disillusioned that is not similar.

Experiences and feedback during this excavation led volunteers to suggest, "people prefer talking rather than looking at notice boards" (GR). This was seen in that people would briefly glance at the notice boards next to the trenches, but spend more time looking into the trench. For some this gave them the opportunity to 'ask the questions I want to know' (AV) which not only opened up dialogue between the archaeologists and the public, but also made the professionals discuss amongst themselves what the public were really interested in. For many, they realised it was the 'instant archaeology', for example the finds they were interested in. Many of the public stopped and looked in, and in many cases seemed to want to ask questions, but failed to do so. They appeared to open their mouths to say something, looked quizzically, tried to get the attention of one of the excavators', but then changed their mind and walked away tentatively, looking back frequently. This would indicate the need for either one of the volunteers or archaeologists to be specifically put in place outside the excavation area and around the fences to talk to and engage with the public, rather than waiting for the public to make the first move.

Since the public archaeology programme in Chester, like Mitchell, South Dakota (US), there has been a reported increase in tourist numbers. "A tourist survey said that the (amphitheatre) excavation was the second tourist attraction in Chester next to the cathedral: we jumped up from nowhere' (MM). This could through indicate that the same number of tourists merely changed their preferences.

7.3 York

The City of York is located in the county of North Yorkshire, North East England. It is known as one of the best preserved walled cities in the United Kingdom. The city itself has a population of just over 18,1094; with an ethnicity of 95% white British (national average is 87%) (2001 census, http://www.york.gov.uk/content/45053/ 64877/64880/Census_information/York_2001_census_pr ofile). Politically, the city council is currently under no

overall control, but the liberal democrats have the most seats.

Over a two-day period in March 2008 I carried out formal interviews, casual conversations and participant observations. This investigation took place on the community excavationat Hungate, at the DIG at the Archaeological Resource Centre, at the offices of York Archaeological Trust and also included casual conservations in the city's cafes, bars, restaurants and shops. I formally interviewed Peter Connelly (Director of the Excavation (PC)), Jon Kennedy (Community Archaeologist for YAT (JK)) and Pam White (Volunteer Coordinator of the Community Excavation (PW)). Informal conversational style interviews were carried out with members of public, staff members and volunteers.

Local Attitudes to Archaeology

The research revealed a very positive connection to the archaeology of York by the local people. Many of the local public appeared to be proud of "their heritage", even saying that its heritage made it a beautiful city this was one of the reasons for moving to the area. The residents' positive associations with heritage also, in part, related to the economic benefits of 'heritage tourism' to the City of York. This was substantiated positively by comments from tourists. The heritage is seen as an important tourist draw to the City, which is something that local govern-ment had built on, with the support of the tourist industry, leading to investment in large and internationally renowned projects, including creation of the Jorvik Viking Centre, DIG, the Castle, and York Dungeons.

The City of York's specific interest and investment in heritage is also reflected in the drawing up and passing of Section 106, which is a non-statutory guidance to supplement the planning policies for the City of York (http://www.york.gov.uk/environment/Planning/guidance/ S106_Obligations/). This specifies the need to consider heritage 'education provision' as part of planning consent for the development of open spaces, and a financial contribution from the developer for this can be built in at the planning stage (S106).

Context

The site of Hungate is located of in the centre of York, within the city walls. It is private land owned and being developed by (York) Regeneration Ltd. This regeneration project is joint venture between Crosby Lend Lease, Evans Property Group and Land Securities Group PLC (www.jorvik-viking-centre.co.uk/hungate/abouthungate/ about1.htm). It will result in a large number of houses being built to meet the increasing demand for housing within the city. The developer-funded archaeological research and community archaeology programme being carried out on site is a requirement of planning consent under PPG16 and S106 (Connelly et al 2008).

The excavation carried out by York Archaeological Trust commenced in 2007 and it is planned to run until 2012 (www.jorvik-viking-centre.co.uk/hungate /abouthungate/ about1.htm). The archaeological site is comprised of a large open area excavation, with fencing around the edge of the site, and public walkways running through the middle and around, so that the public can view the archaeology (See Fig.7.8).

Figure 7.8 Photograph of Hungate
(Faye Simpson)

History

The site of Hungate is outside the original Roman fortress; it is believed that archaeology on this site is more likely to the medieval, dating from the Norman Conquest (www.jovik-viking-centre.ac.uk/hungate/history/ medieval.htm). Documentary evidence suggests that this was a medieval rubbish dump. From the 16th -18th centuries, map evidence from John Speed's map (c.1610) and others, indicates that there was a wide street running through this area alongside the River Foss (www.jovik-viking-centre.ac.uk/hungate/history/postmed.htm). There was a massive development of the area in the 19th century, with new streets and buildings being laid. In the 1840's Hungate became known as a poor glass-working area and in 1901 Seebohm Rowntree referred to it a one of the main slum districts of York. Industries were established in the area, such as a sawmill and flourmill, but these were cleared in 1930's along with slums and the area was redeveloped for light industry and warehousing. One of the main aims of the archaeological research is to investigate the urbanisation and industriali-sation of the area (www.jovik-viking-centre.ac.uk/hungate/history/modern. htm)

Background to the Community Archaeology Project

The community archaeology project and publicly viewable excavations started in 2007 as a prerequisite to redevelopment of the site for housing (Connelly *et al*

2008). The aim of the excavation was to reveal and recover the archaeological remains that would otherwise be destroyed by development; it is therefore a 'rescue excavation.' Interestingly, there is not specific clause in PPG16 which specifics public involvement, so the public outreach on this site occurred through pressure from the City Council archaeologist and planning officers, York Archaeological Trust's involvement and the developer's sense of 'corporate responsibility.' In part this was possible because of York's long standing tradition of developing public archaeology projects, and outreach activities, including the Archaeology Resource Centre (www.yorkarchaeology.co.uk) and Jorvik Viking Centre (www.jorvik-viking-centre.co.uk). Subsequently, at Hungate walkways were opened up around the site, with corresponding display panels, and opportunities were created for volunteers to excavate on certain days of the week.

The Hungate project was not the first attempt York City Council and York Archaeological Trust made to make commercial excavations accessible to the public. The Coppergate excavations in the 1979- 1981 had walkways and a museum located on the site, which encouraged the public to visit, but it was perceived by the local residents with some degree of scepticism, as many still did not feel that they were consulted or informed sufficiently about the work and the findings, which is still brought up (http://www.jorvik-viking-centre.co.uk/about2.htm).

It is important to note that the 'community' in Hungate is a constructed one; the community group, Hungate Community Trust, is the result of the developer's need for public consultation during the project. Historically, Hungate has had no resident community since the 1930's, when the last housing was knocked down (Wilson 2007). Therefore, the community participating in the excavation is a specific group of interested people, rather than a truly local and contextual community.

Participation

The surrounding community were able to participate actively in the excavations at Hungate through becoming part of the community archaeology programme, which was done by contacting Jon Kenny, and arranging a taster session. Following this, participation was structured, and focused around Wednesdays and Thursdays each week, and with a later addition of one Saturday a month. The decision to operate on these specific weekdays was based on providing opportunities within the normal working week for of the professionally employed archaeologists employed on the commercial excavation at Hungate. Therefore, this meant that demographically participation was primarily limited to retired and unemployed members of the wider York community. The majority of public's involvement, however, was through taking tours and viewing the site from platforms and walkways, rather than through active participation.

Espoused Values

Professionals: There were two distinct strands of values attached to the project by professional archaeologists. These related to the community and commercial aspects of the project. In both of these strands there was the value of research, and acquiring new knowledge about the site. It was also about "experiencing a commercial dig from a completely [new] way from how they would see it through a training excavation" (JK) and there was a balancing act to be performed. In many ways the commercial project was more important, and the community aspect was ancillary, with professionals having to "fit in extra activities for people to join us in our job" (PW), rather than the community aspect coming first and professional archaeologists being employed to cater for the community.

Some professionals saw it as 'community archaeology validating a profession, getting people out of holes and [therefore] broadening the social context [value]" (Martin). This was of value to the profession as well as to the public "working to attract other professionals to the site" (PC) in order to open their eyes up to the possibly of commercial and community archaeology working together. York Archaeological Trust (which is a charitable organisation but engages in commercial archaeological work, under the remit of re-investing profits from this into its charitable trust) was in charge of the archaeological project, and also the supplier of staff for the community archaeology dig through grants. Therefore the structure of the organisation and its remits of enabling access and education was a key *raison d'être* and keeping up this profile was very important to them as a organisation: "to start with, everybody thought are they going to do this public access that is in the project design? But of course we are, especially with YAT because that is part of our reason for being" (PW) and there has been a long history of such commitment.

This community archaeology project was valued by professionals because of its ability to provide 'access' to archaeology, and because it can 'add value...getting people to come along" (PC). The archaeologists believe that 'encouraging people to do things they wouldn't usually do" (PC) increased values in archaeology through creating new audiences and a new interest in the past, "creating a stimulus across the board" (PC). Although the educational value was emphasised by the project team as an important aim it was not the only one. It was also hoped that this active involvement in archaeology would add values "beyond knowledge" (JK), promoting quality of life: "[we] want to know about how this affects health and wellbeing of people" (JK)

The professionals hoped that this project would change the public's perception of the process of archaeology and understand that it is 'not just about getting down on your trowel for a couple of hours and finding things' (JK). Its aim was that by sharing this knowledge and involving them in excavation it would change and increase the value and respect for archaeology, therefore could have an influence on the public's support for archaeology in the future.

Public/Volunteers: Many of the public and volunteer's views and values about archaeology came from television, "my views come from what I have seen on TV" (David, Volunteer), and many commented that this was what had interested them in coming along, "for a fun day out for the children...something we could all do together....getting to see the real thing" (AV).

During initial consultations prior to the excavation commencing, the volunteers (Hungate Community Group) commented that they "produced a list of aims for Hungate and community archaeology" (Martin). This list included a heavy emphasis on active involvement and participation, educational work with adults and school children, and communication between professionals, developers and the public. Assumptions were also made by the volunteers about the public (perceiving themselves as representatives of this wider public group) that 'the majority of people are interested" and "field work is what people want" (DB). To many of the amateurs and volunteers, the community excavation, and participation in it, was about being able to experience "the physical buzz of digging" (DB)

From a student volunteer perspective, involvement in this project had values educationally and, eventually, economically, as it would be "helpful to them in their future career" (PW). It was believed that the "learning experience" (PW), of being involved in a commercial/community excavation would enable students to gain the relevant skills to get a job in commercial archaeology after volunteering. This also had value to the profession by having already highly trained staff coming into it, and therefore requiring no investment from companies in training. Furthermore, this "positive experience" (PC), would encourage people to go into professional archaeology.

Developers: Interestingly, the value of undertaking this project to many of the professionals and to the clients, York Regeneration Trust (YRT) relates to the '106 agreement' (JK) that "specifies education must be written into the project, [and] the developer has to deliver" (PC). Furthermore, the support for community archaeology work by the client related to the fact that YRT is not a commercial enterprise but rather it is a trust, which works with under a charitable remit (similar to YAT), therefore is require to reinvest profit back into the community.

The value of this project in the initial stages, was seen by the developer as being able to "create a new community in this area" jointly with the archaeologists, who also claimed it could create a 'sense of community" (PC). Critically, this was because the area itself had no local community, therefore the community archaeology project and the setting up of a community trust (of which many of the volunteers are members), enabled a chance to create a community spirit through "community involvement' (PC) Furthermore, "the developers have got involved so they can have feedback about the development" (PC), and they can "get the approval of the community". Many describe the developer's interest relating to the fact they 'didn't just want another faceless flat' (Martin). So, in many senses, this project was also aimed at meeting the 'ethical considerations' of the developers as well as of archaeologists: "It needs to be there for public as it is their heritage" (PC). Therefore, the professionals and developers attached a social and political value to the project: "hopefully each of the companies will get something beneficially out of it, like PR" (PC).

Actual Values

Professionals The excavation aspect of this project, by both professionals and volunteers, was not always an easy balancing act. Although professional archaeologists commented that "we encourage them to do everything" (PW), this idea was recognised as becoming increasingly problematic and they "may get to a point where [the] archaeology will not be suitable for the activities we are currently doing, on health and safety grounds" (PW) A similar comment was also made by the director, Peter Connelly. This is where the professional and public values could clash. Part of the reason for this is that, although it is seen as valuable, socially, politically and educationally by all parties, to get the public 'amateurs' involved in the process of archaeology, the professional archaeologists still perceived, that the volunteers are not capable of complex and fragile archaeology, which is part of the reason why they are generally only 'allowed' (Anon Arch) to dig on areas considered suitable, such as the 19th and 20th century archaeological features and ground surface (as in other case studies, see Mitchell and Chester).

The success in integrating the four different stand of values, 'public outreach and education,' 'research,' 'commercial' and 'community' has been questionable, over the long term. In part this is because, in reality, the archaeologists and the volunteers are not working as one group, but rather on separate areas of the site. It appears that the research value is prioritised over other values, and the public demand and values for this project were not fully maintained. Furthermore, this has not been communicated to the amateurs or the public, and therefore the value of the project in "achieving successful communication…" (L) has failed.

The commercial and community aspects of the project have not been as easy in practice as they are in theory, as written within the section 106 clause. Despite the developer's support, they were not willing to put up any money for the community site: "it's been difficult facilitating community participation here and it is in 106, the financial side was very tight in the end… [We] had to go outside and raise money to do the 106 stuff, so that is

very interesting" (JK). This funding went towards paying for John Kenny's and Pam White's positions on site, without whom volunteer participation would not have been possible. Furthermore, even with this, John has had to make them "trust me as an archaeologist to supervise people, so I did feel as if I was having to push a bit to make it happen". This is also reflected in the volunteers' experiences who feel "there was a lot of archaeology done before the community archaeology became involved, and part of the problem was not the right person was involved" (Martin). This was prior to John Kenny's grant-funded appointment as community archaeologist for Greater York. Many of the volunteers still commented that "YAT has not produced a statement and neither has the Council" (about community involvement and the community aims).

Handing over the 19th and 20th century archaeology aspects of the project to the volunteers was perceived by many of the professional archaeologists as less risky to research values than a Viking or medieval site (which lies underneath), but the work done on the site and the interest and knowledge that has resulted has changed many professional's ideas of the importance of this period, and they were "surprised how attached the public are to the 19th and 20th century archaeology". It is that attachment that has "amazed" the archaeologist (PC), and actually expanded the project to fit these public demands by producing a book on oral history and employing a historian: "we have a fantastic story" (PC). Whether more credence will be shown to this archaeology in the future is yet to be seen. In some senses this project has also changed what archaeologist's value and understand about what the public value, or even, in some cases, validated many of their value claims.

The archaeological work of this project has increased knowledge about the archaeology and history of the area on an academic level. This partly relates the community side of the excavation focusing on material and a time period that would usually have been more quickly recorded and then machined away. The time given to assess this material, and the corresponding historical and oral history research, has increased the indicated to the professionals that not everything is recorded in history, or archaeology and all these strands of evidence can add to a more comprehensive understanding of the past.

The project has also been credited by its organisers, Peter Connelly and Pam White, with positively changing professional opinions of community involvement in archaeology, and increasing the value the profession places on participatory projects and they have had "very good feedback" (PW). It was claimed that it helped shed the misconceptions about the quality of the archaeological work on such projects: "I know that people coming to see the site have been very pleased with the quality of work" (JK), and therefore this encourages the professionals to see the positive value of community involvement in archaeology.

Peter Connelly claims that the number of visits to the site by professionals gives an indication of the level of interest shown by the profession and the government in these type of projects: "people seem surprised by what we are doing, because it's commercial and community, training and volunteers and education, its doesn't happen very often" and people often "express their amazement" (PC). There have been visits from not only local archaeologists and commercial units, but also at a national level. To date, though, there has been no change in local government agenda to uphold more rigorously the 106 clause.

There is admittance by the archaeologists organising the project that this is 'hard work', but they have also discussed "enjoying it" (PC) and that they were "learning a lot from the experience as well" (PW). They also learned about themselves: "I am learning to supervise and co-ordinate...bringing in skills from previous occupations and social activities" (PW).

Volunteers: For the majority of the public and volunteers that came to the site education was a motivation, but the social and entertainment aspect of archaeology, became more prominent. It has encouraged people to "learn more in the future" and to want to find out more about the area. Experiences of digging have changed some peoples' perceptions of archaeology and the profession, "[I] couldn't believe I could get involved in something like this" (Margaret).

Discussions with the public on the walkway and with the volunteers indicate that they value of the work archaeologists do, even if it is not something they would like to do themselves "and seeing the archaeology and in particular working with the archaeologists changes the perceptions of archaeology – it opens your eyes up" (DB). Previous perceptions been largely been formed through popular media and programmes like Time Team: "it [Time Team] seems to simplify it a lot...just digging glamorous parts" (DB). These comments both indicate that involvement in this project, and direct involvement in digging, does change perceptions and the values attached to the archaeological work. Working closely with the archaeologists has led to very positive perceptions of them as people: "the professional archaeologists are wonderful" (DB), and furthermore they have felt, which surprised some of them, that "the professionals [were] treating us with respect", helping to dispel many of the ideas about the insular nature of the profession.

Socially, many of the volunteers have made friends, and "it's really a group of friends with a common interest" (Margaret). Many of them meet up in the pub, for trips and for Christmas dinners "often even if it's raining and there isn't a lot of work to do, turning up just to chat" still seemed worthwhile.

In terms of creating a community, and the social value of this project, it has created a community, but "it is not a geographical community, but it's used physicality to create a sense of unity, there is a pretty tight sense of community but it's a community interested in archaeology" (JK). This community of interested people is apparent when assessing the nature of the volunteers participating in this project. The majority are not residents of York City centre, but rather they live on the outskirts and hinterlands of York. The majority of the people involved are retired, and many had a prior interest in archaeology (i.e. they are members of an archaeological group, or they have been on other YAT community projects). Therefore, they have not been completely successful in 'reaching new audiences'. This tight 'community' of volunteers has also created division as well, many perceiving it, including some archaeologists as keeping "geriatrics off the street" (anon). As well as not being the local Hungate community (since there are no current residents), none of these participants were likely to be buying the new housing that is going up on this site. Therefore, it has failed to attracted new audiences to participate. What has been more successful are the public tours (the majority of these are tourists from outside York), in terms of visitor numbers, which sound impressive: "we have had over 10,000 visitors" (PC).

There was a problem in communicating the opportunities for direct involvement to the public: "It's not general knowledge that you can be involved" (Margaret), and "[I] had no idea there was stuff happening there". Equally, for many, it was just not something they perceived as being interesting to them: "Funny, just don't get round to doing things on your own doorstep," and "[I] haven't been along myself" and "[it's] mainly for children." The public also commented on the fact that they had to email a couple of times and "harass" the organizers before getting a response. Although the project aimed to be all-inclusive, there was a limit to how many people could come to excavate. Some of the other residents of York would have preferred the archaeologists to do something more relevant to them, like look at their back yards, and do something more exciting and personally relevant.

Like many other of the community projects, including Chester, it has challenged the perception that the main value people place on archaeology is the opportunity to dig themselves. The initial professional view was that "they like digging from my experience" (JK), but many volunteers discussed that they "don't enjoy digging as much" as finds work, or were shocked by the reality of what excavation was like, and realised what a hard physical activity it is. Not all experiences of hard digging work were negative: "I sleep at night after a good days work."

The majority of the public did not want to get practically involved, and communications of interest to John indicate that there are a limited number who wanted to take an active role. Many seem happy to come on a tour, or even just hear about it. The majority of the people on the tours were families. Part of this could relate to the fact that the sessions for practical involvement require commitment, training and being available on week-days, which is problematic for most of the residents of York.

Developer: The excavation has raised the profile of the York Regeneration Trust, and also provided them with a community, if not a geographic one, to discuss the development with, but this is a false community and it is (self-)selective. There has been media coverage, both BBC TV's 'One Show' and local press have mentioned the YRT whenever they discuss the project and this has helped them demonstrate their corporate responsibility. The project and the involvement of the public, has provided benefits to the developers; Peter Connelly and David commented that there had not been the big demonstrations about the development that there were at Coppergate, which generated bad publicity and also held up and the development, with negative economic implications for the developer.

7.4 Brayford

Brayford is located in rural North Devon, in South West England and is a village on the edge of Exmoor National Park. It had an estimated population of 400, in 2000, and at present there are 300 on the electoral register (http://www.brayford.org/geography.html). There is virtually no ethnic or social diversity; the majority of residents are white British.

The excavation was directed and funded by the X-Arch Project, run by the University of Exeter, with funding from the HLF. It was organised jointly by Penny Cunningham (X-Arch project manager) and Jim Knight (Amateur Archaeologist).

My research was carried out over a two-day period in April 2008, during the period of week-long community excavation. My presence on site was as a supervisor for X-Arch, but I was able to step back from many of these responsibilities due to the abundance of other supervisors and limited archaeological remains. I formally inter-viewed Penny Cunningham (Director (PC)), Sam Walls (Supervisor (SW)), Ryan Watts (Student Volunteer (RW)) and Jim Knight (Organiser/Amateur (JN)), had other casual conversations and observed the participants both on site during the community excavation, as well as in the village.

Local Attitudes to Archaeology

There is evidence from earlier projects of a strong local interest in archaeology and heritage. There was previous public involvement in the Brayford Millennium Project, completed in 2000, in which members of the local community were involved in landscaping and planting derelict land by the River Bray to be used as a local amenity and focal point (http://www.brayford.org/history.html).

Local interest was also indicated by the survey carried out by Jim Knight, who collected evidence of archaeological smelting activity, including slag from local residents' back gardens. This work indicated that most of the gardens located in the village centre contained evidence for previous iron working.

This small village has been described has having a strong community spirit (http://www.brayford.org/geography.html). There is a thriving Women's Institute but few public amenities other than a church, preschool and primary school, and village hall.

Village History

The village of Brayford was founded around the River Bray. There are recorded references in the 10th century to "Braeg", in the 12th century to "Brai", and in the 13th century to "Hautebray". The name "Hegebregh" has also been recorded (www.brayford.org/history.html). There are 16th century references to "Brayforde" and "Braiford". By the 17th century the Ford provided a stop on a highway route across Exmoor (http://www.brayford.org/history.html).

Context of the Excavation

The site of Welcombe Farm is located on the outskirts of Brayford and is part of a private farm, which is on a platform overlooking the valley (see Fig 7.9). The field, which contains the excavation site, is situated on the edge of a quarry.

Figure 7.9: Photograph of Excavation site at Brayford (Faye Simpson)

The excavation aimed to locate and determine the nature, function, and date of two ditch features identified by geophysical survey. Previously an excavation had been carried out on the site by amateurs, who had recovered Roman pottery, which was believed to relate to a possible Roman settlement of the site. It was believed that the settlement was associated with the Roman iron smelting sites previously identified by the Exmoor Iron Project at Sherracombe Ford, Mill Lane and Bray Vale. This suggested that Brayford could be a major Roman iron production site (http://www.brayford.org/history.html), but much more evidence was needed to confirm this theory.

Background to the Community Archaeology Project

The community excavation on the site started in May 2008, and stemmed from the results of the geophysical work carried out by X-Arch during the previous year, at the request of Jim Knight (a local resident and amateur archaeologist). The X-Arch project is a Heritage Lottery Funded community archaeology project (from 2006-2009) based at the University of Exeter. The X-arch programme organised and directed the community excavation, to tie in with very specific aims laid out in the HLF bid document. These aims included:

- Raising awareness of archaeology

- Empowering the community

- Providing archaeological support for interested individual and groups

- Increasing knowledge and knowledge transference of local heritage

- Promoting long-term appreciation of heritage.

- Encouraging involvement and participation in heritage (where lacking)

The HLF document specified that this should be done through giving people the opportunity to experience the archaeological research process, by providing "doorstep" archaeological training and assistance in relation to "self-seeking" demand, which will increase awareness and benefit the region's heritage management.

The excavation involved one long evaluation trench, aimed at investigating the geophysical results that indicated what appeared to be two ditch features. The trenches were unlike the excavations at York, Chester and Shoreditch, not surrounded by any fencing, as there were no significant health and safety requirements and the site was in a private setting.

Participation

The local community were able to attend the community archaeology excavation at any point during the week of the excavation, when they could have a site tour or, if they specifically asked, to have an opportunity to excavate. There were ten to twelve amateur volunteers attending the excavation, and they were trained in the methods of archaeological excavation and recording (see

Fig 7.10). These volunteers were 'selected' by James Knight, based on them being asked personally to participate by himself, as well them were members of North Devon Archaeological Society (NDAS) or Devon Archaeology Society (DAS); three of these were also student volunteers from the University of Exeter. There were seven organised school visits during the excavation, each spending half a day on site doing four different activities, a site tour, finds processing, making pottery and excavation. At the end of the excavation there was an organised open day, with approximately 30 local residents attending.

Figure 7.10 Photograph of Volunteers excavating at Brayford (Faye Simpson).

Values Espoused

Professionals: The research values of excavating this site were not a priority for the professional archaeologists, which was unusual in relation to the other community projects evaluated, including Mitchell and Chester. Rather, the main aim was to build on the local interest in archaeology by practical engagement. After providing a geophysical survey of the site, at the request and "enthusiasm of one individual [Jim Knight]" (Sam Walls (SW)) "[the] next step really was a small excavation, partly to help train Jim and the other local people in how to excavate properly and to fulfil our outputs" (SW). By involving the public in excavation, it was hoped it would be possible to prevent the mistakes and poor recording that had previously occurred, when excavation had been carried out without any professional input: "[we can] enforce correct excavation methods and techniques because he'd excavated before and obviously not recorded it properly, so the correct thing for us to do was to reinforce and teach him" (Penny Cunningham (PC)). The aim was to prevent the archaeological record being destroyed by training the volunteers in necessary skills. Similar to Hungate, in the future they would have the ability to excavate without professional supervision as well as being able to identify and record archaeology to appropriate standards: "hopefully it will improve their ability and methodology for future excavations" (SW).

Community involvement in the archaeological process was also a requirement for the professionals, as part of their HLF project. The project had to be opened up to encourage engagement with a broad social audience, creating social value, and extending the project's value from one individual member of the community to the village's community at large, involving and encouraging a more diverse local demographic to be involved in their heritage, "to engage with people that had no experience before" (PC). This project was regarded as having educational value for the local schools, offering them the chance to "learn by watching and doing" (RW), fitting into the National Curriculum in learning about their local environment, heritage and a possible Roman settlement site.

It offered a chance of doing outreach work, subsequently other professional organisations became involved in, including Taunton Museum and the University of Exeter. For the museum it provided an opportunity to reach new audiences and encourage an increased number and diversity of visitors to their museum. For the University of Exeter, the project was seen as encouraging wider participation in higher education, and increasing the number and diversity of archaeology university applicants. These aims were perceived as having economic, political and social value.

Amateurs: The research agendas of this project, and the subsequent knowledge value, were most prevalently discussed by the amateurs: "[they are] interested in the site, and the history, or they are interested in the archaeology" (Ryan Watts (RW)). The majority discussed wanting to gain a more comprehensive understanding the site and local area, and ability place it within a boarder historical and archaeological context. It was hoped that this excavation would provide evidence for "living accommodation" (JK) for the area's past iron smelting population. This reflected a very specific local interest in the past, rather than people wanting to gain a broader understanding of archaeology. Only two of the volunteers discussed a more general interest in archaeology, and wanting to gain experience and knowledge. For them, this excavation offered the opportunity of digging: "its not very often you get an opportunity like this" (Volunteer (VOL)). They saw this experience as a chance to gain knowledge without the pressure of academic study: "We don't have the academic back up in this area. I have always been interested in history and I am not an enormous academic, I prefer a hands on experience and archaeology is more that way" (JK).

Jim Knight suggested that the amateurs perceived this project as a chance to working with professionals who would offer them a form of validity, accreditation and recognition for their previous archaeological work. This had a perceived political value for the local archaeological

societies, and it would help in gaining support for future work.

Actual Values

Professionals: The teaching of good excavation practice to amateurs, was felt by the archaeologists to be a partial success: "I think they have a lot better idea of how to excavate...I still don't think it will be enough training for them to conduct an excavation on their own to a sufficient standard" (SW). It was therefore questionable whether the educational aims could be achieved in the limited time span of one week. Part of the problem with the educational value aims was that some volunteers did not see the worth of them personally, as they believed that they already knew how to excavate correctly, because they had dug here themselves before this project. "We did our best to show him [Jim]...whether or not he will take that on board is another completely different matter" (PC).

A example of a problem was the inability of the project directors to communicate to the volunteers the archaeological preservation reasons for backfilling trenches after excavations were finished: "we agreed the trench would be closed as soon as we finished, and he hasn't done that" (PC). There were further problems over the use of different excavation techniques. For instance, there was an argument on site during the open day, about the use of mattocks to dig trenches, and the amateurs felt that the archaeologists were destroying the archaeology, and missing the finds (all soil was sieved and finds were retrieved).

It was felt by the professional archaeologists that the amateurs did not understand the research motivations for the positioning of the trenches: "I don't think we have clarified why we...have chosen where we are well enough to all of them" (PC). Furthermore, the amateurs often did not believe the interpretations of the professionals, especially those relating to the date of the ditches. There appeared from conversations to be confusion about the date of the site, with the archaeologists saying it was Roman, but difficult to date due to lack of dateable evidence, and the amateurs and volunteers telling the public it was 'Iron Age'.

The academically trained archaeologists who aimed to become professionals felt there was a knowledge value, with RW reflecting that they had been "working with different kinds of people, and working with a closer team, and then passing on knowledge reinforced my own knowledge". Furthermore, like Annapolis and York, this experience had given them vital experience that would help with job prospects, by providing them with the opportunity to perform "a more supervisory role" (RW).

The social value of this project was discussed at length, "its good fun working with people" (SW), something that many were not expecting. There was a surprise at the standard of excavation amateur and volunteers were able to achieve: "they have done a good job...that ditch is much cleaner than I would have got it...things are getting done" (SW), and that the hard work was balanced with fun and enjoyment. This positive experience of community archaeology excavation changed and broadened the archaeologists' opinions of the nature of the archaeological experience and public involvement: "it taught me that there are people out there who are just interested, they play an important role, the dig wouldn't have been done without members of the community" (RW).

The major issues raised related to the time span, and it was for many of the professionals a learning experience in balancing the needs of the amateurs getting things done: "the quality of work is still good, but because of the time span you have work to get done, some stuff we did here with a mattock, it wouldn't of got done [otherwise]" (SW).

Amateurs: The research values for the volunteers of finding the settlement during this excavation were not completely achieved, as the two ditches found and the few sherds of Roman pottery did not really indicate of settlement, but they did get "some good dating of the enclosure" (SW), even though it was not totally conclusive. Despite this, the amateurs were still optimistic, if slightly confused about dating: "having dug it we now know, yes, whatever was here was backfilled in the Roman period; we have made some progress to finding the settlement in the Roman period" (JK). On reflection many were aware this was because the dig was only for a week, but this lack of conclusive evidence did fuel the volunteers' desire to learn more, and possibly excavate again, with or without professional support.

The work on this site developed a very strong sense of ownership for the people involved, especially Jim and the landowner, who were very keen to have "it done properly" (RW). This ownership meant that the Jim was heavily involved in the planning of the excavations, with the advertising and getting the volunteers. "[The] community side wasn't so bad because that was quite easy in a sense because Jim was keen to do that" (PC), which took some of the pressure of work off the professionals and made it more community led which was not only an aim of the project, but also potential allowed the "community side to be a success" (PC).

The strong sense of ownership also had negative implications, in part because of the exclusive nature of volunteer selection, but also in terms of the "very high level of expectations (that were placed on the archaeologists), and what we can do for him, post-excavation...he is going to be really disappointed" (PC). This resulted in disagreements between individuals and the archaeologists both prior to, during and after the community excavation, including the mentioning of promises or agreements not being adhered to on both fronts: "he still hasn't backfilled the trench, so I feel that

is a bit worrying" (PC). Whilst there was disappointment with the museum for not producing the display that they promised, the county archaeologists "were quite happy for us to do excavation...[but] didn't actually see the excavation... they were going to come and put on a display for general interest...they didn't do that" (PC). For some professionals (including the county archaeologists and academics), the status of this project as a community excavation was questionable due to one individual having control over who was involved and his selectively (Anon).

The experience of excavation was described has having a long term social and knowledge value, encouraging future involvement in archaeology. One volunteer said that archaeology "got me hooked" (VOL) and "[I'm] now going to do a course in archaeology, as [I] want to learn more" (VOL). Some of the volunteers who were not already members of a local archaeology society were "now going to join NDAS" (SW), and since the dig "subsequently joined NDAS" (Jenny), therefore it was believed that "we [professionals] have opened it up and got a lot of positive response from people that want to joint DAS/NDAS, and come back to help at Hartland (a subsequent community dig)" (PC).

A further social value was that "friendly people" on the team, had built the confidence of the volunteers. Some who started saying "I don't feel confident enough to dig" (VOL) later gained this confidence. During the course of the week one of the volunteers, who was very nervous and had a learning disability changed from hardly speaking at the beginning to teasing the archaeologists by the end and wanting to come on more excavations and join NDAS: "she has gone from being quite shy to being confident" (RW).

Local Residents: The aim of reaching a diverse cross-section of the community was not achieved, with the exception of school groups visiting. This was because many of the volunteers participating in the excavation were selected by Jim Knight, of which the majority had previous experience of working with him on an archaeological excavation: "the selection of people working here has been chosen very carefully, for very specific reasons. Jim wants certain people here and doesn't want certain others" (RW). The rural location of the site meant that effort was required to visit and participate, and "the problem is that in such a busy farming community people, haven't got the time to participate in the dig, the only people are retired people really" (JK). The retirees' involvement was something that was foreseen in the HLF document, and targeted by the project. The volunteers in this age group discussed this project providing a social value to the community: "when you retire you have to look for new interests...when you find its going on in your own door step and you can become a part of it, it becomes an attractive thing" (JK), furthermore the academic involvement and thought involved in archaeology "disciplines the mind" (JK), this was a similar pattern that emerged at York.

The lack of visually exciting archaeological remains and finds on the site proved problematic in transferring knowledge and communicating archaeology to the public. It proved difficult for archaeologists and the volunteers to explain the ditches to the public, as there was little visual stimulus, and few finds to back up assertions about dating. This problem with communicating knowledge was prevalent in people without any prior experience of the past or the area: "some of them come up and they had some knowledge and history of the area, so they were quite excited and could place this in with other bit they know about, other people come up and had no real understanding at all and found it quite difficult, I think, to see what we were doing" (PC). It was therefore felt that "they would have got a lot more out of that when they were actually finding things" (SW). School children "get a bit bored, understandably when they aren't necessary digging anything interesting" (SW). For the majority of the visitors, there was very little to see and it required someone to show them around, and explain what was going on. If this did not happen, members of the public usually walked away slightly confused after looking rather bored. The local television station that visited actually left, in part due to the rain, but also as there was little to see, it was not visually entertaining.

Things were different for those involved in the excavation process throughout the week, who discussed enjoying it despite of the lack of finds: "yeah enjoyed it, just wish we found more" (VOL). Furthermore, one of the children revisited the site on the weekend with her mother, who was a volunteer. She had changed her perceptions of archaeology and instead of wanting to find treasure, told her mother that the best find would be a bit of pottery.

Of other members of the local community who visited, the majority were friends or relatives of the volunteers. They had made a specific visit to see them socially, and to have a cup of tea and piece of cake. The Women's Institute held their meeting on site on the Saturday. Rather than wanting to learn about the archaeology and the excavation, this became a social venue for the some of the villagers. When discussing what kept other villagers away from the site, it appeared that the limited time span meant that many members of the local community could not come due to "other commitments" or they "didn't realise the excavation was happening this week". Another reason seemed to be because it was regarded as an individual's project rather than the community's project.

Five groups of school children attended and participated in the excavation and other activities. They were described as "all super-excited" (RW). The children had a good understanding of what archaeology was, and many mentioned, "it's like Time Team", or, when trying to help each other, said "do it like they do on Time Team". They were aware of the time periods, and did archaeology was undertaken, and this was very unlike many of the children I conversed within the United States. For many, however, it seemed that they were more interested in playing: "I think most of it was it was a trip out, something different to do… [the] fact it was an archaeological dig was neither here nor there" (RW). They enjoyed making pots rather than the digging, and it was felt that, due to the short time period and nature of site, "they haven't learnt a lot (from digging)" (RW). When discussing the excavation and experience with the teachers they were all positive about the experience, discussing "really enjoying it" and it being "great fun", for both themselves and the children. It was felt that it was the other activities, especially the pottery making, that were more successful at educating and engaging, but this depended on who was supervising.

8. AUDIT OF COMMUNITY ARCHAEOLOGY CASE STUDIES IN THE UNITED STATES

8.1 Mitchell

Mitchell is a city located in Davison Country, South Dakota, in the northern mid-west of the United States, which is a largely Republican state. Mitchell has a population of 14,558 (http://www.idcide.com/citydata/sd/mitchell.htm), and its ethnic demographic consists of the vast majority being white (just under 96%) with a small Native American population (just under 3%). The average income is just over $31,000, which is well below the national average of $48,200 (http://www.idcide.com/citydata/sd/mitchell.htm). It is described as a 'stop-off' city for American tourists, with the site located just off the main interstate running through the centre of South Dakota. This interstate (I90) is the main route for America tourists heading to national historic and natural landmarks including the Badlands, the Blackhills, Mount Rushmore and Yellowstone, beyond. There are four primary tourist attractions in Mitchell, the Prehistoric Indian Village, the Corn Palace, Dakota Discovery Museum and the Enchanted Doll Museum (subsequently closed).

Research was carried out in Mitchell from the 6th July to 5th August 2007, during which I attended the public archaeology excavation directed by Professor Adrien Hannus (AH) and Dr Alan Outram (AO). My role was site supervisor overseeing the work of twenty undergraduate students from the University of Exeter. My presence as site supervisor enabled me to attend for the full programme of activities, and to live in Mitchell for the month. This allowed me to spend time in the community with local residents, and draw on the perspectives from the local community, the students, professionals and politicians. The length of time and direct involvement in the project enabled friendships and trust to be built up and subsequently more open conversations and interviews.

This approach had drawback of balancing research with the many duties of site-supervisor, and this direct involvement in the project and excavation made objectivity difficult to maintain. The experience on this excavation provided a pilot study in preparation for the core case study planned for 2008.

State Legalisation

South Dakota was one of the first of twenty-two states, to sign up to reserving exclusive ownership of archaeological resources on state land in 1966 under the National Historic Preservation Act (as amended in 2000) (McGimsey 1972, 91). It was required to support and maintain any archaeological site on state owned land, something that was progressive in the 1960's. The responsibility for this work, including research, outreach, archives, and permits is done within the Department of Tourism and Economic Preservation, based at Pierre, with support from South Dakota Historic Preservation Society, which formed an official relationship with the state in 1901 (www.SDhistory.org, 2005). The state therefore employs a total of 11 staff archaeological staff, and at total of three State Historic Preservation Officers (SHPOs) working within this huge state, much of which is national park land and therefore falling under federal jurisdiction. The SHPOs have responsibility to represent South Dakota and its citizens in the preservation of cultural heritage, and also to maintain to federal and state laws, providing advice and assistance (2005, 2).

Legally, Federal and State Laws govern the heritage of South Dakota. Federal land is protected by the National Historic Preservation Act, Section 106, and State land by the South Dakota code, of Codified Laws, sections 1-20 through to 1-20-16 (although at present these have been repealed) (www.legis.state.sd.us/statues/DisplayStatute.aspx?type=statute&statute=1-20, 2005, 2) and by the Administrative Rules of South Dakota, Chapter 24, Section 52 (www.legis.state.sd.us/rules/DisplayRule.aspex?Rule). Both of these are mitigation procedures, which promote public consultation and public comment, in which the public also has right to appeal, but can still, proceed with no public involvement. Furthermore, The South Dakota code states within a desire for public archaeological programs and outreach, and the ability to allow public participation in projects. Yet, despite this the Codified Law states in quite a contradictory manner that "archaeological field work shall be done by qualified individuals" (1-20). The state also has the provision of an authoritarian official department to redistribute archaeological material (i.e. finds) around the state to different locations to safeguard it to be of greater benefit to the public (McGimsey 1972, 96).

The site at Mitchell was previously city owned land, rather than state, and furthermore was turned over the citizens' board, making it private land. Therefore, neither federal, state nor city governments have any legal jurisdiction on the site, and subsequently are not required to provide funding or support for the sites (similar to Muncy). This has some positive implications, as it enables to site to be controlled and developed by members of the local community (those on the board), without having to go through the official channels.

Local Attitudes to Archaeology

Attitudes to archaeology by the population of Mitchell varied vastly and were not always positive. To understand local attitudes it is vital to first recognise that this is Republican state and like much of the American Mid-West, it has traditions of highly conservative politics and philosophical mindsets lending itself to patriotism, individualism, and economic strength and handing over control to states. It is worth mentioning that the politics and the attitude towards archaeology in Mitchell are also affected by the nearby city of Sioux Falls. This is a largely democratic city, where the focus is more on education, arts, and culture; subsequently the democratic state senators have backed the intellectual research and supported the public archaeology programme at Mitchell Prehistoric Indian Village. This educational value of archaeology has further been supported by Augustana College, Sioux Falls. The public of Sioux Falls has given the facility volunteers, including those from the local historic society.

Since the majority of the local residents are white, with relatively low incomes, there has been, and still is, some resentment towards state budgets being spent on the public archaeology facility, even through this funding came from the I90 fund for developing tourism along this interstate, rather than directly for the archaeology. Too many people regard the excavation as solely a tourist attraction, and therefore perceived it of being of no benefit to local people, except for the increased tourist trade that this could produce. This was especially prevalent because many did not perceive themselves as having an interest in archaeology. This negativity to the facility also related to the nature of the site. Because it is a Native American site, some of the population did not regard it as 'their' heritage and therefore did not regard it as 'their responsibility'. Subsequently, many were resentful of public money being spent on this facility.

This partly related to the previously discussed political history relating to Native American sites. Since 1990, because of tensions between Native Indians and non-native archaeologists, many states have shied away from supporting or promoting these types of sites. This has been the case in this site, even though the local native Indian population, both visitors to the site and in the local area, have no concerns and support this facility. The Native Americans that I talked to suggested that this was because they do not regard it as their tribe, and not their heritage.

The Mandan are believed to be the Native American tribe associated with this settlement. From conversations during visits to the site by Native American groups, and with board members of Native American descent there was support for the archaeological activity. Had the archaeological remains related to a sacred site (for example, had burial mounds and bodies been found), there would have potentially been more interest, but also considerable conflict over the archaeological excavations.

There are many people in Mitchell who support and value the facility and archaeology, furthermore, offer their time to the facility through volunteering for the board and in the facility. Despite the lack of support for site perceived by some people, there was a general liking for the site, rather than dislike for it.

Context

The archaeological site of Mitchell Prehistoric Indian Village is on the outskirts of the City of Mitchell, situated on the banks of Lake Mitchell. The site is located on City owned land, which was subsequently turned over to the board; it holds dual statutes on the national register and national landmark site. This responsibility for the site has been handed over to a Board of Governors, which is made up of 'native and non-native civic, business and cultural leaders' (www.mitchellindianvillage.org). This board in a non-profit-making organisation, and operates from membership, sponsorship, admission, gift-shop sales, contributions from individual and corporate donors, as well as receiving some limited federal, state and private foundation funding (www.mitchelllindianvillage.org). Therefore, in legal terms, both the federal and state government have a duty of care towards the preservation and presentation of this site, as specified in section 1-20 of South Dakota State Code, of Codified Law (McGimsey 1972, 178). The aim of this is that, the government hands over responsibility for the site, enabling it to become self-supporting. Therefore, although a large proportion of the initial funding for the site came from the state, through the I90 tourism development initiative, a large proportion of financial support for the buildings including the Archeodome has come from private investment. In the past, it has received some funding from the state, through local senators ear-marking budgets in Washington DC. Mitchell Chamber of Commerce has also supported the project, regarding it as vital part of the tourist economy.

History

Archaeologically the site is a native Indian prehistoric village dating to the start of the second millennium AD. It is extremely finds-rich and a long-lived, complex settlement site with archaeological features comprising of multiple of earth lodges, cooking pits with cooking debris and rubbish (Hannus 1976). Excavations on the site started in the 1960's, and the Indian remains are associated with what later became the Mandan tribe in North Dakota. The Archeodome was placed over a proportion of this settlement site, incorporating at least two earth lodges in the excavation area, and two covered underneath the building (see Fig 8.1).

Figure 8.1 Photograph of Archeodome at Mitchell (Faye Simpson)

Background of the Community Archaeology Excavation

The public archaeology programme was based around the Thomsen Centre Archeodome. This was completed in 1999, and commissioned from various funding sources, including an I90 tourism grant and a large percentage from a private donor, Gordon Thomsen (a Mitchell local businessman).

The public archaeology project has involved in-kind support from Augustana College (Sioux Falls), and its commercial archaeology unit, which is directed by Adrien Hannus. The prehistoric Indian village, in its present incarnation can be largely accredited to the endeavours of local individuals and Adrien Hannus. The public archaeology programme focuses on a month long publicly viewable excavation, which is supported by the University of Exeter, UK. This collaboration finances staff and supports the excavation.

Participation

Although the site did not allow general public participation in the archaeological excavation, there were occasional volunteers, the majority of whom come from Sioux

Falls, but there is not an active local history society. The focus of the excavation enabled undergraduate students to experience excavation and the public participation is restricted to viewing from a raised walkway during the one month student excavation and then engaging in finds processing work, including washing and sorting objects under supervision in the laboratory (see Fig. 8.2). The site complex also has a museum, including a life size reproduction of a Native Indian earth lodge, and other kinds of activities include the 'kid's dig' (a sandpit in which finds are placed and found) and the chance to try throwing a dart with an atl-atl. The participation of the public with these activities was varied, and often limited as it depended on the guidance and presence of a tour guide, who where local volunteers, or occasionally an archaeology student. The use of casual volunteers or students as guides meant that there were not always tour guides available, and often a discrepancy in the ability and knowledge of the guide, and misinterpretation had become a problem (AO/AH).

Figure 8.2 Photograph of students excavating inside the Archoedome at Mitchell (Faye Simpson)

Demographically the participation in this project was socially and economically varied and outside the usual white middle class visitors of many of the other projects in the United States. This can be seen when one asked the visitors what encouraged them to visit. They tended to mention the ambiguity of the title and advertising boards on the highway: none of these used the word 'excavating'. Many thought they were going to be visiting a reconstruction of a site, which would have tepees. The majority of visitors were family groups, stopping off along the interstate tourist route on their way to Mount Rushmore or the Badlands. Interestingly there was also a smaller group, of local visitors, who were well informed and generally falling into the well educated, white middle-class bracket. Many of these individuals were return visitors. There were also a lower number of Native American visitors to the site, often grandparents bringing along grandchildren, as well as in tour groups.

Espoused Values

Professionals/Academics: The main value attached to this site for Augustana College and University of Exeter staff was primarily "academic research" and training students. The site provided an opportunity for personal and professional research and investigation of a well-preserved Indian settlement site of the late first millennium AD. It was hoped that this would promote 'legitimate and academically-sound research' and 'a credible level of research in a public setting, and furthermore that this work would not get drifted into creating a Disney type program,' (AH), therefore aiming to balancing public outreach within this research framework (Hannus 1973).

To the archaeologists this public archaeology initiative enabled the Archeodome to be built, which was perceived as vital in preserving and investigating the archaeological record. The building enabled excavation in a controlled environment 'an opportunity to control a range of elements' (AH), in which this site could be best 'preserved' and 'protected', from seasonal changes in climates and from the loss of information due to the constant opening and re-opening of the site for excavation.

Educationally, it was believed that the controlled climate within the Archeodome would encourage visitors to the site and enable excavation on the site to continue throughout the year. This would enable the public to see the archaeological remains in context, 'providing a better education' (AH) and inform them about the process of excavation, "to make research translational' (AO) and 'encourage the public to understand' (AH). It was hoped seeing the process and progression of the excavation would encourage a 'higher level of interest' (AH) from local visitors, and to 'serve in the interest of the public at large' (AO). It is believed by the organisers that this is an environment in which public can interact with the archaeologists, ask questions, and see the passion and dedication of the investigators, all of which will be transferred to the visitors. Many of the organisers and academics suggested that this offered a 'unique experience', and this would be something that drew people in to archaeology

This site provided the University of Exeter with a location for one of their summer training excavations, introducing first year undergraduate students into field archaeology, teaching them the process of archaeology and basic excavation and finds skills. Besides educational aims it was hoped that communicating archaeology to the public the students would get social value by being able to 'gain some skills for dealing with people," (AO), and also a understanding the multitude of values attached to archaeology by the public outside the academic realm, realising that people 'perceived archaeology for very different reasons' (AO). It was hoped that this would provide economic value in the future for students when pursuing careers, both inside and outside the archaeological professions.

City and State: The City's chamber of commerce and the Board's reaction to this project have been described as a 'mixed bag' (AH). They supported this project as a tourist attraction, potentially providing more visitor numbers, which would form quantitative evidence of its value. As the City owns the site, it is regarded as their responsibility. The site encourages people to stop-off the interstate and stay in local motels; eat in restaurants and therefore supports the local economy. More negatively, support for the Archeodome has varied dependent on who was on the Board and in the Chamber of Commerce and who is on the council. In other words, it depends upon who regards the investment of public money in the project as a "drain on resources", taking money away from education, and other public amenities. This view seems to be predicated upon idea that this was not part of their heritage. Although this was described as personal opinions of a few, it also represents some more general local and national philosophical mindsets in America towards Native American sites.

The senator for the State, and particular refereeing to a visit from Tim Johnson's (Democrat) secretary, supported the Archeodome, based on ideas that it was of economic and social value, and provided visually marketable commodity to produce a positive effect on their election campaign. This recent visit demonstrated the political interest, which could, or had the potential to encourage the public to understand the past and report archaeological discoveries. Furthermore, the politicians wanted to know how it was more broadly socially and economically valuable, and what qualitative evidence there was for this value (anonymous government official/ AO).

Actual Values

Archaeologists: The experience of this project has made the archaeologists realise that the public values differ from their own "they don't necessary see what we see as interesting" especially in terms of material culture. There was a realisation the 'you can't take interest in archaeology for granted' (AO).

The research values of this project were achieved, as it gave the archaeologists an opportunity to investigate the zones between houses that had been largely ignored in the past and open-area excavation without time-pressures has proved of benefit. There have been more negative effects of this being a training dig and a public archaeology facility. These included the need to leave some delicate features and finds on view to the public when this prolonged exposure could cause the deterioration of the remains. The concentration on the importance of excavation has meant that the Indian Village, and its board have overlooked post-excavation work. There is a lack of funding and support for non-excavation research and conservation of the finds.

Students: The values attached to the project by the students were not primarily associated with education despite the aims of the organisers. However, it was described in casual conversations by all students, who explained that they now know a lot more about the period and archaeology, both pre and post excavation, than previously.

Interestingly, for many of the students the main value in coming to the excavation seemed to be associated with experience, and entertainment. They mentioned the excitement of coming to the United States, and the adventure of working abroad, especially in "cowboy country" (anonymous student). The 'experience' did change their perceived values of archaeology, as the majority of the students had not received field experience prior to this excavation. Many of the students: "thought it would be more interesting" (anonymous student), and there were comments and complaints about the hard work and being tired. This experience was not always positive, but it did give them a frame of reference, and for many either led to them describing an aspiration to pursue a career in archaeology, particularly field archaeology. Alternately, others mentioned that it gave them the motivation to seek out another path. As Alan Outram suggested, the dig was; "key to whether people go into professional archaeology or not."

It did, as hoped, encourage communication between archaeologists (students) and the public, but it did highlight that it could not encourage people to have good social skills, it could only teach them what not to do. This was particularly evident when observing outdoor activity sessions and finds washing, in which each of the students had to take part. Students who were naturally sociable and outgoing were good at talking and engaging with the public, whilst students who were more introverted and unsure failed to engaged with the public. The Kid's Dig was particularly successful in getting students and the public to engage with one another. Conversational feedback with the students afterwards involved discussing directly what public values and comments were. This was valuable in making them reassess their perceptions of the public, but also defined the public's perceptions of them, and furthermore they were able to discuss what interested the public most.

The project has had a direct impact to the Department of Archaeology at Exeter. It has increased the numbers of students taking the Zooarchaeology course taught by co-director Alan Outram: because: "people that participate in fieldwork tend to follow their lecturer through the rest of the years' (AO). This indicated an increased interest as well as a breaking down of some of the lecture/ student barriers and helping the learning process.

The social value of this project can be further seen in the friendships that students developed during the month, including with some of the local American people. Evidence for these friendships, and the maintenance of

them following the excavation, can be seen through them becoming 'Facebook' friends, inviting each other to parties when back in Exeter, and attending as a team to events such as Exeter Archaeology Society's pub quiz. This gives some indication that 'fieldwork is a bonding experience' (see Fig. 8.3).

Figure 8.3 Photograph of Students at Mitchell (Faye Simpson)

Public: This project highlighted the numerous confusions about expectations 'where are the tepees?' to 'do you have Native Americans in England?' by the public visiting the site. This has highlighted the lack of public knowledge about this specific period of America past to the archaeologists, and giving them a better insight as to what level to pitch public education. Furthermore, many visitors had not expected to see digging, similar to Muncy (see below). It has been described as a unique and rare experience, so coming along thinking it would be a reconstruction but finding a dig was described as a 'happy' and positive 'surprise' for people to see a real archaeological dig. In some respects not all is positive since it raised high expectations with 'many mentioned wanting to get closer" (BF), and 'what I really want to do is digging' which could also be seem as sparking new interest in young children.

To some degree this lack of being able to participate in the actual archaeological excavation was compensated for by providing 'Kids Dig' area outside the Archeodome, which, during the archaeology weekend, was highly popular, in part due to it being staffed by archaeologists and students. The children seemed to enjoy finding things, and digging in the sand, and even some teenagers had a go, spurred on by the promise of a getting a replica flint arrowhead for finding artefacts in the sand (see Fig. 8.4). In some respects this satisfied many of the children's interest more than the archaeological excavation itself, and they spent longer on this activity than watching the excavation. Although they found this entertaining it failed to increase knowledge about the site itself, although the children did learn to identify bone and flint.

Figure 8.4 Picture of the Kids Dig at Mitchell
(Faye Simpson)

Interestingly, the children who got involved in finds work picked up typology of objects easily, but were still very confused about chronology, including references to the 'like the film "Ice Age"'. These questions gave the archaeologists the opportunity to educate in a way that one mother describes as 'more memorable than a textbook" (anonymous mother). This seemed to relate to the fact that it did not just provide a forum for questions, but also engaged and entertained children. This gave archaeologists a friendly, less intimidating manner to pass on correct knowledge, partly because people did not feel intimidated. It also provided a forum for questions, especially in the laboratory. Educationally, the hands-on laboratory work worked well with children who were more willing than adults to touch, wash and sort finds.

This project indicated that by opening up the archaeological process and enabling the public to handle finds, there were some changes in perceptions and values associated with archaeology, "I was surprised that a kid of four could do finds work, surprised to see them handling finds" (KMIT TV presenter). This broke down some of the barriers, and made it more family-orientated and friendly. This had other knock-on effects including people bringing finds into the museum for archaeologists to identify them. This was something that was experienced at Muncy too, with metal detectorists bringing finds to the archaeologists to identify, encouraging relationships to be built.

During the project, a mother and teenager daughter were allowed to excavate, this provided them with an interesting experience. They had contacted Alan and Adrien, and made it clear that the daughter wanted to be an archaeologist. After experiencing the dig, the reality caused the child to have an initial change of heart. She

stated that she was: "very tired, its hard work, hadn't realised it would be so dirty". Often the reality of excavation is not as exciting as the fantasy. Indeed, this was a similar experience to that of some Exeter students. It did make visitors aware of "what hard work it was" (AO) and some were "amazed at the patience involved, I couldn't do it, it looks quite boring" (anonymous visitor). This indicated a certain amount of respect for archaeologists, even though they did not necessary want to be archaeologists themselves. Therefore the Archeodome shed light on US stereotypes for the archaeologists and created an experience that challenged the public to revaluate these.

In some senses the project failed to deliver, as some visitors' expectations were very high, especially after visits to other sites including the Mammoth Site at Hot Springs. One visitor stated that "the Mammoth site was 250% better" (anonymous 10 year old), and people were '"disappointed at not being able to dig" (anonymous parent). It became clear that the sand pit was not enough of a digging experience for some. These comments were in the minority.

City and State: The project was has undoubtedly been of economic value to the city and state. There has been a rise in local tourism to Mitchell since the opening of the Archeodome, especially during Exeter students' visits. Exeter's month-long stay in Mitchell had further economic benefit to the city, accommodating and feeding twenty-four people in a motel, and buying supplies from local shops, bringing direct economic benefits to the local businesses. This in turn led to a more positive view of the project by the local community, changing some of the more negative perceptions of archaeology. Media interest increased the profile of the site, although not necessary for archaeological factors but rather based on British connections, and the idea of terrorism occurring in England and the US.

The public interest worked to change some of the negative perceptions and misconceptions about the site, including the idea that it 'isn't their responsibility.' The Board and Chamber of Commerce are now actively looking for new sources of funding to continue and build on the public archaeology programme in the future, including private investment, and to start to tackle getting more state budget ear-marked for the project.

8.2 Muncy

The town of Muncy is located in the largely Democrat state of Pennsylvania, in Lycoming county, just inside the East coast of America. It has a population of just over 2,600. Demographically it has little ethnic and social diversity, with a population of 98% white, with a medium income of $33,000 (below national average) (http://www.citytowninfo.com/places/pennsylvania/muncy). Furthermore, it has some of lowest tourism rates in the country, with only 2.1% of the local income generated by this (http://www.citytowninfo.com/places/pennsylvania/muncy).

The community archaeological excavation was directed by Bill Poulton (Chair of Muncy Historical Society) and Robin Van Auken (Independent Archaeologist). Research into this project was carried out over a two-day period in August 2007. It involved visiting the site, observing and conversing with people, who were both participating and not participating in an evening community excavation session, touring the surrounding landscape and spending time in the town and surrounding areas talking to local residents. During this period I formally interviewed Bill Poulton (Site Director (BP)), and Robin Van Auken (Principal investigator (RVA)). Casual interviews through conversations with participants were noted, though not recorded as previous work at Mitchell and Chester indicated that the public found this intimidating, and therefore were less willing to talk honestly in this context. There were also fewer participants so this was a more practical approach. The lack of visitors during my time there required further comments and statements to be taken from the project website and online dig diaries of the volunteer diggers and students.

State Legalisation

The state of Pennsylvania has been described as having minimal funding for archaeological programmes, which are based within the state museum (McGimsey 1972, 84). The State does have a pro-active State Historic and Museum Commission, which is the main agency supporting archaeology research (www.portal.state.pa.uk). Furthermore, the Historical and Museum commission has a duty to carry out prehistoric and historic archaeological research, and 'report this work to the public'. The state also has very strong laws prohibiting vandalism and fraud (collecting, taking material from archaeological, historical sites). The State Archaeological Service's website has pages dedicated to public benefits and values of archaeology and ways for the public to get involved in archaeology. (http://www.paarchaeology.state.pa.us/pub_1right.htm).

The relative lack of state and federal funding in Pennsylvania is not uncommon in the US and means that much of the archaeological research relies heavily upon university funds and local societies who are very proactive in this practical research role (McGimsey 1972, 90).

The state of Pennsylvania was, in colonial times, a Quaker state and known for having very moral and strong public voices. It was one of the "keystone states", one of original thirteen to form the United States and sign the Declaration of Independence (http://www.legis.state.pa.us/WU01/VC/visitorinfo/pa_history/pa_history.htm). The state was among the first to speak up against slavery and it played a pivotal role in its abolition (http://www.legis.state.pa.us/WU01/VC/visitor_info/pa_history/pa_history.

htm). There is limited historical and archaeological evidence of American Indian settlement in Pennsylvania, as research on these types of sites are feared for political reasons, and, therefore, this part of the past is largely ignored and not the focus of archaeological research (RVA).

It is worth mentioning that the excavation took place on private land, rather than state or federal land, and as it is not a registered historic site, there is no legal obligation for the state historic and preservation service to support the work at Muncy or provide any guidance.

Local Attitudes to Archaeology

There appears to be a strong sense of patriotism in the town, with majority of houses flying the national flag. It has been described as a town proud of its rich heritage (see Fig. 8.5) and this is support by the existence of a thriving and proactive local history group. This has set up its own museum, holds regular meetings and is in the process of designing and applying for funding to create a heritage park of which the public excavation will form a part.

Figure 8.5 Photograph of Muncy town centre
(Faye Simpson)

Interesting aspects of Muncy's rich heritage include the first Gristmill in Muncy Creek with associated canal system. Muncy also has the only railroad that is a state registered site. However, despite this, the state appears to consider Muncy as low priority for research. This could be partly due to its relatively low local population (anonymous local resident). There is little mention locally of Native American Indian remains or archaeology, which still appear to be a politically and socially contentious subject, and so largely an ignored part of Muncy's heritage.

Context

The rural canal site is located approximate two miles from the town centre of Muncy, down a single road track in woodland close to the bank of Muncy Creek (see Fig. 8.6). The land, including surrounding fields, is privately owned by the family of the chair of the local historical society, Bill Poulton. The site is only accessible by car, or a long walk down narrow road. Without knowledge of the site and having directions, it would be very difficult to find, as there were no signs or directions posted on the road sides.

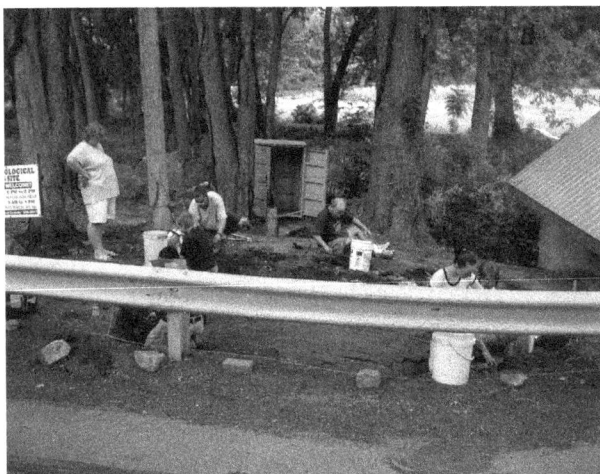

Figure 8.6 Photograph of Excavation at Muncy
(Faye Simpson)

History

The site is that of a canal dating to the 19th century, and in the 2007 excavation the lock keepers lodge was being excavated. The canal was finished in 1834 and became a thoroughfare for exporting goods around the region. A small trench of approximately four by four metres was opened over the predicted central area of the lodge. Previous archaeological work on the site revealed a waste pit, and a well, which are believed to be contemporary with the lodge. The well has remained open after excavation was complete and is now under cover, with the intention of making it a permanently accessible visitor attraction.

Background of the Community Archaeology Excavation

This project could be described as a 'grass roots', as it was initiated and funded by the owner of the land, local resident and president of the Muncy Historical Society, Bill Poulton, who had a 'vision' for the site. The project has been supported and funded by the local historical society and through private funding from the owner. The

project worked through the support of a few interested and passionate local individuals, with little or no state support, either financially or professionally. A single independent archaeologist Robin Van Auken supervised the excavation, with support from local historical society volunteers.

Similar to other sites, including Chester, the first couple of weeks were funded and supported by providing a training dig for the local Lycoming College students. The following weeks were supported by Muncy Historical Society, providing evening and weekend drop-in facilities for the public and local society members to come along and do excavation work and occasionally some finds processing in the barn down the road. In addition, they provided valuable research and evidence about the site in order to get it state registered and gain funding for the larger heritage park initiative application.

Participation

The first couple of weeks of the excavation was run as a training dig for students, and then opened up to local people to participate at weekends. It was also open every day, in the evenings from 5pm to 7pm for drop-in visitors and volunteers from the local society (www. muncyhistoricalsociety.org/dig /index.html; see Fig. 8.7).

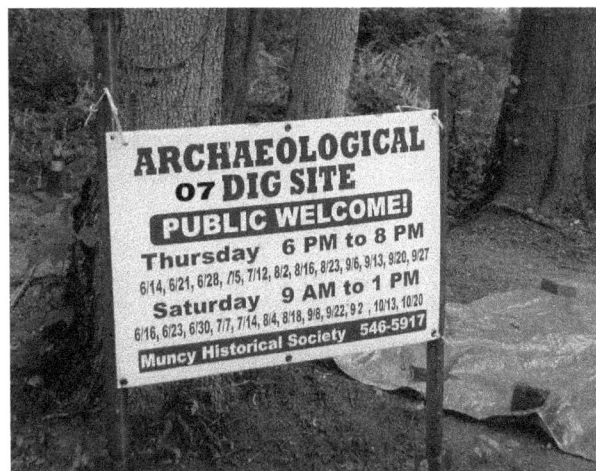

Figure 8.7 Photograph of sign next to excavation
(Faye Simpson)

Participation in this project was varied but largely white and middle class. The site was open to a 'loose schedule' (RVA) but, principally at evenings and weekends, 'encouraged' children and families to attend and also enabled local society members to come along, many of who have jobs during the day. The local society employed an independent archaeologist to supervise the excavation. During my visit there were three families, one teenager (whose mother stayed in the car), two members of the local society and Bill giving tours and supervising. Two of the families has been previously, and both of these where local, whilst the other family and teenager had travelled a couple of hours to specifically visit and dig at the site. All of these people were white middle class families. All of them engaged in digging and sieving, although not in finds work, and stayed the full two hours.

Espoused Values

Professional/Amateur: The perceived primary values of this project were twofold. The amateurs regarded the research value and knowledge value as the most important, similar to that espoused in Brayford (UK). This research focused on the excavation's ability to provide information, including finds that would tell the story of the mill site. This information would then be used to interpret and present the site to the public and provide educational material for local schools. The investigation of this site was spurred on by the personal interests of Bill Poulton, who was the driving force behind the excavation and the local society's involvement. This also served as part of an individual's 'vision,' "if I were king for a day" (BP), with this excavation providing a "golden opportunity" to add to the knowledge of the site (again similar to that of an individuals' vision at Brayford). The site also provided an important "element to the proposed heritage park" (BP), which had the support of the town.

To the local history society this project also had political value, it aimed to raise the profile of the town's archaeological heritage to the state "this site isn't even listed" (BP) and to the public "it all promotes archaeology and anthropology" (RV). This was in part aimed at dispelling some of the perceived governmental issues with lack of the balance of protection and access, proving that this type of project could do both: "the public having access to archaeology is getting better…however the government and certain chapters, quazi state organisations like to think they can protect every site…. Who they protecting it from? I think archaeology is more accessible not because they are making it accessible but because they can't prevent its accessibility," (RV). In relation to this, "the project could enable controlled accessibility and it was something that should be encouraged, rather than discouraging it, as this would also protect the site through the 'community having a connection" (RVA). The loss of control by the state was regarded as a very positive thing. The project was, therefore, also perceived as having the ability to create emotional links, and therefore social values, by enabling a connection with the site through "being there no matter what" and "making yourself available" deconstructing the barriers between the professional and archaeologists.

For both the local historical society and the principal archaeologist, the espoused values of the project focused on encouraging education and involvement of the public in local heritage "we're here to educate and train anyone who wishes to participate, this is a great opportunity for everyone especially students" (RV). In part, this educational focus related to Robin's connections with the

local Lycoming College. This experience and knowledge of the archaeological process was aimed at providing a core component of the work involving local college students in the project as part of their summer fieldwork. This was something which was the primary reason why college students enlisted in this dig, as well as the fact it was local. Furthermore, there have been some school visits to the site, but these have been more restricted, usually allowing them to watch and have a tour of the site. These restrictions were also due to the number of children in a class and the size of the excavation. For the public, involvement in the project appeared to be a secondary aim of the project "giving them something to do" (RVA).

Actual Values

Professionals: It has yet to be seen whether this project will have an impact on the state (professional) attitudes toward public excavation and public involvement in archaeology. Robin and Bill feared that a recent visit from the State Historic Commission and State Historic Protection Officer, which occurred a couple of days prior to my visit, may not been positive. It was described by Bill as an 'interesting state attitude' and Robin referred to their comments about the quality of excavation, 'that they did not seem impressed'. Furthermore the state's negative comments focused on the problematic nature of the on-site recording strategy. This comment and an overall negativity relating to professional standards may, following my observations of the site and its recording strategy, have been justifiable concerns by the state officials. In many seasons the research value of the site and the value of the archaeological record may have been overlooked in order to provide an opportunity to excavate, and this is partly because of the lack of coherent supervision.

There has been a social value personally for Robin in this project, conversations with people about their relationships, and by watching people, it has provided her with characters and ideas for her romance novels.

Amateurs: The excavation of this site did reveal evidence and new knowledge about the lock keepers' lodge. It provided physical remains, evidence of walls for the position of the lodge and furthermore artefactual evidence of "finding lots of domestic artefacts" (www. muncyhistoricalsociety.org/dig/index.html). This work has located the situation of buildings and defined their usage, and providing artefactual evidence to support historical and social knowledge about the site, providing a more complete record of the past. Furthermore, this evidence has been used in the bid and it has been planned that the finds will be displayed.

As previously mentioned, this project was initiated through the 'vision of one individual" and this individual vision has now become the "vision of 60 people condensed into this piece of paper." They have developed a formal proposal for funding for the heritage park, which has received widespread backing from other society members and the wider Muncy community, even if it is still, not officially supported by Pennsylvania SHPO.

Both Bill and Robin mentioned learning things personally and academically from working with the public, being made aware of features in the surrounding landscape that they would otherwise have been missed "come up with different explanations" (RVA), such as the conversation with the school group where they recognised a bridge over the canal, hidden in the forest that no one had noticed before. Subsequently they feel they have learnt things as well through communication.

Students: Educationally the project did have value to students, as was indicated from the changing depth and type of questions asked of students (both college and children) over the course of the excavation experience that it did increase their knowledge and understanding of the past, and of archaeological methods. The questions became increasing complex, focussing on archaeological features and identifying archaeological finds without the assistance of the archaeologists. There was also an indication that students and school children felt more able to speak up, and give opinions and have the confidence to interpret their surrounding landscape: "Why was there a bridge here?" (anonymous 9-year-old child). This was similar that the growth in personal confidence that was experienced at Brayford. Bill stated that personally he was very excited about this as he felt the child had learnt, and taught him something that he had missed, because of his over familiarity with the site "missing the clues that are right underneath your nose" (BP).

The excavations also served to change the relationships and perceptions towards archaeologists. This was highlighted with regard to the college students' perceptions and relationships with teachers, "don't look at www.ratemyprofessors.com; she is so easy, she is so fun, which is good" (RVA) (note: she is not on website). This was an indication of a more friendly and open relationship with teachers which being out of the classroom situation and adopting a 'flexible' approach seems to enable, which corresponds to the positive effects that field work had at Mitchell on staff-student interactions. The students seem to form a more tangible connection to the past and their local area: "they get very excited about this, also possessive" and comments were made that they were "very proud of uncovering the history of this area" (KB). This pride in doing this work was the main reason why many students came back after the training excavation had finished.

The majority of the students comments about the dig related to the entertainment and social value of getting involved "I am very excited about this class and all the possibilities that will come from it" (KB), and that "this is going to be a really interesting class" (GT) and "really exiting" (SS). The primary reason for this excitement and interest was that it was 'hands on' and that they got to dig

and "find new stuff," (GT), mentioning when they could not dig because of bad whether or having to do some other activity "I missed digging" (LR).

Public: The majority of the people visiting the site had made a specific effort because this was such a unique site "it is so rare that the public are allowed to dig." All of the visitors had some knowledge of archaeology, and all three of the families and teenager mentioned had pre-existing interests in archaeology. "This is our third visit" stated one family (anonymous family of four). Another family discussed this being their second visit and stated that they were: "already interested in archaeology" (anonymous family) and "interested in becoming an archaeologist, interested in history" (anonymous teenager). The site did not change perceptions; rather it encouraged pre-existing interests and the desire to learn more about the site. After the visit they felt they had learnt a great deal and wanted to learn more.

The majority of the visitors to the site expressed their motivations for coming to the site as being an after school educational activity for the children: "great after school activity". This was similar to Mitchell visitor's expectations in this related to the educational value of attending the excavation, and doing hands on activities. The majority of these people attending (during the excavation there were two families and one teenager and mother, as well as two local volunteers from the local historical society), had previous knowledge and interest in archaeology and wanted to learn more, and pass on and "encourage" this interest on their children (see Fig. 8.8).

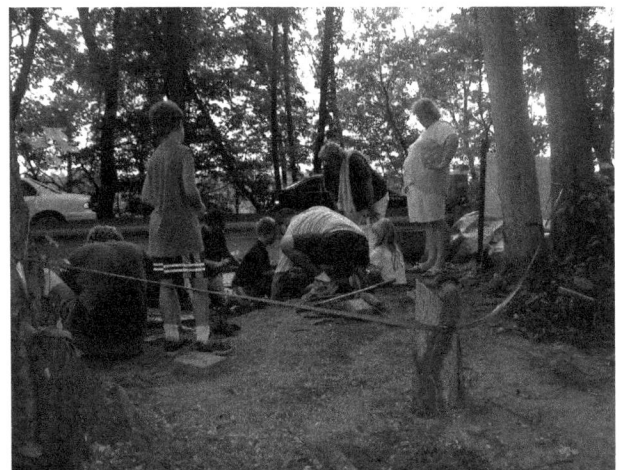

Figure 8.8 Photograph showing community excavating at Muncy (Faye Simpson)

They also discussed its social value for the family, enabling the family to do activities together, and therefore bond. Then the teenager and one of the older children expressed an interest in archaeology and wanting to become a professional. The mother of the teenage girl had brought her along to give her a practical experience to "help her decide if this was really wants she wanted to pursue at college" (anon. mother).

Enjoyment and entertainment was also a value attached to archaeology after the visit to the site. It was described as "fun", "exciting" as well as being described as "a great after-school and holiday activity" (anon. parent). The parents and children described 'enjoying it' which encouraged them to come back again. To many parents this was a surprise as they had not expected the children to respond so well, and had come along initially for educational value, but kept coming back because of entertainment and enjoyment value. This excitement and enjoyment from the participants was backed up with observations. All stayed the full two hours digging, children worked with their own families and appeared to be excited by finding artefacts, and showing them to people around them. The social value was also evident, with children showing finds to other people around them, and strangers talking with one another. Robin also mentioned 'this type of project encourages team work in students, working in groups, and communicating' observational evidence backs up this statement.

The public seemed to regard finds work as boring and tedious. When asked, none of them wanted to go and do finds processing and they were reluctant, and uninterested. Instead they discussed wanting the 'excitement of finding things' and 'if we wanted to do finds stuff we could go to a local museum'. Perhaps this was not helped by the fact that the finds processing took place off-site. To many of the public, the main value was the 'excitement' of digging, and discovering, 'something that is special'.

Metal detectorists: Robin regarded this project as having a positive effect on both the reporting and relationships between metal detectorists and archaeologists, something this has been a problem in the area. Metal detectorists initially stopped off in cars and asked what was being found and whether it was Indian: "I get them engaged and I tell them they are welcome to come out here and work with us... the next time I see them, they come out here and bring their artefacts out here for me to identify." (RVA). This had the potential to build relationships, and tell them about codes of conduct for metal detectorist on sites, and hope they gain respect and understanding: "the idea is you want to convert them, it's like a religion" (RVA). This has the potential for increasing archaeological knowledge and encourage these finds where recorded formally. This situation was similar to that discussed at Mitchell.

8.3 Annapolis

The City of Annapolis is located in the state of Maryland, and situated on the East Coast of the US. It is known by the population of America for it colonial heritage and its naval academy (see Fig 8.9). It has a population of just over 36,000 (http://annapolis.areaconnect.com/statistics.

htm), and at present it is under a Democrat council. The public archaeology programme is directed by Mark Leone (University of Maryland), and project managed by Matthew Palus and Matthew Cochran.

Figure 8.9 Photograph of Harbour at Annapolis
(Faye Simpson)

Research was carried out over a two day period in May 2008, in which formal interviews, casual conversations and participant observations were carried out in and around the community excavation. Casual conversations about the project took place in the city; with both residents and visitors (including tourists), in hotels, bars, coffee shops, shops, restaurants, museums and the local tourist information centre.

Formal interviews were carried out in person with Matthew Cochran (Project Managers (MC)), Matthew Palus (Project Supervisor (MP)) and over the phone with Mark Leone (Director (ML)). Informal conversational interviews were carried out with members of the public, staff members (including Stephanie Duensing (SD), John Blair (JB), Cinday Change (CC), and Jessica Mundt (JM)).

State Legislation

The State of Maryland has a state-financed archaeology programme, providing funding for salaries for state archaeologists, and a state museum, and at present employed 78 individuals (www.marylandhistoricaltrust. net/aboutmht.htm). The archaeological programme itself was set up within the Geological Survey Agency and is now run out of the Department of Housing and Community Development; rather than as a separate agency specifically for archaeology (McGimsey 1972, 91; Shaffer and Cole 1994). This lack of ring fencing of funding has in Maryland's case resulted in more money for archaeology, including enabling over 78 staff to be employed and various public archaeology initiative including the newly funded web-basing of 'grey literature' (www.marylandhistoicaltrust.net/arch-res.htm). This is, in part because individuals involved were political active, although with less effective advocates for archaeology this lack of ring fencing could have resulted in less funding than other states (Leone *et al.* 1987). Subsequently, this allowed for archaeology to receive more funding, support and growth than has been seen in states where archaeology was separated. Furthermore, this has made it easier to work with universities to receive more support, including the University of Maryland (Potter 1994).

Maryland has long standing, strict regulations regarding archaeological work being done by "properly qualified" persons or institutions (McGimsey 1972, 153), requiring that 'all archaeological investigations are conducted by or under the direct supervision of individuals meeting appropriate professional qualification in archaeology (Shaffer and Cole 1994, 61). This has undoubtedly restricted public involvement in the archaeological process, including excavation on any state land. There are similar stringent laws regarding antiquities requesting "assistance and corporation of citizens and landowners" (McGimsey 1972, 96), which furthermore requires the public to report and hand in any artifacts found of state land to be placed within the state museum.

The State of Maryland has a proactive HPO; Maryland Historical Trust was set up in 1961 "to assist the people of Maryland in identifying, studying, evaluating, preserving, protecting, and interpreting the state's significant prehistoric and historic districts, sites, structures, cultural landscapes, heritage areas, cultural objects, and artefacts, as well as less tangible human and community traditions" (http://www.marylandhistoricaltrust.net/aboutmht.html)

The City of Annapolis has numerous laws protecting its historic and archaeological heritage. The historic preservation zoning for the Annapolis historic district is established in the city's code, Title 21 (Planning and Zoning), Chapter 56 (Historic District) (http://bpc.iserver. net/ codes/annapolis/) this protects the archaeological remains, and historic building, and integrity of the city from being destroyed by development. There are other laws that apply which apply to the specific aesthetic integrity of this historic city; for instance, there is a ruling on signs that was implemented to limit the use of neon within the historic district. Maritime zoning is also used to accomplish historic preservation in the Eastport neighbourhood, without calling it historic preservation *per se*. This preserves the city aesthetically as a historic city, which is vital to its tourist economy.

Many of this city's regulations are enabled by state level legislation, for example there is legislation enabling the designation of municipal historic districts (www. marlandhistorictrust.net/aboutmht.html) There is also an act of the Maryland State Legislature that created underground utilities districting, specifically for Annapolis and for the town of Frederick further north, which is part of

the motivation of this mitigation and archaeological investigation at Annapolis.

Local Attitudes to Archaeology

Annapolis has built much of its tourism on its colonial past, subsequently Annapolians appeared on the whole proud of their heritage, and are nationalist. This is in part a reflection of the Naval Academy's base there. During the period of my visit it was the graduation ceremony of the Naval Academy, and many of the visitors were family members of these students. Furthermore, these students make up a large percentage of the population of Annapolis, and are very visible in their uniforms.

The tourist industry of Annapolis consists of numerous guided tours, walking through the historic streets, buildings and to the museums. Many of these buildings are recreated or reconstructed rather than being original. Conversations with the residents of Annapolis suggest that there is an understanding and respect for the past, and the archaeology, much of which is learned from local newspapers, or from school trips. Despite this knowledge, there is little desire to become more engaged with this past. In some sense, being surrounded by the past appears to have made my Annapolians blasé about it.

The longevity of the relationship and its economic benefit has led to schemes and partnerships including the creation of Archaeology of Annapolis, and Historic Annapolis Foundation, both of which have supported archaeological work and public engagement in heritage. This relationship, and often the personal relationship have enabled the beginnings of the creation of a preservation ethic in the city, for example, in the historic inns of Annapolis the owner created a glass floor over the 1720's hypocaust system, which is now the coffee room in the hotel.

Local attitudes are mixed through, many of the African American population still feeling disenfranchised from 'archaeology' despite the recent efforts with displays in the Banneker-Douglass Museum and outreach work at Eastport. Part of this relates to the fact many believe there is nothing new that archaeology can teach them that stories and relatives cannot teach them, and part of this may also relate to archaeology and the archaeologists of Annapolis all being white Americans, trying to study 'their past'.

Context

The City of Annapolis has a higher then national average racial and ethnic diversity, with 62.66%, white as opposed to 72.1% average for the US, and 31.44% Black African American, as opposed to 12.4% the national average, and over 8% Hispanic (http://annapolis.areaconnect.com/ statistics.htm). This is an interesting fact given the focus on colonial and white history which is predominately the focus of heritage industry in Annapolis, rather than native and Black history.

In the city's age demographic is spread out with 21.7% under the age of 18, 9.3% from 18 to 24, 33.4% from 25 to 44, 23.7% from 45 to 64, and 11.9% who were 65 years of age or older (http://annapolis.areaconnect.com/statistics.htm). The median age was 36 years. In 2008 the medium income for a household in Annapolis is $49,243, which is slightly higher than in 2006, the median annual household income was $48,201.00 (http://profiles.nationalrelocation.com/Maryland/Annapolis/)

The sites for Archaeological in Annapolis were located on Fleet Street and Cornhill Street, located just of Market Square, which is the main focus of activities in Annapolis (see Fig. 8.10). Both of these streets are residential streets, which have three shops nearest Market Square (including a tea shop on the intersection between the two streets, and two boutiques nearest Market Square). Cornhill Street also offers some short-term parking. Subsequently, these one-way streets are frequently busy with passing cars, which go right by the side of the trenching.

Figure 8.10 Photograph of Excavations on Fleet Street (Faye Simpson).

The excavations of these streets took place over a two-month period from April to May 2008, and occurred at 10 locations along the sidewalks, adjacent to the houses.

History

Fleet and Cornhill Street were believed from historic records to be built around 1770. This land, which is situated between the historic areas of the state circle and the city dock, has been identified from these historical record as reserved for Colonial Governor Francis Nicholson in his 1695 plan for Annapolis, but it was not until it was sold to Charles Wallace in 1770 that the land

was subdivided and urban development was initiated, including the building of residential houses, workshops, taverns and inns.

The census records from 1880-1930 indicate that in 1880 the houses in Cornhill Street were pre-dominantly white households, whilst interestingly it appears Fleet Street was mostly African American. It also identified that the majority of the occupants were born in Maryland or the Adjoining States. The 1910 census indicated an influx of immigrants on the street, with a number of Jewish Russian families on Cornhill Street.

Background of Community Archaeology Excavation

Public archaeology programmes has been happening in Annapolis for over 25 years, directed by Mark Leone, who has over this time built up relationships with the members of the city council, museums, and the Historic Annapolis Foundation

The archaeological work on Fleet Street and Cornhill by Archaeology in Annapolis (a partnership between the University of Maryland, The Banneker-Douglass Museum, the City of Annapolis, and the Historic Annapolis Foundation, for the department of Public Works and the City of Annapolis) was principally a commercial exercise led by a CRM firm affiliated with the University of Annapolis. This work was undertaken as a result of putting in underground services. Initially, another CRM firm won the contract, but pressure from the City Archaeologist and some members of council about that company's ability to communicate with the public, on what could be a highly sensitive contract, led to the current situation.

Participation

The excavators at Fleet and Cornhill Street allowed the public to watch the excavation process although, for the majority of the time, not actively participate in it. Volunteers where taken on for the summer school, which did allow experience for newly graduated students to do commercial archaeology, which is similar to that participatory experience offered at Hungate (UK). Access to the site was more open to the public than many of the other excavations, including Chester, Hungate and Mitchell. The trenches' close proximity to the road and houses meant that the barrier between the trench, archaeologists and the public was only a wooden plank, rather than a formal fence (see Fig. 8.11).

Espoused Values

Professionals: The research values of this project were perceived by some of the archaeologists as the most fundamental values of the project: "excavations are always guided by questions" (leaflet 2008). They wanted to find the early land-use history of the city, to identify historic the community of Fleet Street and Cornhill Street, focusing on the historic communities of African

Figure 8.11 Photograph of excavation outside house in Fleet Street (Faye Simpson).

Americans, immigrant and Jewish immigrants, and to understand the early historic street paving and infrastructure changes in these two streets, linking this to the historical records (leaflet 2008).

It was also believed at the beginning that "everybody loved old stuff" (MC), but because of this there was a new research drive which "oriented toward the archaeology of African Americans" (MP), shifting the research aims of the project away from the 'power building' of Annapolis, to something more socially valuable, that reaches new audiences, as well as making archaeology more relevant by "moving Mark (Leone) toward the 20th century" (MP). It also provided a new way of conducting research, and engaging in a new research topic, which also assisted the personal research of the PhD students who where supervising and managing the project.

It was hoped that this would have a social benefit, opening up communication, "trying not to be didactic when you try and talk to people, I mean trying to explain our excitement about it and get a reaction" (MC). In some respects the archaeologists wanted to engage and pass on knowledge and excitement and make people passionate about 'their past.' Through this it is hoped to "achieve some sort of buy in" (MP) to the archaeological record and "create a sense of ownership, that's like the best case scenario" (MP), and subsequently enable a preservation ethic and perhaps even stop the archaeological record from being destroyed from underground works through public support for archaeology, or even force the council to excavate 100% of the archaeological record before it is destroyed. "[It] gives us a change to come up with a mitigation plan, come up with some sort of management strategy and resources" (MC), and furthermore "[it] gives us further potential to call for more archaeology to really hold the City accountable."

Students: The graduate students who where employed on this project hoped that this would offer them valuable

work experience helping them get a job after this project was completed or having the offer of more work on another aspect of Archaeology in Annapolis. "It's a professionalizing experience for them, with this much experience they really can do this for a living" (MP) The project was also aimed at "supporting graduate students" (MP), including doctoral students, in gathering material and case studies for their research.

Council: In part the council's agreement to support the extra cost of this mitigation process, was to win public support for the underground works and the massive amount of disruption it would cause the residents of the streets, hoping that the archaeologists would be the "shinny happy face for whatever is going on here" (MC). Therefore, it was essential that since the works were "imposing on these peoples' neighbourhoods, so we should try and act like guests" (MC). It was for the council, as Matthew Copran described it, "a little political" and it was the city that suggested, "there had to be public presence."

The winning of this contract by the University of Maryland was also "a little political" and required "a negation process" (MC), with a "little lobbying, we were able to convince the council of the worth of this project" (MP).

Actual Values

Professionals: In terms of the knowledge and research values of doing this project, it has outperformed many of their initial hopes. The excavation provided evidence for the earliest occupation in Annapolis in the form of a wooden road and preserved water logged remains. "No one had any idea this was down there, we didn't know, nobody [knew]" (MP). It has offered evidence of African American Archaeology; with preserved offerings in one of the ditches (although it is worth mentioning the archaeologists have some reluctance in publishing this information, at present). This offering was clay "bundle" filled with small pieces of common metal, including nails, lead shot and pins, which has been associated to African religion, distinct from hoodoo and other later practices blending African and European traditions.

Over the course of the excavation, relationships between the local residents and the archaeologist have developed, breaking down many of the social barriers and perceptions of what archaeologists are like, e.g. "smoking joints and hippies" (local resident), and led to the public engaging with them with "friendly responses, good rapport; [they] stop and talk like friends" (Digger). In part this is due to the close proximity of the archaeologist to the residents "digging right on their doorsteps" (MC). Still, it has not broken down the barriers in terms of people feeling that they can become archaeologists or have a right to actively engage in 'their' heritage: "It's like they almost don't feel they have a right to stop us [doing archaeological investigation and digging up there streets], and the same is true for what is under the streets, as far as they are concerned it [is] our domain" (MP).

It has also led to the archaeologists "feeling responsible" (MC), and direct involvement with the public forced them to reconsidered their methods and ethics: "I am a lot more reflexive...I have had to come back on some of my beliefs...Do we owe the city and their under-funded project [to finish of the work we have started], or do we owe the residents to produce more of a base [information] to show them heritage of this neighbourhood and really effect some political change" (MC). It appears from this quotation to have been a difficult balancing act, and one that has forced commercially funded unit and its staff to question who they are working for, and examine the pay-offs of being more public minded, rather than so economically driven. It has made the professional archaeologists more aware of the political potential of involving the public in archaeology: "[it] gives us further potential to call for more archaeology, to really hold the city accountable" (MC).

Students: The project did provide a research value for the graduate students "Archaeology in Annapolis has gone through a series of PhD students" (MP), with one PhD using the work to research the anthropological study of the values of heritage. Furthermore previous community excavations provided research for another PhD student.

Graduate students' values about the project related to physical and social values rather than educational and knowledge values. Motivations, beyond mere employment, and its clear economic value were described thus: "I just like to dig" (JB). Socially, the students felt they had a positive experience of archaeological excavation, and described their experience as better than a commercial excavation due to the more social and friendly atmosphere: "The atmosphere is great; people are a team; its very friendly and lots of talk" (SD). Furthermore, students described this as useful in enabling them to communicate with the public and teaching them the importance of that: "I enjoy it here ... you actually get to talk to people" (SD). All of the students attending the excavation intended to get or had jobs lined up for after the project finished, which supports the claim: "...with this experience they really can do this for a living" (MP).

Professional partnerships have come about from this work: "...our research partners are the museum, and there is [also] a strong partner in the Historic Annapolis Foundation...we love the idea of community partners" (MP).

Public: The public response has been described as "great" with "everybody being really psyched" (MC). Furthermore, although there are friendliness and sociability values attached to the project the project, the following describes the value that the public placed on knowledge and the relevance they feel it had to them: "the African American Community have very little interest,

not in us personally, but in archaeology as a way to learn their past; they had living people who were able to tell them everything that was important about their past" (MP). Therefore, the project failed to engage with one of the communities of Annapolis.

The excavation was successful in changing the attitudes of the public towards archaeological professionals and opened up dialogues and produced more informal ways of communicating knowledge. The majority of people who stopped off to talk to the archaeologists and got involved in the project were local residents, whos houses the archaeologists were working outside. When discussing the project with them, their main comments were about the people involved, rather than the archaeology, describing them as "amazing people." Furthermore, they used "have you found anything interesting?" (Anon.), as a conversational icebreaker before more social discussions. This initial interest was often superficial interest in what had been have found, many people paid little attention to the answer or started walking away immediately. It appeared that the "generally bored, [were] not that excited" (Anon.) by the answers, in a sense indicating that the public "want to know what large things [we have] found rather than piddly [things]" (Anon. Archaeologist).

The excavation also had some negative connotations to some of the local residents and businesses. In part, this often related to the frustration with the under-grounding project, and, in some circumstances, confusion over the archaeologists' role. Many people considered them to be the under-grounding contractors, with direct links to the council. Such people tended to "just wish they would finish up" (Anon.). Other businesses, including a local teashop and boutique, described the work as a bit annoying: "it's kind of interesting but kind of intrusive" (Anon. business). These concerns were about aesthetic and business disturbance caused by digging holes outside their shops and there were further complaints raised directly about the archaeologists and the "volume of noise and disturbance on the side walks" (MC). Furthermore, some of the residents were frustrated by having to manoeuvre cars around the diggers, who been "almost hit by cars; they appear to hate us" (MP), although this was a minor problem, and I did not observe any open animosity. These negative impacts, although felt by a minority, meant that specific people were less interested in finding out more about the archaeology, or in talking to the archaeologists about what had been found.

In terms of the value of excavation, and the public actually digging themselves, it appears that children were generally keener to dig: "I want to dig, I want to be an archaeologist," (Anon.). The adults didn't want to get involved quite so much, but perhaps saw the excavations as a "baby sitting service" (MP). The majority of people did not show any interest in getting physically involved in excavation and in some sense "I was doing excavations; I got very little interest" (MP). In part this related to the type and nature of the archaeological remains: "I don't think they would jump in there even if they could. I think its because its deep, we are filthy… all of that looks like a mess and no one wants to get involved; they don't want to get dirty" (MP). Part of this related to the aesthetics of this particular excavation and the issues with seeing the archaeology and understanding it from the very small hole in the ground (see Fig. 8.12). The public's lack of direct involvement in excavation further relations to the relationship between the archaeologist and public, the public respecting the professionalism involved in doing archaeological fieldwork.

Figure 8.12 Photography of Archaeologist Excavating Test Pit in Fleet Street (Faye Simpson).

There were problems with knowledge transfer to the public. In part, this related to the actual involvement and participation that the council allowed on the archaeological mitigation project. The majority of information communicated to the public came from three information boards; one was positioned at the corner of Cornhill and Fleet Street, and the other two by the sides of the trenches. There was also a leaflet that the archaeologists had to give to the public, if they were asked, but as the majority of the visitors were local residents from the two streets, or people that had already visited; these were not given out very often. Information about the dig was passed on through conversations with archaeologists, who had been encourage to, and were all, according to my observations, eager to talk about what was happening, and what had been found. This had produced a friendly atmosphere for leaning about archaeology through more casual conversations, which even took place in the bar later on in the evening. A point MP considered unfortunate was that most of the residents were short-term let and holiday tenants, although many were encouraging and positive towards that archaeology, it "means very few of these folks are going to know what we did a year or so from now" (MP).

The excavation was less successful in reaching new audiences, in particular the aims of engaging the African

American community in their past. The experience of trying to engage with African Americans, and Jewish residents was described as failing: "the African American community [had] very little interest, not in us personally, but in archaeology as a way of learning their past, they had living people that were able to tell them everything that was *important* about their past and that is why I accept this kind of indifference" (MP). This response has made the some of the archaeologists involved more cynical about the potential of public archaeology: "public archaeology fails as often as it succeeds, actually it fails more often then it succeeds, and I say that having failed to generate any excitement in Eastport" (with the African American community) (MP). The African American community have not seen the relevance of this project; when discussing the excavation with the Africa community they told me the facts about what was happening, but when asked if they intended to visit or had visited, showed no interest in visiting the site, saying " [I] haven't been there myself" (Museum Attendant).

When discussing with the majority of people in the town, both in the Banneker-Douglass Museum, in which there is an exhibition relating to the archaeology of Annapolis projects, and at the tourist information centre, there was still, after 8 weeks of digging, confusion over what was actually being excavated. Many cited the newspaper report, which mentioned the wooden structure, the bridge/walkway in Fleet Street, although they often remembered it wrong (as it was actually a walkway), although all did say the 'oldest' in the city suggesting as Matthew Copran did a form of "Fetishising archaeology." The majority had not visited the site. Part of the issue was that they were aware where it was, but it was along a side-street down which there was little other reason to go.

The incorporation of some information into the tour guides walks was, in part, more successful. Although independent to the dig, some of the tours, incorporated a visit and provided information on the excavations, "there are tour groups and some of them are really interested" (MP). However, just as many tours were described as actively avoiding the excavations.

The occasional tourists, described as "stumbling across the site", were interested and stayed around chatting to people. The majority of such visitors I talked too had not heard of the site, and were in Annapolis because of its military connections. In some respects, many were not interested in the local archaeology and mentioned being around for a graduation ceremony, but were taking the opportunity to look around a historic and beautiful town.

To a certain extent the excavations and other programmes from Archaeology Annapolis have brought economic benefit, building on the pre-existing interest of the town in exploiting its heritage. Examples include tour groups using it in guides of the city, and the historic inns of Annapolis preserving the 1720's hypocaust system in their coffee room, in order to draw in more tourists to stay somewhere unique. Furthermore, in this particular case "the owner paid for it out of [their] own pocket" (MP).

Local Council: Initially the public archaeology excavation gained a very positive response from the council, their support was obtained, in part, due to the "historical relationship of the project with the government and there has been adequate support for this to happen" (MP), but also due to personal relationships of Mark Leone with the government official "someone, somewhere along the way intervened to make sure that this was handled right" (MP), suggesting that the council saw the political benefits, and community benefits from doing archaeological work, and outreach.

This project has also had a politically value, with the archaeological work being used by the City Council to justify the delay to the under-grounding work (which was in part due to financial trouble): "on one hand they say how progressive we are, on the other hand they point the finger and say we are holding them up" (MC). There

appears to be a mixed response, described by MC as "seemingly disinterested", but I observed some awareness by local government when one of the state's senators stopping by and talked to the archaeologists in the bar asking: "found any neat stuff? [I'll] have to come along tomorrow" (SS). There appeared to be some very close, personal relationships that had developed between the archaeologists and politicians

The work has had some negative impact upon what the public and archaeologists think of the City Council: "They [the council] invite us to this meeting to present a nice window dressing, and then try and light us on fire afterwards…but this didn't work" (MC), in this meeting the archaeologist where used firstly to highlight the community work that the council was involved with, and then later accused of delaying in the under-grounding work. This some sense soured the relationships on both sides producing more negative views of "the process of archaeology as civic engagement…it just doesn't work" (MC).

9. DISCUSSION

9.1 Introduction

Over a two-year period, seven community archaeology excavations were analysed using the self-reflexive and ethnological methodology outlined in Chapter 6. Three sites from the US and four sites from the UK were assessed, allowing the espoused and actual values to be established and compared, both within and between case studies. This critical analysis of community archaeology excavations highlighted key value themes and differences, relating to the espoused and actual values, and the inputs and outcomes. Furthermore, conclusions from this study enabled values to be reassessed in a more contextually specific manner. In many cases there were more values attained from community archaeology than had been assumed, but some of the key assumptions of community archaeology, that had been academically based, were unsubstantiated.

9.2 Methodological Issues

During the course of this analysis there were some potential problems that emerged in relation to the types of community archaeology projects that were available to study. In the initial stages of research there were many community archaeology excavations in the UK which were open to the public to participate in, the majority of which where HLF funded, including large scale projects in Manchester, Shoreditch and Hull, and small scale projects in Brixton and Merton. During the course of this research many of the community projects finished and after this few seemed to secure further funding. This related to funding for heritage being diverted to the Olympics and a severe economic downturn.

In the US a similar pattern emerged, with many projects that had state or government backing being closing down, including Balitimore and Florida, or reducing their staff (e.g. South Dakota), as well as the number of volunteers and excavation projects they could cope with (e.g. National Parks Authority). This appeared to relate to 'the

credit crunch' in the US and funding for the 'war on terror'.

This is a trend that is likely to continue for the foreseeable future, with increasing financial pressures on both the UK and US. This has been reflected in the UK already, with growing assessment of the value of projects, and audits of their cost-effectiveness.

9.3 Summary of Case Studies

Shoreditch

It is apparent that the project was successful in meeting its research aims, and producing knowledge value. In many respects it exceeded these goals, in part due to the oral history research and personal research of some members of the community; this also occurred in Hungate, Brayford and Annapolis.

Socially, the project had a benefit to the older population in giving them the chance to become engaged with other members of the population and tell their stories. It gave many of them a renewed sense of pride in the local area and their past. This was to some degree transferred to some of the younger population, who got involved in the project through school trips, or by chance. This also happened to a limited extent at Chester and Hungate.

A clear limitation of the project's wider social impact was that interest in the project waned after the excavation finished. This was not a problem in relation to the initial application for the Big Lottery Fund's 'Their Past Your Future' grant which focused its funding upon the commemoration of the 60th anniversary of the end of World War II, and only hosted the exhibition at the Museum of London for a short period only in June and July 2005. From the perspective of this application, sustainability was not a primary output. However, in terms of the subsequent bid for funds, it was an explicit objective to encourage further interest in the heritage from the Hackney community and build on the work of the excavation. More positively, local people taking part in 2005 did return to get involved in the subsequent year's excavation, but this indicates that the excavation itself was a draw. It was therefore disappointing that there was a lack of participation in subsequent non-excavation activities, or visitations to the Museum of London, after the project had finished.

The drop in visitor numbers, and problems with attendance in the post-excavation outreach activities, gives an indication that, for many people, it was the excavation that was the key to their interest in this project. Whether that consisted of simply watching the process or practically engaging in it, once the digging ended, local interest evaporated. The theatre of the excavation was subsequently memorialised in the Time Team project and local people may have benefited from the experience of being there and (for some) of taking part. However, it is difficult to evaluate whether there was any concrete and enduring influence on community knowledge and engagement with their heritage, never mind any influence upon individual and group identities.

The project also highlighted major financial issues for this type of externally funded community project. The grants had finite timescales and therefore, without further funding, subsequent projects had a very limited time span and have proved unsustainable to date. Like many other community archaeology projects, it relied upon being supported by a large organisation, to get off the ground and be successful. This enabled many of the costs for staffing and resources, including that of paying for a community archaeologist, to be covered: "I think it would come out as a relatively expensive project...not just in terms of money we spent but in terms of number of people we impacted" (HS).

The success of this two-year project was assessed quantitatively by the Museum of London and the Lottery Fund, through visitor numbers. Figures indicated that the project attracted over three thousand visitors, with over seven hundred local people participating in the excavation, and subsequently it was claimed by the organisations and sponsors that these figures indicated clear interest in archaeology and local heritage by the community. Critical analyses indicated that these high numbers were, in part, due to the excavation's urban location, situated in one of the few open spaces in the area, surrounded by housing tower blocks. This was supported by the fact that the park was a thoroughfare for the community's city workers. The focus upon relatively recent history, within the living memory of the oldest members of the community, and perhaps also the association with the war (a popular topic not least for local school groups), also enhanced the popularity of the project. A limited qualitative survey was focused on participatory visitor enjoyment of the project (Streeter 2005). The results of this survey suggested a resoundingly positive response. However, this survey did not assess the

opinions of the majority of people who visited, rather only those who got involved in the excavation. Similarly, like the quantitative surveys, the qualitative survey gave no indication as to whether opinions changed and what impact this project had on people's values regarding their heritage.

In critical terms, assumptions were made, in part by me, that excavation was key to successful outreach. This reflected my colleagues' and my own background in field archaeology and our experience of excavation. There was public and political consultation prior to the excavation, in which support was voiced, but critically this was really a matter of marketing an idea already in place. Ideas were drawn together for peripheral activities beyond the excavation influenced by the public themselves, but the core of the project was designed by, and for, the research and community agendas of professional archaeology and influenced by agendas and financial support from various tiers of government.

Chester

In some respects, this project failed to excite the public in the way the other projects investigated did. This could be related to the type of archaeology, size of excavation, publicity, and the presence of fencing. Visually, unlike Shoreditch and Hungate the archaeology was not exciting, which was similar to Muncy. However, the lack of digging opportunities and public interaction on the site meant that, unlike Mitchell and Muncy, (even though this was a rural site) the feedback from the public and the values achieved were less apparent. In some cases, the impacts were negative; there was disappointment in what archaeology really involved. Subsequently, it should be questioned whether, if one cannot fully commit the time and money to a community archaeology project, then it may be better and less detrimental if one does not try at all.

This project was principally research based. The archaeologist's response to the public was mixed. The combination of research, first, and public, second, was really the case in this project and the results do indicate this. If one looks back at previous years, there was a definite interest and pride among local people in their heritage ('Chester is a magical place'), and tourism figures show that archaeology is interesting. The high number of repeat visitors indicated that they wanted to see and experience archaeology. It was just that this project did not live up to the expectations raised by the earlier amphitheatre project and was not what many of the public wanted. Perhaps it has been most successful in changing the perceptions of the archaeologists regarding the public, particularly in changing assumptions of what the public's values are.

Hungate

This project met the needs of amateurs, but not necessarily those of the general public. This is because the general public and amateur archaeologists were regarded by the professionals as one entity, with shared values, when in reality they had different needs.

Educationally, many of the aims of the project were fulfilled for a select group of people (excavation volunteers who were largely already members of archaeology societies). Whilst the wider community was able to attend tours, there was, in part due to health and safety concerns, and lack of outreach, an inability for many of the public to actively participate. During discussions with the public (both volunteers and people on tours), it became evident that the majority of people (especially adults) were not interested, themselves, in excavating, but did want to see the reality of excavation and interesting finds. Children seemed more excited by the prospect of getting their hands dirty.

Socially, the impact of this project has been very positive for a select demographic. It is questionable whether it created a community in Hungate, rather than a community who are interested in archaeology but live elsewhere. It gave the development a higher public profile, and people seemed more accepting of the development as a result, but they did not necessarily regard this project as relevant to them, as it was not in their own back yard.

Interestingly, one of the more positive aspects of this project was the social (rather than educational) activity it provided for retired people. Professionally, it enabled archaeologists to consider the integration of commercial and community aspects of their work. In reality, however, these were really two separate strands in this project, which did not overlap significantly. The professionals merely accommodated the wider York community, and it appears that (like Annapolis) the commercial and research aspects overshadowed what the community wanted.

Brayford

The community excavation at Welcombe Farm produced some interesting results. Like Muncy, this was a project initially led from the bottom up, a 'grass roots project' initiated and led by the enthusiasm of one individual. It therefore had research and knowledge value to select members of the community and, in some senses, an individual political and social value. X-Arch's involvement attempted to broaden the values of this project, and interlink them with their own.

This project indicated that the process of excavating sites with community volunteers could be slow (like Muncy and York). The nature of this site, the organisation and the 1:4 ratio of experienced to inexperienced excavators (similar to that at York and Chester), meant that, unlike Muncy, it maintained a high standard of archaeological practice: "I don't think there is anything we did wrong or that we made archaeological mistakes" (PC).

All stakeholders frequently discussed the limited time span of one week for excavation. This produced tensions

between the archaeologists and amateurs in the techniques used to excavate, and the goals that were obtainable. It was perceived as 'leading to disappointment' and a feeling of lack of commitment from the archaeologists. If given the choice all stakeholders would have "excavated for a longer period" (PC) and it was believed if this had occurred, more sustainable values would have been achieved.

Both the amateurs and professionals had high expectations as to the values this project could achieve, which were unachievable given the time, location and nature of the site. There were issues relating to individuals relinquishing control, which was similar to Chester and Mitchell. One of the more successful aspects of this project was its social value. There were long-term sustainable values, capturing the excitement of the archaeological process and increasing knowledge of those who already had an interest in archaeology. It failed, though, to capture the excitement and interest of those who did not have a previous interest in archaeology. Similarly to Hungate, Chester, Shoreditch and Annapolis, rather than the knowledge value that was espoused, it was the social value that was most prevalent for the individuals involved.

Mitchell

This project did have proven economic values to the community; increasing tourism and visitors stopping off the Interstate for a break. It indicates that through the presence of archaeologists and an English university group, it changed public attitudes and perceptions of archaeology and England, breaking down some public stereotypes whilst re-affirming others. This was also true regarding archaeologists' and English students' perceptions of the American public. Yet many of the local people in Mitchell had not visited the project, and were not particularly interested in the archaeology. Many were more interested in England and hearing English accents.

Educationally, this project has proven beneficial to the students, visitors and even the professionals. It has enabled people to see the archaeological process and, for some, to get involved with the process. This was most successful when the archaeologists themselves talked to the public and therefore broke down stereotypes and enabled the public to ask more questions. Comments from the public did indicate that it had been enjoyable. They saw it as interesting, not boring, 'watching' people dig. Yet they wanted more interaction, to get closer, and parents did comment that it sparked an interest, especially in children, to dig and find things.

It is still questionable whether this project really served the public and their values or merely acted as a platform to be able to carry out research. Part of the problem is that it failed to address what the public wanted and, for some, their desire to participate in the excavation. Nor did the Archeodome provide transferable skills to the public. Interestingly, especially with the adults, they did not express a desire to dig. They were more than happy letting others carry out the hard work, like at Chester. In some respects the reality of digging put some people off. It did successfully change attitudes towards archaeologists, and alter the view of some archaeologists towards the importance of the public.

Muncy

This project had some interesting results in getting some local residents more involved and engaged in the archaeological process, although the majority of people attending the excavation had a previous interest in archaeology, and were members of Muncy History Society (see Brayford), or came along as part of the summer placement with the college. Interestingly many visitors returned and some of the students also returned to carry on excavating after their placement was over, providing some evidence that this project had been successful in creating a sense of ownership in the past.

The project did have knowledge value as it enabled interesting and important research about the mill, regarding its function and date. This would not have happened without the private interest and investment. The private ownership of the site, and its rural context, meant the project lacked state support, and limited the project's outputs, and actual values to the wider public.

The public attitudes toward the site were, on the whole, positive, but most people did not themselves want to excavate (as at Mitchell, Chester and Annapolis). Many local residents respected the work and effort of the individuals involved, but did not want to participate, nor visit the site. In terms of educational value, it augmented knowledge, but it is questionable whether the participants learnt a great deal more about archaeology.

This public archaeology excavation was only part of a larger bid and, like Chester, the future of the project has yet to be secured, but it has the potential to build on initial interest, and in 2008 a third year of public excavation occurred. This is only likely to materialise if it succeeds as part of the larger heritage park, and if the site becomes state registered, as this will allow for the application of grants to continue with the future 'vision' of a research strategy.

The most important value for this project was social, with people's views and perceptions of the archaeologists changing and become more positive, similar to Brayford and Mitchell. The close working relationship and personal approach gave the public the opportunity and experience of talking to archaeologists and working with them placed the archaeologist in a more positive light, and gave the public more confidence in their own ability to understand and connect with the past.

Economically the project has had very little impact on the local economy, but the future plans could be more beneficial, if the project brings more tourism and larger investment. The main shift in values was the realisation by the participants that archaeology was entertaining and enjoyable, and that archaeology is accessible and not just about science. However, this perception has yet to be transferred to the local community in general.

Politically it did raise awareness of the site; the local SHPO visited the site, although it is questionable whether awareness of the community excavation actually changed the state archaeologists' values.

Annapolis

The project itself has successfully developed strong political relationships and has provided valid political values for both the local council and archaeologists. It has built up friendships and relationships with local residents and positive responses to archaeologists as people, though it is debatable whether there has been an actual increase in interest in archaeology; it has rather become a part of the background noise for the city. This project successfully enabled archaeologists to increase their knowledge of the city's past, but the transference of this to the public has been more questionable, and is not something that many of the public regard as important, but interesting. It is the social interaction between the public and archaeologists that seemed more valued. These relationships and friendships have facilitated the longevity of the project.

The archaeologists had managed to communicate their findings through newspaper reports and the population of Annapolis were aware of the project, and could locate it. Even if there was some confusion as to what it all meant, people were more aware of archaeology and were positive towards it. Interestingly, despite this, the public felt no or little want to visit the site unless they were passing by.

Like other projects, including Mitchell, Chester and Hungate, the majority of the public where not interested in participating in excavation, and it was frequently seen as something that was 'not for them', but for professionals. There were stereotypes about what archaeologists should be like. Although residents and the public were willing to talk to the archaeologists, most were being polite rather than engaging with what was happening. It appeared that there was a psychological, if not physical, barrier to getting involved, even if the social barriers had been broken down and communication opened up.

9.4 Espoused Values

The analysis of the espoused values indicated that, regardless of the different contextual situations of the seven case studies from both the UK and US, all involved similar assumptions (Table 9.1). These related to social, educational, economic, and political values within the profession (Darvill 1995; Lipe 2007) and engaging with

Table 9.1 Summary of major findings of research

Values	Espoused Value Claims	Actual Value Outcomes
Social	• Encourage proactive and direct involvement by members of the community in their heritage.	• Involvement was often superficial: only select demographic (amateurs, retirement age), e.g Brayford, Grosvenor Park, Hungate.
	• Encourage a more diverse audience and participation in Archaeology	• In the majority of cases diversity was not achieved. It was achieved in Shoreditch though it was not comparable to the population demographic.
	• Build communities (pride of place)	• Did not build communities. Led to demographic separation between those involved and not e.g Hungate, Muncy.
	• Meet public desire to dig	• Frequently did not meet public desire to dig: The majority of the public did not want to dig. e.g Mitchell, Grosvenor Park, Annapolis.
	• Reduce Crime (specifically at urban sites Shoreditch, Hungate and Chester)	• Reduced crime rates (graffiti, vandalism) during excavation in specific urban areas e.g Shoreditch and Chester.
		• Provided entertainment and social activity, e.g Brayford, Hungate, Shoreditch.
		• Opened up dialogues between archaeologists and the public.
Education	• Increase knowledge and awareness of archaeology.	• Increased knowledge and awareness of archaeology for those participating.
	• Increase desire and ability to learn	• Increased/ maintained desire and ability to learn, in those actively participating in excavation and in a select demographic: school children/students/local volunteers (amateurs).
	• Research of site	• Enabled new archaeological research.e.g. Mitchell, Annapolis.
Economic	• Save the community the cost of commercial excavation	• Saved the community the cost of commercial dig e.g Muncy, Brayford
	• Increase tourism (specifically at urban sites, Mitchell, Chester and Hungate)	• Did increase tourism in certain urban locations e.g. Grosvenor Park, Shoreditch.
Political	• Increase political awareness of importance of archaeology: change agendas, support and increase funding for archaeology.	• Created political interest, awareness and appreciation of archaeology locally in urban location e.g Shoreditch, Mitchell.
	• Increase awareness/ support for local government by communities.	• Has not (to date) directly affected political agendas and financial support for archaeology.
		• Met corporate responsibility/patrimony agendas, e.g. Hungate

the public as a justification for the archaeological profession and its internal research agendas.

At the core of all 'values' was the concept of proactive engagement of the community with 'their' past. For instance, engagement with excavation would change and increase the values attached to heritage (Table 9.1). This concept evolved out of the growing discourse relating to the public relevance of archaeology (Little 2002; Jameson 2002), which was, in part, due to increasing political and economic pressure to justify the use of public funds for archaeological activities.

There was evidence of superficial differences in the priorities projects placed on the various espoused values. Principally these related to the context of the projects and the dichotomy between rural and urban settings. Projects in urban areas, with large-scale excavations including Hungate and Shoreditch, perceived, and to some extent focused on, the social and political value of the project in creating a sense of community, and pride in 'their'

heritage, bringing people together in a common goal. This would suggest that, as Start (1999) asserts, political value becomes the principal espoused value attached to community archaeology, with research value secondary. This could be related to the increasing need for archaeology in general to be publicly accountable, and justifiable when subjected to cost-benefit analysis (Carman 2002). Therefore espoused values often reflected current political agendas.

Furthermore, these projects made broad claims to reduce crime and re-offending rates from public engagement in archaeology, through the creation of pride and a sense of community. In some senses these projects were attempting to not just prove themselves to the public, but also political paymasters, as was apparent at Annapolis, Hungate and Shoreditch and, to some extent, Mitchell.

Whereas, the rural community projects, including Muncy and Brayford, and, to some extent Mitchell, placed value precedence on the ability to create educational value and knowledge about the place to the public. In these cases social value was rarely considered. In part, this was because it was believed there was already an established sense of community.

The espoused value attached to these projects focused on use value as defined by Darvill (1995) and suggested by Carman (2002). They failed to identity the relevance of other values including option and existence value, perhaps, in part, because these are less understood, and is not tangible in the present. This could relate to an inability to think beyond the archaeological and consider anthropological, social and philosophical influences on the value of heritage (Potter 1994).

9.5 Actual Value Outcomes

The espoused values of community archaeology projects are often different from the actual values attained as outcomes (Table 9.1). This is partly because the various stakeholders and communities have different objectives, critically not all of which were considered prior to projects' commencement. As a result, projects have adapted, producing different outcomes, which hold equal if not higher prominence than the values initially espoused. This adaptability of community archaeology projects, relates to the breadth of its definition, which is highlighted by the variability of the projects in this study. Furthermore, it is this ability to be flexible and organic, within different contexts, which makes each of the projects valuable.

Participatory involvement in excavation has been regarded as vital to understanding and valuing the past (Holtorf 2006). This research has found that participation in excavation is not vital to creating and maintaining public values (also see Simpson & Williams 2008). There was an indication, however, that it did produce social values, including psychological values.

Education

Participation in excavation was key to the learning potential of organised groups, such as schools and amateurs, in sites where a multi-disciplinary approach was taken. This educational success related to the type of archaeology on the site; it was the archaeological rich 19th and 20th century sites i.e. Shoreditch, Hungate and, to some degree, Annapolis, that were able to incorporate oral history and historical research that appeared to offer the best learning experience for both the community and the archaeologists. These sites offered a temporal framework, which the community could relate to and understand, and, therefore, they had more cultural relevance.

Conversely, the prehistoric site Mitchell, the Iron Age/Roman site of Brayford, and the 17th century site of Chester had issues with public understanding of the archaeological remains. This related to the lack of

obvious standing remains, and, at Mitchell, a lack of public awareness and understanding of Native American Indian remains, and their relevance to local agendas. All of these sites were from periods rarely taught in schools.

Social

This research indicated that the majority of the public who visited these projects did not want to dig, but came to visually experience an excavation, and principally attended in order to be entertained, rather than to be educated. It was the social value of being entertained, and making friends that was perceived to be the most significant value that these projects had to the communities, both by the communities themselves and by the professionals, after the excavation had finished. This was highlighted in the UK examples of Brayford, Chester, Hungate and Shoreditch, but interesting not discussed in the US examples, although there was evidence of this for students and professionals at Mitchell.

These findings back up Holtorf and Williams (2006, 249) concept that community excavations could act as 'theatres for memory', backing up the theory that they act as performances in the landscape, which engaged and entertained the public in the past. This assertion has also been further supported in research carried out by Moshenska (2007). Therefore, these projects were, particularly in the UK, perceived as Fowler (2002, 62) principally as a leisure activity. It can therefore be surmised that the past has become entertainment, as Hewison (1987, 83) suggested earlier.

In the majority of the case studies, involvement in excavation had negative implications for future desire to be involved actively in digging. It was described as boring, tedious, and tiring, which is very different from the pre-conceived perceptions of archaeology as exciting and fast paced as portrayed on popular television programmes (e.g. Time Team). Conversely, in the select demographic of amateurs, involvement in excavation increased the desire to be involved in further excavation. These results offer confirmation of society's desire and demand for immediate gratification (Holtorf 2006), something that involvement in the long process of archaeological excavation does not provide and may have a negative impact on values attached to archaeology.

A further interesting social benefit was the reduced crime figures and lack of graffiti and vandalism in the local areas of the projects, at both Hungate and Shoreditch. This was something that was previously asserted by Dig Manchester's work, claiming to see a 1/3 reduction in crime in the local area (Norman Redhead pers. comm.). This could relate to the fact that in Shoreditch they took on youth offenders and adults on probation as work experience and physical involvement and engagement with their local area enabled people to feel a sense of ownership and respect for the park, therefore reducing vandalism.

Economic

It has been claimed that community excavation can save the commercial costs of excavation, or enable the excavation of an area, which would otherwise not have had the financial support to excavate it. This was true for all the case studies with the exception of Hungate where additional finances were needed to support community excavation from the commercial sector. Here, it was claimed that this project and the extra costs were legitimised by the provision of free marketing for the housing development and contractors. The archaeological project made local and national press, in which the area and the people were all branded with logos of the respective contractors. This is something, which was claimed to be worth tens of thousands of pounds (Swain pers. comm.). It has also been claimed that this type of work, and involvement of the public in their open spaces and their heritage can increase the house prices of the area (CABE space). To date, none of the digs in public spaces in the inner city have legitimised this claim.

Critically, if justifying these projects in terms of market economics (Carman 2002), using cost-benefit analysis, i.e. *investment* (input) versus *values* (output). the smaller projects, or those with less capital investment, had equal if not more benefit to the community then more large-scale, controlled projects. In part, this was because they required more support, assistance and involvement from the community (mainly amateurs) to both initiate them and to run them. Therefore, these projects had a greater sense of community involvement and ownership.

Political

The espoused moral and ethical ideals of incorporating local values into the practice and interpretation of these archaeological projects, have been less successfully achieved. Archaeologists were, on the whole, still reluctant to embrace multicultural, intangible, social and psychological values attached to the heritage. This appears particularly true of the community projects in the UK. This is unlike the US, which had the political impetus and Acts (i.e. NAGPRA, 1990) which required archaeologists to listen to the multiple voices of communities, and incorporate these into cultural resource management. Critically, it is this difference that gives an indication of why some of the value claims in the UK are not being achieved.

This research highlighted the political influence on the espoused value claims and on the actual values. This backs up Start's (1999) assertion that it was political motivation and then research that was key to espoused values of the community archaeological projects. Yet he specifically mentioned this was only true of the UK, whilst the US was more democratic, and Marxist, and controlled by the public. This is something that this research indicated was false. In reality, both the UK and US projects were principally driven by political and research agendas outside the public domain.

Specifically, the comparative analysis between the UK's political situation of a Labour, and relativist philosophical and political stance, versus the previous US political situation of a Republican and absolutist mindset meant that the theoretical values and achieved values were different. The more quasi-socialist political framework affected the values people attached to heritage over the last 10 years (ref chap 2), with values primarily being associated with entertainment, socialisation, and leisure. Whilst in the US, conservative framework has focused on education and the pushing of national identity, in some senses excluding and simplifying certain periods of history (including indigenous and pre-civil war archaeology). For the public, it was the extra-curricular educational value of visiting community projects that was predominantly mentioned. Therefore educational values were not just predominant but also different to the UK where children attended as part of organised school trips. Therefore, there were common themes across the case studies as well as critical differences that give an indication of the strong effect that politics has on the formation of identity and the values people attach to the past.

Location

The location of the community archaeology project was critical to its success. For instance at Mitchell, its political location within a largely Republican area had direct impact on the support both locally, in terms of visitors to the site, but also in terms of volunteers and financial support. It has been suggested that if located within Sioux Falls, with its more Democratic leanings, it would have enabled more visitors and volunteers, and therefore increased support and donations for the project. This site had some of the most impressive archaeological remains and facilities of all the community archaeology sites investigated, yet its semi-rural location and its political location was a hindrance, unlike Annapolis whose Democratic government and urban location enabled them to gain political and community support. Despite Muncy's rural location, its Democratic state government, and progressive archaeological outreach, which the State has championed, also enabled it to gain support. In the UK, Brayford's rural location spurred many amateurs and locals to take a more proactive role, and Hungate's, Chester's, and Shoreditch's urban locations enabled them to gain more political support, and increased interest from those outside the community.

In the UK, politics and political location of community projects can be seen to have had an effect on their ability to gain support. Both Shoreditch and Chester were, in 2008, in Labour constituencies; this helped these projects gain financial and political support from the outset. Hungate was under Liberal Democrat control, which is the only political party to have an archaeology policy, and this could have helped the planning office to incorporate more archaeology and outreach into the planning agreement with the developer.

10. CONCLUSION

The case studies from both the UK and US offer some interesting and controversial insights into the practice of community archaeology. This research has indicated that community archaeology has the potential to have an impact on society's values and understanding of archaeology. Archaeological theories need to be re-assessed in accordance with, not just professional views and values, but those of society, and the multiple communities within it.

The results of this research have highlighted the importance of the self-reflexive approach promoted by Hodder (2000), and the wealth of information that can be gleaned from taking a critical approach, which parallels the conclusions of Potters (1997) and Jones (2004) work. It has led to similar conclusions to Edgeworth (2006) about the importance of ethnological research and taking a more anthropological stance, something that was also highlighted by Dalley (2004) and Pyburn (2003).

The duration of the study indicated the direct effect that politics have had on community archaeology and its ability to perform a meaningful role to various communities; academic, professional, amateurs, interested and uninterested public. The changes in government agendas in the UK highlighted that the community and social partnerships in the late 1990s enabled the initial funding of Chester, Shoreditch, Hungate and Brayford projects. Whilst the US, the Republican government of the early 21st century, saw decreased support for community projects.

It highlights critical problems with the assertions made by academics, professionals and politicians about values attached to the heritage, including those of Hunter (1996), Darvill (1995) and Lipe (1984; 1989). In many cases these espoused values hold little relevance to what is happening, and experienced by the public on the ground. It is therefore not that community archaeology is not valuable, but it does not have the same values that are espoused.

The analysis of these community archaeology projects has formed a similar, if not slightly more complex conclusion of that suggest by Derry (2003), that community archaeology should not take a linear approach but rather a 'double helix approach' (i.e. value strands should be interwoven). Although academics, professionals and amateurs often regard projects as having a simple beginning, middle and end, with specific outcomes, in reality the many different groups that form the community archaeology partnerships, have multiple aims, and outcomes, that alter during the course of the project; the helix has a plethora of interlinked value chains.

10.1 Key Themes

- Though often viewed as a critical component, in many cases involvement in excavation is not key to actual value outcomes.

- Social values were attained more readily than economic, political, and educational ones. It was the espoused qualitative (intangible) values rather than the quantitative (tangible) values that were actually achieved.

- Political context directly affected values espoused and actual values attached to community archaeology projects.

- Knowledge value of community archaeology projects was overestimated, whilst social value was underestimated.

- Rural locations were more successful in achieving social values.

- Urban locations were more successful in achieving political, economic and knowledge values.

- The UK can learn important points from the US: Both Swain (2007) and Carman (2002) suggest that community archaeology needs to be embedded into institutions, enabling broader support and permanent funding. In the US incorporation of community archaeology programmes into the university system has created sustainable projects (e.g. Binghamton).

10.2 Future Research

This research has highlighted fundamental problems with the theoretical value assumptions that are placed on community archaeology, but in order to revise these theories further in-depth work is needed. This research only investigated values relating to community archaeology excavations, but did draw out wider values attached to other community archaeology activities.

Future research agendas could include:

- More extensive research into community archaeology projects, looking for thematic patterns at a global level.

- Research on the values of different types of community archaeology projects, moving beyond excavations, conducting a comparative analysis of the relative values of excavation versus other activities.

- Analysis of long-term community archaeology projects, to understand what make such initiatives sustainable.

10.3 Suggested Guidelines for Community Archaeology

- Context and location are vital to setting objectives, as these are essential to understanding and attaining the values. Political environment plays a key role to these values.

- Produce a cost-benefit analysis before initiating projects.

- Projects should be designed based on an ability to adapt to stakeholder values that emerge through consultation and engagement during the lifetime of the project.

- Marketing and communication are paramount in achieving project values.

- Projects should be embedded in an existing organisation, which can provide sustainability. Projects entirely dependent on time-limited funding are not as cost effective as the values achieved are short term. A smaller number of sustainable projects may deliver better value for money than many short term initiatives whose values are quickly lost.

- Excavation is a key component; but physical involvement in it is not for the wider public, but is a key concern for amateur archaeologists.

10.4 Concluding Remarks

The difficulty in meeting the theoretical aspirations of community archaeology projects often relates to balances of power and in particular the different agendas of the local community and archaeologists. This research has indicated that excavation taking place under the guise of a 'community' project, frequently struggles with serving the public and archaeologists simultaneously, often seeing one group's value overshadowing the other. Achieving the aimed outputs and values of community archaeology projects, and longer term management of the archaeological resource, requires a more sustainable approach. This requires a very different mindset from both funding bodies and institutions that engage in community archaeology projects. Evaluation of projects needs to extend beyond simple 'tick box' targets to encompass longer term qualitative values.

Bibliography

ACENTURE. 2006: Capturing the public values of heritage: looking beyond the numbers. In K. Clark (ed.), *The Public Value of Heritage:* The Proceedings of the London Conference 25-26 January 2006. Swindon: English Heritage, 19-22.

Advisory Council on Historic Preservation. "National Historic Preservation Act of 1966. As Amended through 2000," 26 April 2002. See <www2.cr.nps.gov/laws/NHPA1966.htm>

AITKEN, R and SIMPSON, F. 2005: Shoreditch Park Community Excavation. In: *MOLAS 2005: annual report.* London: Museum of London.

AINSWORTH, S. and WILMOTT, T. 2005: *Chester Amphitheatre: From Gladiators to Gardens.* Chester: Chester City Council and English Heritage.

All-Party Parliamentary Archaeology Group. 2003: *The Current State of Archaeology in the United Kingdom.* London: The All-Party Parliamentary Archaeological Group (APPAG).

ANDERSON, B. 1983: *Imagined Communities: Reflection on the Origins and Spread of Nationalism.* London: Verso.

ANTHONY, D. 1996: Nazi and eco-feminist prehistories: ideology and empiricism in Indo-European Archaeology. In P. Kohl and C. Fawcett (ed.), *Nationalism, Politics and the Practice of Archaeology.* Cambridge: Cambridge University Press, 82-98.

ARNOLD, B. and HESSMENN, H. 1993: Archaeology in Nazi Germany: the legacy of Faustian bargin. In P. Kohl and C. Fawcett (ed.), *Nationalism, Politics and the Practice of Archaeology.* Cambridge: Cambridge University, 70-81.

ASCHERSON, N. 2000: Editorial. *Journal of Public Archaeology* 1(1): 1-4.

ASCHERSON, N. 2004: Archaeology and Television. In N. Merriman (ed.) *Public Archaeology.* London: Routledge, 145-158.

ASTON, M. Forthcoming: Publicizing Archaeology in Britain in the Late Twentieth Century – A Reflective, Personal, Biographical View.

ASTON, M., COSTON, A., GERRARD, C and HALL, T. 1997: *The Shapwick Project,* Volumes 1-8 (ed.). Bristol: The University of Bristol Department for Continuing Education.

Australian Heritage Commission. 2002: Ask First: A guide to respecting heritage places and values.

BAHN, P. 1996: *Archaeology: A Very Short Introduction.* Oxford: Oxford University Press.

BANKS, I. 1997: Archaeology, Nationalism and Ethnicity. In J. Atkinson, I. Banks and O'Sullivan (ed.), *Nationalism and Archaeology.* Glasgow: Cruithne Press, 1-11.

BEAVIS, J. and HUNT, A. 1999: Bill Putnam: An Appreciation. In J. Beavis and A. Hunt (ed.), *Communicating Archaeology.* Bournemouth University School of Conservation Sciences Occasional Paper 4. Oxford: Oxbow books, 1-10.

BENDER, B. 1998: *Stonehenge: Making Space.* Oxford: Berg.

BERGMAN, C.A. and DOERSHUK, J.F. 2003: Cultural Resource Management and the Bunisness of Archaeology. In L.J. Zimemerman, K.D. Viteli and J. Hollowell-Zimmer (ed.), *Ethical Issues in Archaeology.* Oxford: Altamira Press, 85-97.

BINFORD, L. 1983: *In Pursuit of the Past. Decoding the Archaeological Record.* London: Thames and Hudson.

BLACKBURN, S. 2006: *Truth: A Guide for the Perplexed.* London: Penguin Books.

BOWDEN, M. 1991: *Pitt Rivers: The Life and Archaeological Work of Lieutenant-General Augusts Henry Lane Fox Pitt Rivers,* DCL, FRS, FSA. Cambridge: Cambridge University Press.

BRADLEY, H., DAWSON, T. and LELONG, O. 2008: Saving Sandwick. British Archaeology, March/ April 2008: 5 (99), 34-37.

CABE. 2004: *The value of public space: how high quality parks and public spaces create economic, social and environmental value.* London: Commission for Architecture and the Built Environment.

CARMAN, J. 1996: *Valuing Ancient Things: Archaeology and Law.* London: Leicestershire University Press.

CARMAN, J. 2002: *Archaeology and Heritage: An Introduction.* London: Leicestershire University Press.

CARMAN, J. 2006: *Against Cultural Property: Archaeological Heritage and Ownership.* London: Duckworth.

CARMAN, J. 2006: Digging the Dirt: Excavation as a Social Practice. In M, Edgeworth (ed.), *Ethnographies of Archaeological Practice: Cultural Encounters, Material Transformations.* Lanham: Altamira Press, 95-102.

CARVER, M. 2007: On Archaeological Value. In L.J. Smith (ed.), *Cultural Heritage: Critical Concepts in Media and Cultural Studies* (Vol. I). London: Routledge, 342-360.

CATLING, C. 2007: Archaeology and Politics a personal view. *The Archaeologist* 63), 40.

CHAMPION, M. 2000: *Seahenge: A Contemporary Chronicle.* London: Barnwells Publishing.

CLACK, T. and BRITAIN, M. 2007: *Archaeology and the Media.* London: UCL Institute of Archaeology Publications.

CLEERE, H. 1984: Introduction. In H. Cleere (ed.), *Approaches to Archaeological Heritage.* Cambridge: Cambridge Archaeological Press.

CONINGHAM, R. COOPER, R. and POLLARD, M. 2006: What value of unicorn's horn? A study of archaeological uniqueness and value. In C. Scarre and G. Scarre (ed.), *The Ethics of Archaeology: Philosophical Perspectives on Archaeological Practice.* Cambridge: Cambridge University Press, 260-272.

CONNELLY, P., KENDALL, T., HUNTER-MANN, Kurt. and MAINMAN, A. 2008: The Archaeology of Modern Urban Poverty. *Current Archaeology* (215), 24.

COPELAND, T. 2006: Presenting Archaeology to the Public: Constructing insights on-site. In N. Merriman (ed.) *Public Archaeology.* London: Routledge, 132-144.

COPPER, D. 2006: Truthfulness and 'inclusion' in Archaeology. In C. Scarre and G. Scarre (ed.), *The Ethics of Archaeology: Philosophical Perspectives on Archaeological Practice.* Cambridge: Cambridge University Press, 131-147.

CRESSEY, P.J. 1987: Community Archaeology in Alexandria, Virginia. *Conserve Neighbourhoods*, No. 69. National Trust for Historic Preservation.

CRESSEY, P.J., REEDER, R. and BRYSON, J. 2003: Held in Trust: Community Archaeology in Alexandria, Virginia. In L. Derry and M. Malloy (ed.), *Archaeologist and Local Communities: Partners in Exploring the Past.* Washington D.C: Society for American Archaeology, 1-18.

CRIST, T.A.J. 2002: Empowerment, Ecology, and Evidence: The Relevance of Mortuary Archaeology to the Public. In B.J. Little (ed.), *Public Benefits of Archaeology.* Gainesville: University Press of Florida, 101-120.

CROSBY, A. 2002: Archaeology and Vanua Development in Fiji. *World Archaeology*, Vol. 34 (2), Community Archaeology, 363-378.

CROUCH, D and PARKER, G. 2007: 'Digging Up Utopia? Space, practice and land use heritage. In L. J. Smith (ed.), *Cultural Heritage* (Vol II). London: Routledge, 338-360.

CUNLIFFE, B. 1981: Introduction: The Public Face of the Past. In J. Evans, B. Cunliffe, and C. Renfrew (ed.), *Antiquity and Man: Essays in Honour of Glyn Daniel.* London: Thames and Hudson, 192-194.

DALLEY, C. 2004: *Control and Power in Australian Community Archaeology: Case Studies from Waanyi Country, Northwest Queensland.* Queensland: University of Queensland.

DARVILL, T. 1995: Value Systems in Archaeology. In M. A. Cooper, A. Firth, J. Carman and D. Wheatley (ed.), *Managing Archaeology.* London: Routledge, 40-50.

DARVILL, T. 1999: Reeling in the years: The Past in the Present. In J. Hunter and I. Ralston (ed.) *Archaeological Resource Management in the UK: An Introduction.* Stroud: Sutton Publishing, 297-315.

DCMS, 2006: *Better Places to Live: Government, Identity and the Public Value of Heritage. Summary of Responses.* London: Department of Culture, Media and Sport.

DENNELL, R. 1997: Nationalism and Identity in Britain and Europe. In J. Atkinson, I. Banks and O'Sullivan (ed.), *Nationalism and Archaeology.* Glasgow: Cruithne Press, 22-34.

DERRY, L. 2003: Consequences of Involving Archaeology in Contemporary Community Issues. In L. Derry and M. Malloy (ed.), *Archaeologist and Local Communities: Partners in Exploring the Past.* Washington D.C: Society for American Archaeology, 19-30.

DERRY, L. 2003: Concluding Remarks. In L. Derry and M. Malloy (ed.), *Archaeologist and Local Communities: Partners in Exploring the Past.* Washington D.C, Society for American Archaeology, 185-188.

DEUNERT, B. 1996: *Modern Archaeology and its Reflection in the Value System of Contemporary Culture. Based on anthropological/ archaeological research conducted in Australia.* BAR International Series 648.

EDGEWORTH, M. 2006: Multiple Origins, Development, and Potential of Ethnographies of Archaeology. In M, Edgeworth (ed.) *Ethnographies of Archaeological Practice: Cultural Encounters, Material Transformations.* Lanham: Altamira Press, 1-19.

EMERSON, R., FRETZM R. and SHAW, L. 1995: *Writing Ethnographic Fieldnotes.* Chicago: The University of Chicago Press.

English Heritage. 2000: *Power of Place: The Future of the Historic Environment.* London: English Heritage for the Historic Environment Steering Group.

English Heritage. 2006: *Heritage Counts: The State of England's Historic Environment* 2006. London: English Heritage.

ERIKSEN, T.H. 1993: *Ethnicity and Nationalism: Anthropological Perspective.* London: Pluto Press.

FAULKNER, N. 2000: Archaeology from below. *Journal of Public Archaeology* (1), 21-33.

FAULKNER, N. 2008: Flagship national archaeology scheme faces crippling cuts. *Current Archaeology* (215), 49.

FREDERICKSEN, C. 2002: Caring for History: Tiwi and Archaeological Narratives of Fort Dundas/ Punata, Melville Island, Australia. *World Archaeology*, Vol. 34 (2), Community Archaeology, 288-302.

FOUCAULT, M. 1980: *Power and Knowledge.* Brighton: Harvester Wheatsheaf.

FOWLER, P. 1986: The past in the public: roots for all or life with dried tubers? In C. Dobinson and R. Gilchrist (ed.), *Archaeology, Politics and the Public.* York: York University Archaeology Publications, 6-13.

FOWLER, P. 1992: *The Past in Contemporary Society: Then, Now.* London: Routledge.

FREUD, S. 1961: Lecture II: Parapraxes [1915]. *In the standard ed. Of the complete psychological works of Sigmund Freud*; Vol. 15, ed. J. Strachey, 23-39. London: Hogarth.

FREUD, S. 1964: Constructions in Analysis [1937]. In the standard ed. *Of the complete psychological works of Sigmund Freud.* Vol. 23, ed. J. Strachey, 255-69. London: Hogarth.

GATHERCOLE, P. and LOWENTHAL, D. (ed.) 1994: Introduction. *The Politics of the Past.* London: Routledge. 7-17.

GATHERCOLE, P., STANELY, J. and THOMAS, N. 2002: Archaeology and the media: Cornwall Archaeology Society – Devon Archaeological Society joint symposium. *Cornish Archaeology* (41-42), 149-160.

GERRARD, C.M. and ASTON, M.A. 2007: *The Shapwick Project, Somerset. A Rural Landscape Explored.* Leeds: Society for Medieval Archaeology.

GREER, S. 1995: *The Accidental Heritage: Archaeology and Identity in Northern Cape* York. Doctoral dissertation. Department of Anthropology and Archaeology, James Cook University Townville.

GREER, S., HARRISON, R. and McINTYRE-TAMWOY, S. 2002: Community Based Archaeology in Australia. *World Archaeology*, Vol. 34 (2), Community Archaeology, 265-287.

HANUS, L.A., LUECK E.J. and R.P. WINHAM. 1987: *Mitchell Prehistoric Indian Village: Summary of Studies and Excavation Through 1986.* Sioux Falls: Archaeological Lab of the Centre for Western Studies, Augustana College.

HARKE, H. 2002: *Archaeology, Ideology, and Society: The German Experience.* Frankfurt: Peter Lang.

HASSAN, F. 1995: The World Archaeology Congress in India: Politicizing the Past. *Antiquity* (69), 874-877.

HAWKINS, N. 2000: Teaching Archaeology Without the Dig: What's Left? In K. Smardz and S.J. Smith (ed.), *The Archaeology Education Handbook: Sharing the Past with Kids.* New York: Altamira Press, 209-216.

HENSON, D. 1997: *Archaeology in the National Curriculum.* York: Council for British Archaeology.

HENSON, D. 2004: The Education Framework in the United Kingdom. In D. Henson, P. Stone, and M. Corbishley (ed.), *Education and The Historic Environment.* London: Routledge, 13-22.

HENDRY, H. 1999: *An Introduction to Social Anthropology: Other Peoples World.* London: Macmillan Press Ltd.

HENRY, P. 2004: The Young Archaeologists' Club: Its Role Within Informal Learning. In D. Henson, P. Stone and M. Corbishley (ed.), *Education and the Historic Environment.* London: Routledge, 89-100.

HEMS, A. 2006: Introduction: Beyond the Graveyard – Extending Audiences, Enhancing Understanding. In A. Hems and M. Blockley (ed.), *Heritage Interpretation.* London: Routledge, 1-8.

HEWISON, R. and HOLDER, J. 2006: Public value as a framework for analysing the value of heritage: the ideas. In K. Clark (ed.), *The Public Value of Heritage: The Proceedings of the London Conference 25-26 January 2006.* Swindon: English Heritage, 14-18.

HEWISON, R. 1987: *The Heritage Industry: Britain in a Climate of Decline.* London: Methuen.

HILLS, C. 2001: The Dissemination of Information. In J. Hunter and I. Ralston (ed.) *Archaeological Resource Management in the UK: An Introduction.* Stroud: Sutton Publishing, 215-224.

HODDER, I. 1986: *Reading the Past: Current Approaches to Interpretation in Archaeology.* Cambridge: Cambridge University Press.

HODDER, I. (ed) 2000: *Towards Reflexive Method in Archaeology: the example at Çatalhöyük* Cambridge: McDonald Institute for Archaeological Research, University of Cambridge.

HODDER, I. (ed.) 2001: *Archaeological Theory Today.* Cambridge: Polity.

HODDER, I. (ed) 2005: *Excavations at Çatalhöyük: the 1995-1999 seasons.* Monograph of the McDonald Institute and the British Institute of Archaeology at Ankara.

HOLE, F. 1979: Rediscovering the Past in the Present. Ethnoarchaeology in Luristan, Iran. In C. Kramer (ed.), *Ethnoarchaeology: Implications of Ethnography for Archaeology*. New York: Columbia University, 192-206.

HOLTORF, C. 2005a: *From Stonehenge to Las Vegas: Archaeology as Popular Culture*. Oxford: Altamira Press.

HOLTORF, C. 2005b: Beyond crusades: how (not) to engage with alternative archaeologies. *World Archaeology* Vol. 37 (4): 544-551.

HOLTORF, C. 2006: *Archaeology is a Brand! The Meaning of Archaeology in Contemporary Popular Culture*. Oxford: BAR Publishing.

HOLTORF, C. 2007. Can you hear me at the back? Archaeology, Communication and Society. *European Journal of Archaeology*, Vol. 10 (2-3), 149-165.

HOLTORF, C. and HÖGBERG, A. 2005-6: Talking People: From Community to Popular Archaeologies, *Lund Archaeological Review* (11-12), 79-88.

HOLTORF, C. and WILLIAMS, H. 2006: Landscapes and Memories. In D. Hicks and M.C. Beaudry (ed.), *The Cambridge Companion to Historical Archaeology*. Cambridge: Cambridge University Press, 235-254.

HOWARD, P. 2003: *Heritage, Management, Interpretation, Identity*. London: Continuum.

HUNTER, M. 1996: *Preserving the Past: The Sense of Heritage in Modern Britain*. Stroud: Sutton.

HUNTER, J. and COX, M. 2005: *Forensic Archaeology: Advances in Theory and Practice*. London: Routledge.

ICOMOS. 1990: *Charter for the Protection and Management of the Archaeological Heritage*. International Council on Monuments and Sites.

IFA. 1995: *Draft Regulations for the Registration of Archaeological Organisations*.

JAMESON, J. 2004: Public Archaeology in the United States. In N. Merriman (ed.), *Public Archaeology*. London: Routledge, 21-58.

JAMESON, J. 2003: Purveyors of the Past: Education and Outreach as Ethical Imperatives in Archaeology. In L.J. Zimemerman, K.D. Viteli and J. Hollowell-Zimmer (ed.), *Ethical Issues in Archaeology*. Oxford: Altamira Press, 153-162.

JEPPSON, P.L. 2008: Doing Our Homework: Rethinking the Goals and Responsibilities of Archaeology Outreach to Schools. In J. Stottman (ed.), *Changing the World with Archaeology: Activist Archaeology*. Greenville: University of Florida Press, 1-58.

JEPPSON P.L. and G. BRAUER. 2007: Archaeology for Education's Needs: An Archaeologist and An Educator Discuss Archaeology in the Baltimore County Public Schools. In J.H. Jameson and S. Baugher (ed.), *Past Meets Present: Archaeology and the Public. Archaeologists Partnering with Museum Curators, Teachers and Community Groups*. New York: Springer Press, 231-249.

JEPPSON, P.L. and G. BRAUER. 2003: "Hey, Did You Hear About The Teacher Who Took The Class Out To Dig A Site?": Some Common Misconceptions About Archaeology in Schools. In L. Derry and M. Malloy (ed.), *Archaeologists and Local Communities: Partners in Exploring the Past*. Washington, D.C: Society for American Archaeology Press, 77-96.

JOHNSON, M. 1999: *Archaeological Theory: An Introduction*. London: Blackwell.

JOHNSON, E. 2000: Cognitive and Moral Development of Children: Implications for Archaeological Education. In K. Smardz and S.J. Smith (ed.), *The Archaeology Education Handbook: Sharing the Past with Kids*. New York: Altamira Press, 72-90.

JONES, A. 2004: Using Objects: The York Archaeological Trust Approach. In D. Henson, P. Stone and M. Corbishley (ed.) *Education and the Historic Environment*. London: Routledge, 173-184.

JONES, A. 1995: Integrating school visits, tourists and the community at the Archaeological Resource Centre, York, UK. In E. Hopper-Greenhill (ed.), *Museum, Media, Message*. Leicester: Leicester University Press, 156-64.

JONES, D. 2004: Archaeology in Higher Education. In D. Henson, P. Stone and M. Corbishley (ed.) *Education and the Historic Environment*. London: Routledge, 41-46.

JONES, S. 1997: *Theory of Ethnicity: Constructing Identity in the Past and Present*. London: Routledge.

JONES, S. 2004: *Research Report: Early Medieval Sculpture and The Productions of Meaning, Values and Place: The Case of Hilton of Cadboll*. Edinburgh: Historic Scotland.

JORDON, P. 1984: Archaeology and Television. In H. Cleere (ed.), *Approaches to Archaeological Heritage*. Cambridge: Cambridge University Press, 207-214.

JOWELL, T. 2005: *Better Places to Live: Government, Identity and the Value of the Historic and Built Environment*. London: Department of Culture, Media and Sport.

JOWELL, T. 2006: The Consultation to Conversation: The Challenge of Better Places to Live. In *Capturing the Public Values of Heritage: The Proceedings of the London Conference 25-26 January 2006*. Swindon: English Heritage, 7-13.

JUNG, C.G. 1989: *Memories, Dreams, Reflections*. New York: Vintage Books, USA (edited by Aniela Jaffe and translated by Richard and Clara Winston).

KRAMER, C. 1979: Introduction. In C. Kramer (ed.), *Ethnoarchaeology: Implications of Ethnography for Archaeology*. New York: Columbia University Press, 1-20.

KRAMER, D. and, KRAMER, C. 2001: *Ethnoarchaeology in Action*. Cambridge: Cambridge University Press.

LAMMY, D. 2006: Community, Identity and Heritage. In *Capturing the Public Values of Heritage:* The Proceedings of the London Conference 25-26 January 2006. Swindon: English Heritage, 65-69.

LAYTON, R. (ed.) 1989: *Who Needs the Past? Indigenous Values and Archaeology.* London: Unwin Hyman.

LAYTON, R. and WALLACE, G. 2006: Is culture a commodity? In C. Scarre and G. Scarre (ed.) *The Ethics of Archaeology: Philosophical Perspectives on Archaeological Practice.* Cambridge: Cambridge University Press, 46-68.

LEONE, M., POTTER, P.B. and SHACKEL, P.A. 1987: Toward a Critical Archaeology. *Current Anthropology* 28 (3), 283-302.

LIDDLE, P. 1981: Community Archaeology? *RESCUE* (28). PG.

LIDDLE, P. 1989: Community archaeology in Leicestershire museums, In E. Southworth (ed.), *Public Service or Private Indulgence*? The Museum Archaeologist 13, Liverpool: Society of Museum Archaeologists: 44-46.

LIPE, W. 1984: Value and meaning in cultural resources. In H. Cleere (ed.), *Approaches to the Archaeological Heritage: a comparative study of world cultural resource management systems.* Cambridge: Cambridge University Press, 1-11.

LIPE, W. 2007: Value and meaning in cultural resources. In L.J. Smith (ed.), *Cultural Heritage: Critical Concepts in Media and Cultural Studies* (Vol. I). London: Routledge, 286-306.

LITTLE, B.L. 2002: Archaeology as a Shared Vision. In B.J. Little (ed.), *Public Benefits of Archaeology.* Florida: University Press of Florida, 3-19.

LOCK, G. 2004: Rolling Back the Years: Lifelong Learning and Archaeology in the United Kingdom. In D. Henson, P. Stone and M. Corbishley (ed.), *Education and the Historic Environment.* London: Routledge, 55-66.

LOWENTHAL, D. 1989: *The Heritage Crusade and the Spoils of History.* Cambridge: Cambridge University Press.

LOWENTHAL, D. 1985: *The Past is a Foreign Country.* Cambridge: Cambridge University Press.

LUCAS, G. 2004: Modern Disturbances: On the Ambiguities of Archaeology. Modernism/Modernity 11, 109-120. Available on http://muse.jhu.edu/ journals/modernity/v001/11.lucas.pda

MACKENZIE, R. and STONE, P. 1990: Introduction: A concept of Excluded Past. In P. Stone and R. Mackenzie (ed.), *The Excluded Past.* London: Unwin Hyman Ltd, 1-14.

MARSHALL, Y. 2002: What is Community Archaeology? *World Archaeology*, Vol. 34 (2) Community Archaeology, 211-219.

MARSHALL, Y: forthcoming (2009): Community Archaeology. In B. Cunliffe, C. Gosden and R. Joyce (ed.) *The Oxford Handbook of Archaeology.* Oxford: Oxford University Press.

MANELY, J. 1999: 'Old Stones, New Fires' – the local societies. In J. Beavis and A. Hunt (ed.), *Communicating Archaeology.* Bournemouth University School of Conservation Sciences Occasional Paper 4. Oxford: Oxbow books, 105-112.

MATTINSON, D. 2006: The Value of Public Heritage – what does the public think? In K. Clark (ed.), *Capturing the Public Value of Heritage- The Proceedings of the London Conference.*

McCLANAHON, A. 2006: Histories, Identity, and Ownership: An Ethnographic Case Study in Archaeological heritage Management in the Orkney Islands. In M, Edgeworth (ed.), *Ethnographies of Archaeological Practice: Cultural Encounters, Material Transformations.* Lanham: Altamira press, 126-136.

McDAVID, C. 2003: Collaboration, Power, and Internet: The Public Archaeology at the Levi Jordan Plantation. In L. Derry and M. Malloy (ed.), *Archaeologist and Local Communities: Partners in Exploring the Past.* Washington D.C: Society for American Archaeology, 45-66.

McGIMSEY, C. 1972: *Public Archaeology.* New York: McGraw Hill.

McKAY, D. 2001: *American Politics and Society.* Oxford: Blackwell.

McMANAMON, P.F. 2002: Heritage, History and Archaeological Educators. In B.J. Little (ed.), *Public Benefits of Archaeology.* Gainesville: University Press of Florida, 31-45.

MERRIMAN, N. 1991: *Beyond the Glass Case: The Past, the Heritage and the Public in Britain.* Leicester: Leicester University Press.

MERRIMAN, N. 2004: Introduction: Diversity and Dissonance in Public Archaeology. In N. Meriman (ed.), *Public Archaeology.* London: Routledge, 1-18.

MESKELL, L. 1998: Archaeologies of identity. In I. Hodder (ed.), *Archaeological Theory Today.* Cambridge: Polity Press, 187-213.

METCALF, F. 2002: Myths, Lies, and Videotapes: Information as Antidote to Social Studies Classrooms and Pop Culture. In B.J. Little (ed.), *Public Benefits of Archaeology.* Gainesville: University Press of Florida, 167-175.

MOE, J.M. 2002: Project Archaeology: Putting the Intrigue of the Past in Public Education. In B.J. Little (ed.), *Public Benefits of Archaeology.* Gainesville: University Press of Florida, 176-186.

MOSER, S., GLAZIER, D., PHILIPS, J., El NEMER, L., MOUSA, M., RICHARDSON, S,. CONNER, A. and SEYMOUR, M. 2002: Transforming archaeology through practice: strategies for collaborative archaeology and the Community Archaeology Project at Qusier, Egypt. *World Archaeology*, Vol. 34 (2) Community Archaeology, 265-287.

MORRIS, M. 2007: In Search of Cholmondeley's Mansion. The Past Uncovered: Chester Archaeology, *Design and Conservation News*, June 2007, 1. Chester: Chester City Council.

MOSHENSKA, G. 2005: 'The Sedgeford Village Survey: digging for local history in the back garden'. *Local Historian*, 35 (3), 159-67.

MOSHENSKA, G. 2006: The Archaeological Uncanny. *Public Archaeology* 5 (2), 91-99.

MOSHENSKA, G. 2007b: Oral history in historical archaeology: excavating sites of memory. *Oral History* 35(1), 91-97.

MOSHENSKA, G, DHANJAL, S, DOESER, J. PHILLIPS, S. and ALLEN, S. 2007: Community Archaeology against the odds. Manifesto for Community Archaeology, *Current Archaeology* (35), 213.

MUNJERI, D. 2006: Tangible and Intangible Heritage. In L.J. Smith (ed.), *Cultural Heritage: Critical Concepts in Media and Cultural Studies* (Vol. 4). London: Routledge, 323-330.

MURRAY, T. 1998: *Archaeology of Aboriginal Australia – A Reader*. Sydney: Allen and Unwin.

NDORO, W. 1994: The preservation and presentation of Great Zimbabwe. *Antiquity* (68), 616-623.

NEUMANN, L.: The Politics of Archaeology and Historic Preservation: How our laws really are made. (www.nps.gov/history/sec/protecting/html/201-neumann.htm)

NEWMAN, W.L. 1995: *Social Research Methods: Qualitative and Quantitative Approach*. Boston: Allyn and Bacon.

NEWMAN, A. and McLEAN, F. 2007: Heritage Builds Communities. In L.J. Smith (ed.), *Cultural Heritage* (Vol. IV). London: Routledge, 99-111.

NIETZSCHE, F. 1967: *The Will to Power*, Walter Kaufmann (ed.). London: Weidenfeld and Nicolson.

Oxford English Dictionary. 2002: Oxford: Oxford University Press.

OSWALD, A. 2007: Involving the Community in Field Survey. *The Archaeologist* (63), 20-21.

PALMER, N.E. 1981: Treasure Trove and the Protection of Antiquities. *Modern Law Review* 44, 178-87.

PAPAZACHOS, B, PAPAIOANNOV, C., D. PAPASTA-MATIOU., MARGARIS, B. and THEODULIDIS, P. 1990: On the Reliability of Different methods of Seismic Hazard Assessment in Greece. *Natural Hazards* (3), 141-151.

PARKER PEARSON, M. 2001: Visitors Welcome. In J. Hunter and I. Ralston (ed.) *Archaeological Resource Management in the UK: An Introduction*. Stroud: Sutton Publishing, 225-231.

PEARSON, V. 2001: *Teaching the Past: A Practical Guide for Archaeologists*. York: Council for British Archaeology.

PICCINI, A. and, HENSON, D. 2006: *Survey of Heritage Television Viewing 2005–2006*. London: English Heritage.

PITTS, M. 2007: Archaeology the Blair Years. *British Archaeology* (July/ August 2007), 10-13.

PLUCIENNIK, M. (ed.) 2001: Introduction: *The Responsibilities of Archaeologist: Archaeology and Ethics*. Lampeter Workshop in Archaeology 4. BAR International Series 981, 1-8.

POPCORN, F. 1992: *The Popcorn Report. Revolutionary Trend for Marketing in the 1990's*. London: Arrow.

POPE, P. and MILLS, S. 2007: Outport Archaeology: Community Archaeology in Newfoundland. In J.H. Jameson and S. Baugher (ed.), *Past Meets Present: Archaeology and the Public. Archaeologists Partnering with Museum Curators, Teachers and Community Groups*. New York: Springer Press, 169-186.

POTTER, P.B. 1994: *Public Archaeology in Annapolis: A Critical Approach to Maryland's Ancient City*. Washington D.C.: Smithsonian Institute Press.

PRAETZELLIS, A. 2002: Neat Stuff and Good Stories: Interpreting Historical Archaeology in Two Local Communities. In B.J. Little (ed.), *Public Benefits of Archaeology*. Gainesville: Florida University Press, 51-58.

PYBURN, K.A. 2003: Archaeology for a New Millennium: The Rules of Engagement. In L. Derry and M. Malloy (ed.), *Archaeologist and Local Communities: Partners in Exploring the Past*. Washington D.C, Society for American Archaeology, 167-184.

PYKLES, B.C. 2008: A Brief History of Historical Archaeology in the United States. *Society of American Archaeologists*. Vol. 8 (3), 32- 34.

RAGINS, M.G. 2002: Archaeology in Santa Fe A Public-Private Balancing Act. In B.J. Little (ed.), *Public Benefits of Archaeology*. Gainesville: University Press of Florida, 202-207.

RAMOS, M. and DUGANNE, D. 2000: *Exploring Public Perceptions and Attitudes about Archaeology*. Washington DC: Society for American Archaeologists.

REID, P. 2008: Community Archaeology: from the grassroots. *Current Archaeology* (216), 21.

ROWLANDS, M. 1994: The Politics of Identity in Archaeology. In G.C. Bond and A. Gilliam (ed.) *Social Construction the Past: Representation as Power*. London: Routledge, 129-43.

ROSENFIELD, J. 2006: *Bruce Castle Community Dig; Consultation and Evaluation*. London: Museum of London (internal document).

RUSHDIE, S. 1983: *Shame*. London: Picador.

SCARRE, C. and SCARRE, G. 2006: Introduction. In C. Scarre and G. Scarre (ed.), *The Ethics of Archaeology: Philosophical Perspectives on Archaeological Practice.* Cambridge: Cambridge University Press, 1-14.

SCHADLA-HALL, T. 2004: Appropriate Archaeology. In N. Merriman (ed.), *Public Archaeology.* London: Routledge, 255-271.

SCHADLA-HALL, T. 1999: Editorial: Public Archaeology. *European Journal of Archaeology* 2(2): 147-58.

SCHULZE, G. 1993: *The Experience Society. Pie Erlebnis – Gesellschaft: Kultursoziologie de Gegenwart. 3rd ed. Frankurt and New York: Campus.*

SELKIRK, A. 1997: *Who Owns the Past?* London: Adam Smith Institute.

SERRILL, M. 1998: *Hindu Pride: India's ruling B.J.P. has a nationalist agenda that frightens religious minority, and it sees its neighbours as rivals.* Time, May 25th, 35.

SHACKEL, P.A. 2007: Public Memory and the Search for Power in American Historical Archaeology. In L.J. Smith (ed.), *Cultural Heritage* (Vol. II). London: Routledge, 307-330.

SHAFFER, G.D. and COLE, E. 1994: Standards and Guidlines for Archaeological Investigations in Maryland. Ed by D of H a C Development. Maryland: Maryland Hisotric Trust Research Report.

SHANKS, M. and TILLEY, C. 1987: *Social Theory and Archaeology.* Oxford: Polity Press.

SHENNAN, S. 1988: 'Introduction.' In S. Shennan (ed.), *Archaeology Approaches to Cultural Identity.* London: Unwin Hyman, 1-32.

SHULL, C.D. 2002: Irreplaceable Heritage: Archaeology and the National Register of Historic Places. In B.J. Little (ed.), *Public Benefits of Archaeology.* Gaines-ville: University Press of Florida, 195-207.

SKEATES, R. 2000: *Debating the Archaeological Heritage.* London: Gerald Duckworth & Co. Ltd.

SKOCPOL, T. and CAMPBELL, J.L. 1995: *American Society and Politics: Institutional, Historical and Theoretical Perspectives.* New York: McGraw-Hill.

SILBERMAN, N.A. 1999: Is Archaeology Ready for Prime Time? *Archaeology Magazine* (May/June 1999), 79-82.

SIMPSON, F. 2009: Cumwhitton Norse Burial. In S, Thomas and P, Stone (ed,), *Metal Detecting and Archaeology.* Newcastle: Newcastle University Press, 137-146.

SIMPSON, F. 2009: Community Archaeology Under Scrutiny. *Journal of Conservation and Management of Archaeological Sites,* Vol. 10(1), 3–16.

SIMPSON, F. and KEILY, J. 2005: Today's Rubbish, Tomorrow's Archaeology: Using Nineteenth and Twentieth Century Finds. *The Archaeologist* (58), 26-27.

SIMPSON, F. and WILLIAMS, H. 2008: Evaluating Community Archaeology in the UK, *Public Archaeology* 7(2), 69-90.

SLICK, K. 2002: Archaeology and the Tourist Train. In B.J. Little (ed.), *Public Benefits of Archaeology.* Gainesville: University Press of Florida, 219-227.

SMARDZ, K. 2000: Digging With Kids: Teaching Students to Touch the Past. In K. Smardz and S.J. Smith (ed.), *The Archaeology Education Handbook: Sharing the Past with Kids.* New York: Altamira Press, 234-248.

SMARDZ, K. and SMITH, S. J. 2000: Introduction. In K. Smardz and S.J. Smith (ed.), *The Archaeology Education Handbook: Sharing the Past with Kids.* New York: Altamira Press, 25-38.

SMITH, L.J. 2004: *Archaeological Theory and the Politics of Cultural Heritage.* Oxfordshire: Routledge.

SMITH, L.J. and WATERTON, E. 2009: Communities and Archaeology. London: Duckworth.

SMITH, P. 2004: Outreach at Wessex Archaeology. In D. Henson, P. Stone, and M. Corbishley (ed.), *Education and the Historic Environment.* London: Routledge, 161-172.

SMITH, G. and EHRENHARD, J, 2002: Protecting the Past to Benefit the Public. In B.J. Little (ed.), *Public Benefits of Archaeology.* Gainesville: University Press of Florida, 130-145.

SNEAD, J. 1999: Science, Commerce and Control: Patronage and the development of anthropological Archaeology in the Americans. *American Anthropology*, Vol. 101 (2), 256-271.

South Dakota Legislature Statue and Constitution, South Dakota Codified Law SDCL 1-19A-11.1.See </ /legis.state.sd.uk/statutes/index.cfm>

South Dakota State Historic Society. 2005: *Guidelines for Cultural Resource Surveys and Survey Reports in South Dakota* (For Review and Compliance).

START, D. 1999: Community Archaeology; bringing it back to local communities. In G. Chitty and D. Baker (ed.), *Managing Historic Sites and Buildings; Reconciling Presentation and Preservation.* London: Routledge, 49-59.

STREETER, K. 2005: *The Case for Community Involvement.* Unpublished UCL masters Dissertation.

STONE, P. 2004: Introduction: Education and the Historic Environment into the Twenty First Century. In D. Henson, P. Stone and M. Corbishley (ed.), *Education and the Historic Environment.* London: Routledge, 1-12.

SWAIN, H. 2007: *An Introduction to Museum Archaeology.* Cambridge: Cambridge University Press.

TAYLOR, A. 2007: *The Archaeologist* (63), 41-42.

TAYLOR, C. 2001: *The African Burial Ground.* New York: United States General Services Administration (leaflet).

TAYLOR, T. 2000: *Behind the Scenes at Time Team.* London: Channel Four Books.

THOMAS, D.H. 2002: Roadside Ruins: Does America Still Need Archaeology Museums? In B.J. Little (ed.), *Public Benefits of Archaeology.* Gainesville: University Press of Florida, 130-145.

THOMAS, J. 2004: *Archaeology and Modernity.* London: Routledge.

THOMAS, R. 2004: Archaeology and Authority in the Twenty-First Century. In N. Merriman (ed.), *Public Archaeology.* London: Routledge, 191-202.

TIERNEY, M. 1998: Treasures Buried by Layer of Hate. *Times: Higher Educational Supplement* (12 June 1998).

TREBLE, A., SMITHIES, G. and CLIPSON, H. 2007: *The Wider Community's Perception of Archaeology – Elitist or Accessible? Evaluating the Grosvenor Park Excavation.* Chester: University of Chester (unpublished).

TRIGGER, B.G. 1989: *The History of Archaeological Thought.* Cambridge: Cambridge University Press.

TRIGGER, B.G. 1996: Alternative Archaeologies: Nationalism, Imperialism and Colonialism. In R.W. Preucel and I. Hodder (ed.), *Contemporary Archaeology in Theory: A Reader.* London: Blackwell Publishers, 615 –931.

TULLY, G. 2007: Community archaeology: general methods and standards of practice, *Public Archaeology* 6 (3), 155-87.

UCKO, P. 1989: *Academic Freedom and Apartheid.* London: Duckworth.

UNSECO. 1995: *World Commission on Culture and Development, Our Creative Diversity.* Paris: UNESCO.

UNESCO. 2003: *Convention for the Safeguarding Of the Intangible Cultural Heritage.* Paris: UNESCO.

UNESCO. 2004: Linking Universal and Local Values: Managing a Sustainable Future for World Heritage. World Heritage Series 13. UNESCO: World Heritage Centres.

USDA-USFS. 1995: Passport in Time Accomplishments, Region 6. United States Department of Agriculture. Tuscon: United States Forest Service.

WAINWRIGHT, G. 2000: Time Please. *Antiquity.* Vol. 74 (286), 909-943.

WALKER, J. 1988: Community Archaeology and the Archaeological Community: a normative sociological approach. In J. Bintliff (ed.), *Extracting Meaning from the Past.* Oxford: Oxbow Books, 50-64.

WALKER, M. and MARQUIS-KYLE, P. 2004: The Illustrated Burra Charter: good practice for heritage places. Australia: ICOMOS.

WALLACE, J. 2004: *Digging the Dirt: The Archaeological Imagination.* London: Gerald Duckworth & Co. Ltd.

WASSERMAN, G. 1995: *The Basics of American Politics.* New York: Longman.

WATKINS, J.E. 2007: Beyond the Margin: American Indian, First Nation and Archaeology in North America. In L.J. Smith (ed.), *Cultural Heritage* (Vol. IV). London: Routledge, 235-253.

WATKIN, J., PYBUM, K. and CRESSEY, P. 2000: Community Relation: What the Practicing Archaeologist Needs to Know to Work Effectively with Local and/or Descendant Communities. In S.J. Bender and G. Smith (ed.), *Teaching Archaeology in the Twenty-First Century.* Washington DC: Society for American Archaeology, 73-81.

WHEELER, M. 1954: *Archaeology from the Earth.* Oxford: Oxford University Press.

WHITAKER, P. 1995: *Managing to Learn.* London: Cassell.

WHITE, E. 2002. Archaeology and Tourism at Mount Vernon. In B.J. Little (ed.), *Public Benefits of Archaeology.* Gainesville: University Press of Florida, 146-156.

WILLEY, G.R. and SABLOFF, J.A. 1974: *A History of American Archaeology.* London: Thames and Hudson.

WILSON, V. 2007: *Rich in All but Money: Life in Hungate 1900*-1938. York: York Archaeological Trust, Oral History Series 1.

WIWJORRA, I. 1996: German archaeology and its relation to nationalism and racism. In M. Diaz-Andreu and T. Champion (ed.), *Nationalism and Archaeology in Europe.* London: University College London Press, 164-188.

VERSAGGI, N. 2007. Partners in Preservation: The Binghamton University Community Archaeology Program. In J.H. Jameson and S. Baugher (ed.), *Past Meets Present: Archaeology and the Public. Archaeologists Partnering with Museum Curators, Teachers and Community Groups.* New York: Springer Press, 203-216.

VITELLI, K. (ed.) 1996: *Archaeological Ethics.* Walnut Creek: AltaMira Press.

VOLKERT, J., MARTIN, L.R and PICKWORTH, A. 2004: *National Museum of the American Indian:* Smithsonian Institution Washington, DC: Map and Guide. Washington: Scala Publishers (In association with the National Museum of the American Indian, Washington, DC.

ZIMMERMAN, L. 1996: Sharing Control of the Past. In K. Vitelli (ed.), *Archaeological* Ethics. Walnut Creek: AltaMira Press, 209-220.

Websites

www.annapolis.areaconnect.com/statistics.htm

www.bpc.iserver.net/codes/annapolis/

www.brayford.org/geography.html

www.brayford.org/history.html

www.canterburytrust.co.uk/schools/catkitpg.htm

www.chester.gov.uk/amphitheatre/excaprop.htm

www.chester.gov.uk/council_and_democracy.aspx

www.chester.gov.uk/council_and_democracy/research_and_intelligence/chester_in_context.aspx

www.citytowninfo.com/places/pennsylvania/muncy

www.ed.gov/politcy/elsec/leg/esegov/107-110.pdf

www.finds.org.uk

www.hlf.org.uk/english/aboutus

www.http://news.bbc.co.uk/1/hi/uk_politics/4611682.stm

www.idcide.com/citydata/sd/mitchell.htm

www.jorvik-viking-centre.co.uk/hungate/abouthungate/about1.htm

www.jovik-viking-centre.ac.uk/hungate/history/medieval.htm

www.jovik-viking-centre.ac.uk/hungate/history/modern.htm

www.legis.state.pa.us/WU01/VC/visitor_info/pa_history/pa_history.htm

www.legis.state.sd.us/rules/DisplayRule.aspex?Rule

www.legis.state.sd.us/statues/DisplayStatute.aspx?type=statute&statute=1-20

www.marylandhistoicaltrust.net/arch-res.htm

www.marylandhistoricaltrust.net/aboutmht.htm

www.mitchellindianvillage.org

www.muncyhistoricalsociety.org/dig/index.html

www.nmai.si.edu/subpage.cfm?subpage=about

www.nps.gov/history/sec/protecting/html/201-neumann.htm

www.paarchaeology.state.pa.us/pub_1right.htm

www.passportintime.com

www.p-j.net/pjeppson.org

www.portal.state.pa.uk

www.profiles.nationalrelocation.com/Maryland/Annapolis

THE VALUES OF COMMUNITY ARCHAEOLOGY: A COMPARATIVE ASSESSMENT BETWEEN THE UK AND US

www.publicatoins.parliment.uk/pa/cm2)

www.saa.org/aboutSAA/index.html

www.SDhistory.org

www.spiritus-temporis.com/london-borough-of-hackney/demographics-of-hackney.html

www.ukinnl.fco.gov.uk/resources/en/pdf/3190535/insight-uk-ethnic-diversity

www.whitehouse.gov/history/presidents/vc39.html

www.york.gov.uk/environment/Planning/guidance/S106_Obligations

www.yorkarchaoelogy.co.uk

www2.cr.nps.gov/laws/NHPA1966.htm

www-personal.umich.edu/~mejn/election/2008/)

www.ingramcontent.com/pod-product-compliance
Lightning Source LLC
Chambersburg PA
CBHW051304270326
41926CB00030B/4712